KIDWORLD

Rethinking Childhood

Joe L. Kincheloe and Jan Jipson
General Editors

Vol. 16

PETER LANG
New York • Washington, D.C./Baltimore • Bern
Frankfurt am Main • Berlin • Brussels • Vienna • Oxford

KIDWORLD

Childhood Studies, Global Perspectives, and Education

EDITED BY

Gaile S. Cannella & Joe L. Kincheloe

PETER LANG

New York • Washington, D.C./Baltimore • Bern
Frankfurt am Main • Berlin • Brussels • Vienna • Oxford

Library of Congress Cataloging-in-Publication Data

Kidworld: childhood studies, global perspectives, and education /
edited by Gaile S. Cannella and Joe L. Kincheloe
p. cm. — (Rethinking childhood; vol. 16)
Includes bibliographical references and index.
1. Children. 2. Children—Research. 3. Child development.
4. Child development—Research. I. Title: Kidworld. II. Cannella, Gaile Sloan.
III. Kincheloe, Joe L. IV. Series.
HQ767.9.K53   305.23—dc21   00-0487777
ISBN 0-8204-4989-X
ISSN 1086-7155

Die Deutsche Bibliothek-CIP-Einheitsaufnahme

Kidworld: childhood studies, global perspectives, and education / edited by Gaile S. Cannella
and Joe L. Kincheloe–New York; Washington, D.C./Baltimore; Bern;
Frankfurt am Main; Berlin; Brussels; Vienna; Oxford: Lang.
(Rethinking childhood; Vol. 16)
ISBN 0-8204-4989-X

Cover design by Lisa Dillon

The paper in this book meets the guidelines for permanence and durability
of the Committee on Production Guidelines for Book Longevity
of the Council of Library Resources.

© 2002 Peter Lang Publishing, Inc., New York

Printed in the United States of America

■ CONTENTS ■

■ INTRODUCTION ■

CHAPTER 1

Global Perspectives, Cultural Studies, and the Construction of a Postmodern Childhood Studies

Gaile S. Cannella, Texas A&M University

Recent genealogical scholarship in a variety of fields, including history, early childhood education, developmental psychology, and cultural studies, has left little doubt that "childhood" is a cultural invention (Wyness, 2000; Cannella, 1997; Burman, 1994; Bloch, 1992, 1987; James & Prout, 1990; Aries, 1962). Truths inscribed as if within those who are young have been and are created through the "science" of psychology, art, literature, and religion, as well as cultural politics, public policy and legislation, judiciary decisions, pedagogical methods, and historical accounts. Within the "child" construct(s), younger human beings are reified as the "other." This othering labels them as innocent (i.e., simple, ignorant, not yet adult), dependent (i.e., needy, unable to speak for themselves, vulnerable, victims), cute (i.e., objects, playthings, to be watched and discussed), and needing control (i.e., savage, lacking discipline, needing structure), to name just a few. Rather than benefiting human beings who are younger, these constructions often place them in positions in which they are labeled and treated as abnormal, lacking agency and competence, without knowledge, and disqualified, especially when representing nondominant diverse backgrounds and cultural values (Burman, 1994). Connected to the cultural construction of "child," these "others" have been further reified through theories of biology, development, experience, and learning, with surveillance and control over them legitimated.

From within this context that separates those who are younger (children) from those who are older (adults), scholars in education and psychology are calling for the recognition of "child" as a social construction and the critical reconceptualization of our beliefs about, and professional relationships with/for, younger human beings. The purpose of *Kidworld: Childhood Studies, Global Perspectives, and Education* is to further discussions of such reconceptualizations by proposing a "postmodern childhood studies." This rethinking will use the critical discourses of cultural studies and ties to postmodern philosophies and women's studies to illustrate possibilities for an interdisciplinary field of childhood studies that recognizes political and cultural context and challenges the privileging of universal truths. The purpose of postmodern childhood studies would be to generate possibilities rather than limitations.

This introductory chapter (1) provides a brief discussion of the work in interdisciplinary and international cultural studies that can be used as critical perspectives from which to rethink, rename, and relive our relationships with younger human beings; (2) overviews possibilities for the construction of postmodern childhood studies; and (3) describes the work of chapter authors as illustrative of specific areas in postmodern childhood studies research—in this case, (a) corporate/market interactions with human beings and (b) diverse/international perspectives on research and childhood issues.

Cultural Studies and Rethinking Childhood

As an international, interdisciplinary field, cultural studies engages in multiple critical cultural discourses and crosses geographic and knowledge boundaries. From a simplistic perspective, cultural studies is the analysis of culture—however, the concept of culture is itself ambiguous and complex, grounded in attitudes and methodologies that accept culture as belonging to people, as unfinished, as always in process, as unthought-of possibilities, and as always contested. A complete discussion of cultural studies involves detailed analysis of cultural criticism, both historically and conceptually. Additionally, cultural studies can be approached using a broad theoretical standpoint or narrowed to specialized perspectives. For purposes of creating postmodern childhood studies discourse(s), this discussion is limited to basic ideas that would illustrate possibilities for engaging in scholarship with/for younger human beings.

Traversing disciplinary boundaries, the broad-based work in cultural studies has drawn from a vast array of critical discourses to examine cultural institutions, icons, and activities, as well as beliefs, values, and products. Influenced by, but also contradicting, hermeneutics, structuralism, and critical theory, cultural studies uses but is not limited to poststructual, postmodern, and post/neocolonial discourses.

A specific position often taken in cultural studies is the examination of power differentials at the level of daily lived experience (Surber, 1998) as tied to specific cultural ways of being. This focus on issues of domination is often related to race, class, gender, and sexual orientation. The specific positions often found in cultural studies serve as practical orientations toward activism. This activist disposition is well illustrated in the British construction of cultural studies that challenged the eliticism of British literary criticism.

Cultural Studies as Pluralistic and Critical

Although their work has been contested from a variety of locations internationally, British scholars over the past fifty years are credited with at least generating the notion of cultural studies and further supporting and embracing poststructural and postmodern orientations, as well as studies of gender, gay/lesbian/bisexuality, and postcolonialism. In the 1950s, Raymond Williams (1961, 1958) constructed a definition of culture that is dynamic within historical context and daily lived experience, a view in which culture is social and tied to the expression of particular values and meanings. Additionally, Richard Hoggart (1958) illustrated ways in which the working class both create culture and evaluate forms of commercial culture. From working-class backgrounds themselves, the work of Hoggart and Williams challenged the dominant view that culture is privileged knowledge. Finally, foreshadowing future concern that in the identification of specified groups, cultural studies constructs views of people as dependent and without agency, E. P. Thompson (1963) proposed that all groups of people function within a context of social construction and human historical relations. Overall, the early culturalists focused on mass media, working-class cultural production, and the construction of social power relations. The majority of early work was supported by the Centre for Contemporary Cultural Studies, founded in 1964 and first directed by Hoggart.

Soon debates raged between culturalists and structuralists, those who believed in operative structures within culture that limit human agency. Stuart Hall (1981), the new director of the center, formed connections between the two perspectives by insisting that individuals can develop awareness of structural cultural conditions and subsequently become agents of political transformation. From this perspective came scholarship that recognized constructs like subculture, hegemony, and resistance, gave voice to the life experiences of the marginalized and disenfranchised, and focused on ways to challenge dominant cultural forms.

Both poststructural and postmodernist orientations are exhibited by contemporary British cultural studies as the field has expanded to include the examination of subjectivity, popular cultural forms including the contestation of those forms, and the creation and appropriation of cultural texts. Cultural studies scholars have even attempted to avoid the establishment of a discipline, fearing that the construction of boundaries would limit pluralism and the recognition of human complexity (Surber, 1998).

Cultural Studies as International and Contesting Colonization

Not surprisingly, international/diverse perspectives have led to criticism of the "Western," and especially English, domination of cultural studies. As examples, Paul Gilroy (1987) addressed the ethnocentric celebration of "Englishness" through the denial of race in British cultural studies. Using feminist critique, Angela McRobbie (1994) called for going beyond the neo-Marxist structuralism evident in the construction of the concept of subculture. Groups around the world (New Zealand, Australia, Canada, and Taiwan) have conducted cultural studies events with themes that challenge self/other positions and address postcolonial formations (Surber, 1998).

Cultural studies is an international field that crosses interdisciplinary, cultural, and geographic boundaries (Nelson & Gaonkar, 1996) and has integrated with a variety of orientations that challenge universal truth. As examples, structural and poststructural work in France rejected sequential forms of historiography, constructed philosophical and methodological avenues for the exploration of popular culture, and even constructed diverse perspectives on time as related to environment, institutions, and individuals

(Foucault, 1978, 1977, 1965; Braudel, 1949). Introduced in France, the scholarship of Russian-born Mikhail Bakhtin has focused on the inclusion of multiple voices in dialogue, as well as the ways in which the dominant culture can be/is subverted through appropriation of hegemonic discourses and the exposure of repressed desire (Bakhtin, 1984). Finally, cultural studies has emerged as a multidirectional critical discourse in the United States. Literary criticism and critique in fields of communication (e.g., media studies) are common in university academic departments. More importantly, tied to a political focus on diversity, identity, and gender studies, examinations of life experiences of marginalized ethnic, racial, and gendered groups have generated a focus on culturally based scholarship.

Cultural Studies and the Construction of Postmodern Childhood Studies

Cultural studies is a multidirectional (philosophically, methodologically, and practically), international field that is oriented toward a belief in social constructivism. However, scholars from a variety of positions have argued for continued pluralism, the avoidance of universalist truth (even social constructivist, relativist) orientations, and conceptualizations that are not limited by the creation of a bounded field. Further, poststructural, feminist, postmodern, and post/neocolonial discourses have been/are increasingly accepted as not only compatible, but necessary. This tentative, interdisciplinary, and critical perspective generates a location from which postmodern childhood studies can emerge, especially in contrast to scientific, individualistic, deterministic childhood studies orientations.

Scholarship in, or related to, cultural studies has, as would be expected, already included younger human beings. Perhaps most familiar to educators is the work of Heath (1983), Steinberg and Kincheloe (1997), McLaren (1989), and Giroux (2000, 1997, 1996). This scholarship ranges from the joint child/adult construction of values, knowledges, and skills in differing cultural settings to the construction of a corporate "kinderculture" and the generation of possibilities for a political public pedagogy. Further examples include Stephen Kline's (1993) focus on the marketing of children's desires through advertising, and analyses of sexist, beauty-oriented messages ever present for girls, as demonstrated by Mary Pipher (1994) and Valerie Walkerdine (1997).

Explorations of childhood and the media and childhood and corporate culture are the most fully developed. Much of the critique of media and portions of the work examining corporate culture as influencing younger human beings fall into the early cultural studies trap that creates children as the dependent "other" without agency. However, the scholarship draws attention to children as human beings who, like the rest of us, are dealing with hegemonic, power-oriented cultural constructions of themselves generated through capitalist economic and technological perspectives. Further, more recent work integrates the complexities of human agency and identity with political, economic complexity (see as examples, Hughes & Mac Naughton, 2001; Thirugnanam, 1996; Davies, 1993) and with issues of nationalism and globalization (see as examples, Ritchie, 2001; Viruru & Cannella, 2001; Holloway & Valentine, 2000; Mankekar, 1997; Koester, 1997).

Clearly, cultural studies and its variety of critical orientations provide multiple avenues for thought and possibility in the conceptualization of postmodern childhood studies. Recognizing that any discourse can be dangerous and requires continual historical and political examination, the discourses of cultural studies can be used to generate a childhood studies that critiques itself, attempts to decolonize, and struggles to construct partnerships with those who are younger in the generation of human possibility.

Postmodern Childhood Studies

Many of us who are grounded in early childhood education or developmental psychology would ask, "What is meant by postmodern childhood studies? Doesn't childhood studies already exist?" The concept as a field is not new, but has existed historically from at least two fairly oppositional directions. Conceptualized through psychology, sociology, and medicine, a focus on "child and family studies" has generally assumed the enlightenment/modernist belief that science can and will reveal the "nature of the child" and the best ways to "meet the child's needs." Although appearing interdisciplinary and resulting in practices such as counseling, school psychology, play therapy, and even early childhood education, the dominant discourses of both child and family studies have assumed that "child" is distinct and separate from "adult" and that science reveals the truth(s) for all human beings, but especially for children. This dominant construction of childhood studies has, to this point, been mainly limited to discourses of modernist science, rejecting scholarship that challenges generalizations and truth orientations.

Literary criticism and related poststructural critique have recently generated a new orientation toward childhood studies. Increasingly, historians are recognizing "childhood" as historical construction and unmasking political agendas that are/have been legitimated "in the name of" or "for the 'good' of children" (Banerjee, 1996; Rose, 1984). Additionally, the inscription of beliefs about childhood through literary and visual representation has been demonstrated (Tartar, 1993; Cunningham, 1991; Cutt, 1979; Coveney, 1967). Visions of younger human beings are used to represent enlightenment concepts and values, for example—the twins "evil" and "innocence." Finally, an extensive body of literature has challenged the belief in childhood as scientific truth, as well as critiqued dualistic, universalist, stage orientations as applied to children, or anyone else (Wyness, 2000; Cannella, 1997; Burman, 1994; Bloch, 1992; Ariès, 1962). From within these critiques, many scholars remain concerned that younger human beings are the largest group of people who have been othered, marginalized, and colonized, and further, that these oppressive practices continue.

Dominant discourses have designated those who are younger as simple, immature, and lacking—as those who are so vulnerable that we would expect them to be victimized—as requiring protection, like the historical female who could not think for herself or perform physically—as requiring control, like the historical dark-skinned savage who lacked white intellect—as those whose colonization is legitimate. A postmodern childhood studies is needed that challenges regimes of truth, recognizes that younger human beings have not generally had a voice(s) in their own creation, and engages in continual critique to avoid self/other dualisms. Postmodern childhood studies would denaturalize childhood, acknowledging the complexity of all our lives.

The legitimacy of a belief in research (even research that reveals multiple or "lower-case" truths) would be continually examined. Certainly, research questions and problems would be reconceptualized. Minimally, research would be no longer "done to" children, but would be in partnership with younger human beings.

Postmodern childhood studies that intersect with recent work in cultural studies could include, but would not be limited to:

1. Examination of the role of underlying societal beliefs, values, conditions, and historical context on constructions of "child" (including politics, power from various locations, ties to marginalized groups such as women, people of color, and colonized peoples);

2. Interdisciplinary critical inquiry that reveals beliefs about those who are younger in various cultural settings and as exhibited across various disciplines (e.g., psychology, medicine, art, literature, law, business, international and ethnic studies) and how these beliefs have inscribed themselves on/into the lives of those who are younger;

3. Analyses of contemporary issues and actual material conditions that have been imposed on those who are younger and tied to concepts of "child" (e.g., language, culture, living conditions such as poverty, care, education, violence, abuse);

4. Examination of beliefs about "childhood" as constructed and perpetuated by societal institutions (e.g., media, education, business, medicine), dominant official knowledge, and popular culture;

5. Examination of the official and hidden agendas and effects of public policy on the lives of those who are younger, including laws, legislation, court decisions, law enforcement, state/federal programs, declarations and position statements, or political rhetoric (Cannella & Viruru, 1999);

6. Exploration of the multitude of modernist beliefs that have been accepted as truth for all human beings, but most readily imposed on those who are younger (e.g., education, research, voice, morality, religion, social justice), including counteridentification and disidentification with dominant beliefs, as well as radical reconceptualization (McLaren & Giarelli, 1995); and

7. Struggles to generate relationships with younger human beings that are equitable, respectful, and increase life opportunities for all involved.

A discourse that would construct a field of "postmodern childhood studies" is, of course, problematic. Any language that focuses on a particular group—in this case those who are younger—whether developmental psychology or postmodern childhood studies, continues to reify "child," perpetuating the belief in an unquestioned category, and limits life, difference, and possibility for the group of people represented (Cannella & Viruru, 1999). Judith Butler has clearly demonstrated this problem in her discussion of women's studies:

> On the one hand, representation serves as the operative term within a political process that seeks to extend visibility and legitimacy...on the other hand, representation is the normative function of language...set(ing)

out in advance the criterion by which subjects themselves are formed...
(Butler, 1990, p. 1).

Just as many have argued in relation to women's studies, gender studies, and ethnic cultural studies, those who are younger have been historically disqualified and invisible (especially within a context of 2,000 years of patriarchy). Eliminating discourses tied to younger human beings, in addition to being most likely impossible, would also run the risk of silencing, disqualifying, and delegitimating them even further. Additionally, Butler (1990) further proposes that to be constituted (within language) does not mean to be determined. Postmodern childhood studies can have as one purpose the disruption of the adult/child dualism that predetermines people and generates power for one group over the other. Postmodern childhood studies recognizes the concept of "child" as political and would use cultural studies and other critical discourses to challenge universalisms, to "redescribe, reconceptualize, and generate new possibilities" (Cannella & Viruru, 1999, p. 19).

Illustrating Postmodern Childhood Studies

The complex ideas discussed by the authors in this book represent the multiple possibilities of postmodern childhood studies in at least two ways. Chapters 2 through 6 are demonstrations of the inscription of the values of corporate culture on the lives of those who are younger. The complexities of individual and group human agencies, identities, and understandings are illustrated as the culture of capitalism is examined. The last group of chapters represent diverse international possibilities generated by postmodern childhood studies, ranging from illustrations of colonization through physical power, postcolonial and poststructural examinations of institutional constructs tied to "childhood" such as quality and standards, and even to constructions of schooling, education, and human rights. Consistent with a postmodern avoidance of "definition," the reader will also note that concepts (e.g., global/globalization, education, voice, rights) are used in a variety of ways to reveal new possibilities, new limitations, and multiple contradictions placed on "the child" as individual, human group member, and even imagined construct.

Childhood Studies and the Values of Corporate Culture

In Chapter 2, *Making Poverty Pay: Children and the 1996 Welfare Law*, Sue Books reveals the ways in which constructions of "child needs" are used to legitimize market-driven "solutions" through legislation in the United States. She proposes that 1996 reform efforts and the removal of "nonprofit" wording from welfare legislation created poverty (especially of children) as an avenue for profit making. (Some scholars would suggest that this has already happened regarding public housing.) Books discusses the ways that "child needs" have become a discourse for channeling public funds into private hands, especially through foster care and general childcare. She calls for public discourses that (a) hold political leaders accountable for recognizing the complexities of actions and inactions, (b) generate education and critique of child/family welfare knowledge, and (c) challenge market constructions of children, families, or any of us. Her proposals are of special significance as the Congress in the United States faces reauthorization of assistance programs. Will "childhood" be used to an even greater degree as a political and corporate pawn?

In *Constructing Childhood in a Corporate World: Cultural Studies, Childhood, and Disney* (Chapter 3), Sumana Kasturi analyzes how corporate consumptive and profit agendas are manifested in attempts to construct "child" through pedagogies of representation and consumption. The context/content of her explorations are the Disney Web service/sites, specifically sites designed for children that were initially called "Kids" and "Daily Blast." She demonstrates a pedagogy of racist and sexist representation through the use of characters, plots, and activities. Further, a pedagogy of consumption is revealed that uses constructions of child "needs" and "experiences" as necessary for the universal "ideal" child. Kasturi recognizes human agency in her discussion but also demonstrates ways that consumerism is emerging as an unquestioned public desire.

Continuing the discussion of a construction of market desire, Dominic Scott examines the "Beanie Baby" phenomenon in *What Are Beanie Babies Teaching Our Children?* (Chapter 4). Explaining that corporate society views children as both individual consumers and people who influence the buying of others, Scott critiques marketing strategies, globalization, basic economics, and even a form of tourist multiculturalism that is "taught" to children through the marketing of Beanie Babies. Multiple questions can be raised through this analysis. One example includes the possibility that members of corporate culture view children as those that can be manipulated, just like their parents and other adults, but also as people who exhibit agency and make decisions regarding purchases. Does this view limit children more than dominant views of innocence, incompetence, and immaturity? The complexity of multiple and changing identities and views of human beings (as referred to earlier in this chapter) would propose that either explanation places a simplistic, determinist, even dualistic limitation on human beings. Does examining childhood and corporate culture limit, rather than generate, possibilities for those who are younger? But what of the question (and motive) of profit?

In Chapter 5, *The Complex Politics of McDonald's and the New Childhood: Colonizing Kidworld*, Joe Kincheloe uses an analysis of the role of McDonald's as a producer of corporate (profit-driven) knowledge in a media culture to explore the creation of a "new childhood." He illustrates the importance of recognizing and researching corporate power dynamics as related to current public discourses of "child." He proposes the conscious construction of a progressive politics of childhood which involves media and power literacy for children as well as adults that would continually examine power agendas that generate and support particular knowledge(s). Further, this progressive politics and related pedagogy would problematize bodies of knowledge that define and/or reveal "truths about children," viewing them as potentially more advanced and less vulnerable than adults (in addition to questioning concepts of progress and vulnerability). All of the work related to young and old alike would, however, recognize corporate (and other) cultural pedagogies that play increasingly important roles in our daily lives.

The final chapter that deals with childhood and the culture of capitalism could be considered a visual, as well as verbal, study of consumer messages to children juxtaposed with feminist, poststructural thought. In *A Toy Story: The Object(s) of American Childhood* (Chapter 6), Janice Jipson and Nicholas Paley present a vertical dance, a type of poem that illustrates for all of us the multiple value issues tied to profit, consumerism, and representation for young and old alike.

Childhood Studies and Diverse Postmodernisms

The final chapters in this volume represent perspectives from Korea, India, and Australia, as well as languages around the world, displaying the diversity of issues to which postmodern childhood studies is related and can include. In Chapter 7, Mee-Ryoung Shon describes the complex history of Korean views of young children. In *Korean Early Childhood Education: Colonization and Resistance*, Shon explains the simultaneous colonization of Korea, physically by Japan and religiously by Western missionaries. However, since the Japanese refused to allow Korean language and culture to be used in schools, Koreans used the kindergartens of Western missionaries to avoid cultural genocide, performing and enacting Korean language, beliefs, and culture, and sharing these enactments within their communities. This diverse history reveals the complexities of history, politics, and even the need for survival in the worlds and constructions of those who are younger.

Radhika Viruru expands the conversation by questioning the Euro-American notion of "voice" (and research tied to that concept) in *Postcolonial Ethnography: An Indian Perspective on Voice and Young Children* (Chapter 8). In her discussion of qualitative research in a preschool in India, Viruru demonstrates the ethnocentric bias reflected in the construction of the concept of voice, demonstrating Gayatri Spivak's point that speaking belongs to a history and structure of domination. She illustrates how the concept of research, and hearing the voices of others, colonizes Indian teachers, parents, and children. This post/neocolonial perspective results in a major issue for an "academic" field, even if that field would be a borderless postmodern childhood studies: Can we construct research that does not engage in "othering," in creating objects of our gaze? Besides avoiding truth orientations and generalizations, perhaps our constructions of childhood studies research should continually involve rethinking and reconceptualization.

In her research, *A National System of Childcare Accreditation: Quality Assurance or a Technique of Normalization?* (Chapter 9), Susan Grieshaber demonstrates how concepts such as accreditation (as applied to programs for young children in Australia) can become forms of regulation that narrowly define parenting, child experiences, and educational curriculum. In a context in which we would celebrate and appreciate diversity, standardized regulations provide the illusions of both quality and equality while imposing dominant cultural norms on everyone. Divergent ways of dealing with issues or multiple perspectives for viewing the world are silenced. The national, not to mention global, imposition of one standard form can very easily result in placing narrow limitations on everyone.

Possibilities within diversity are well illustrated in Chapter 10. In *Children's Linguistic/Cultural Human Rights*, Lourdes Díaz Soto and René Quesada Inces explore the diverse ways that communities around the world support the acquisition and development of multilingualism in children. They illustrate how English-only movements, an example of one set of standards often common in the United States, deny rights to children. The authors demonstrate multiple options for the equitable and just treatment of linguistic diversity with children, expressing the hope that children themselves will lead in the movement away from oppressive ways of living and interacting with others.

Finally, in Chapter 11, *(Euro-American Constructions of) Education of Children (and Adults) Around the World: A Postcolonial Critique*, Radhika Viruru and I attempt to explore the "most taken-for-granted" modernist belief tied to constructions of child. Usually, even the most "liberal," "radical," "multicultural" educator does not question education as a construct. We attempt to show how education is rooted in colonialist bias and assumptions regarding enlightened, individual intellect and the controlling of savage behavior (the bodies of those who are younger). While many view education as broadening, postmodern childhood studies would approach the concept by considering the life assumptions of those who would educate, the political agendas tied to education, and the knowledge that is not included in educational philosophies and practices.

As with the emerging variety of perspectives that challenge universal truths but engage in a modernist struggle for equity, diversity, and understanding across and among peoples, postmodern childhood studies opens doors for multiple possibilities and new ways of thinking about our lives with everyone, but especially with those who are younger. Challenging fields such as early childhood education, developmental psychology, medicine, or sociology is not easy and may be professionally problematic. Giving up "child development" as a truth may be confusing. Questioning what one thinks one knows (e.g., about a five-year-old, about learning content for children, about how to interact with those who are younger) may be threatening. Deconstructing ideas may (at times) be depressing. Recognizing that younger human beings do not escape the complexities of society may involve examinations of power that are acutely uncomfortable. But childhood studies that would reveal complexity, diversity, and possibility is well worth the discomfort. We hope that you, the reader, will join with the authors of this book in exploring possibilities for thinking about how we live and work with those who are younger, how our lives are tied together, and how we struggle to share and appreciate our diverse values, cultures, and selves while addressing issues of equity, justice, and opportunity.

■ References

Ariès, P. (1962). *Centuries of childhood–A social history of family life*. New York: Knopf.

Bakhtin, M. (1984). *Rabelais and his world*. Bloomington, IN: Indiana University Press.

Banerjee, J. (1996). *Through the northern gate*. New York: Peter Lang.

Bloch, M. N. (1987). Becoming scientific and professional: An historical perspective on the aims and effects of early education. In Popkewitz, T. S. (Ed.), *The formation of school subjects* (pp. 25–62). Basingstoke, England: Falmer.

Bloch, M. N. (1992). Critical perspectives on the historical relationship between child development and early childhood education research. In Kessler, S. & B. B. Swadener (Eds.), *Reconceptualizing the early childhood curriculum: Beginning the dialogue* (pp. 3–20). New York: Teachers College Press.

Braudel, F. (1949). *The Mediterranean and the Mediterranean world in the age of Phillip II*. New York: Harper & Row.

Burman, E. (1994). *Deconstructing developmental psychology*. New York: Routledge.

Butler, J. (1990). *Gender trouble: Feminism and the subversion of identity*. London: Routledge.

Cannella, G.S. (1997). *Deconstructing early childhood education: Social justice and revolution*. New York: Peter Lang.

Cannella, G.S., & Viruru, R. (1999). Generating possibilities for the construction of childhood studies. *Journal of Curriculum Theorizing*, 15(1): 13–22.

Coveney, P. (1967). *The image of childhood: The individual and society: A study of the theme in English literature*. Harmondsworth: Penguin.

Cunningham, H. (1991). *The children of the poor: Representations of childhood since the seventeenth century*. Oxford: Basil Blackwell.

Cutt, M.N. (1979). *Ministering angels: A study of nineteenth–century evangelical religious writing for children*. Wormeley, Herts: Five Owls Press.

Davies, B. (1993). *Shards of glass: Children reading and writing beyond gendered identities*. North Sydney, NSW: Allen & Unwin.

Foucault, M. (1965). *Madness and civilization*. Trans. R. Howard. New York: Pantheon.

Foucault, M. (1977). *Discipline and punish*. Trans. A. Sheridan. New York: Pantheon.

Foucault, M. (1978). *The history of sexuality, Vol. I: An introduction*. Trans. R. Hurley. New York: Pantheon.

Gilroy, P. (1987). *There ain't no black in the Union Jack*. London: Huchinson.

Giroux, H. (1996). *Fugitive culture*. New York: Routledge.

Giroux, H. (1997). *Channel surfing: Racism, the media, and the deconstruction of today's youth.* New York: St. Martin's Press.

Giroux, H. (2000). *Stealing innocence: Youth, corporate power, and the politics of culture.* New York: St. Martin's Press.

Hall, S. (1981). *Culture, ideology, and social process.* London: Open University Press.

Heath, S. B. (1983). *Ways with words: Language, life, and work in communities and classrooms.* Cambridge, England: Cambridge University Press.

Hoggart, R. (1958). *The uses of literacy.* Fair Lawn, NJ: Essential Books.

Holloway, S., & Valentine, G. (2000). Corked hats and coronation street: British and New Zealand children's imaginative geographies of the Other. *Childhood: A Global Journal of Child Research, 7*(3): 335–357.

Hughes, P., & Mac Naughton, G. (2001). Fractured or manufactured: Gendered identities and culture in the early years. In Grieshaber, S. and Cannella, G. S. (Eds.), *Embracing identities in early childhood education: Diversity and possibilities* (pp. 114–130). New York: Teachers College Press.

James, A., & Prout, A. (Eds.) (1990). *Constructing and reconstructing childhood: Contemporary issues in the sociological study of childhood.* Basingstoke, Hants: Falmer.

Kline, S. (1993). *Out of the garden: Toys, TV, and children's culture in the age of marketing.* London: Verso Press.

Koester, D. (1997). Childhood in national consciousness and national consciousness in childhood. *Childhood: A Global Journal of Child Research, 4*(1): 125–142.

Mankekar, P. (1997). To whom does Ameena belong: Towards a feminist analysis of childhood and nationhood in contemporary India. *Feminist Review, 56*: 26–60.

McLaren, P. (1989). *Life in schools.* White Plains, NY: Longman.

McLaren, P. L., & Giarelli, J. M. (1995). Introduction: Critical theory and educational research. In McLaren, P. L. & Giarelli, J. M. (Eds.), *Critical theory and educational research* (pp. 1–22). Albany, NY: State University of New York Press.

McRobbie, A. (1994). *Postmodernism and popular culture.* London: Routledge.

Nelson, C., & Gaonkar, D. P. (Eds.) (1996). *Disciplinarity and dissent in cultural studies.* New York: Routledge.

Pipher, M. (1994). *Reviving Ophelia: Saving the selves of adolescent girls.* New York: Ballantine Books.

Ritchie, J. (2001). Reflections on collectivism in early childhood teaching in Aotearoa/New Zealand. In Grieshaber, S. andCannella, G. S. (Eds.). *Embracing identities in early childhood education: Diversity and possibilities* (pp. 133–147). New York: Teachers College Press.

Rose, J. (1984). *The case of Peter Pan or the impossibility of children's fiction.* London: Macmillan.

Steinberg, S. R., & Kincheloe, J. L. (Eds.) (1997). *Kinderculture: The corporate construction of childhood.* Boulder, CO: Westview Press.

Surber, J. P. (1998*). Culture and critique: An introduction to the critical discourses of cultural studies.* Boulder, CO: Westview Press.

Tartar, M. (1993). *Off with their heads! Fairy tales and the culture of childhood.* Princeton: Princeton University Press.

Thirugnanam, J. (1996). *Pointed noses and yellow hair: Deconstructing children's writing on race and ethnicity in Hawaii.* Paper presented at the Reconceptualizing Early Childhood Education: Research, Theory, and Practice Sixth Interdisciplinary Conference, Madison, WI.

Thompson, E. P. (1963). *The making of the English working class.* New York: Pantheon.

Viruru, R., & Cannella, G.S. (2001). Postcolonial ethnography, young children, and voice. In Grieshaber, S. and Cannella, G. S. (Eds.), *Embracing identities in early childhood education: Diversity and possibilities* (pp. 158–172). New York: Teachers College Press.

Walkerdine, V. (1997). *Daddy's girl: Young girls and popular culture.* Cambridge: Harvard University Press.

Williams, R. (1958). *Culture and society.* New York: Columbia University Press.

Williams, R. (1961). *The long revolution.* New York: Columbia University Press.

Wyness, M. G. (2000). *Contesting childhood.* New York: Falmer Press.

■ PART I ■

Childhood Studies and the Values of Corporate Culture

CHAPTER 2

Making Poverty Pay:
Children and the 1996 Welfare Law

Sue Books, State University of New York at New Paltz

As parenting has become increasingly privatized and costly (Hewlett & West, 1998), children are regarded not only as public investments (Grubb & Lazerson, 1982), but also as public liabilities—a perception that goes hand in hand with policies designed to align their needs with market-driven "solutions." The new welfare law, the Personal Responsibility and Work Opportunity Reconciliation Act of 1996 (Public Law 104–193), is an example of public policy grounded in this perception. The welfare law, which abolished AFDC (Aid to Families with Dependent Children) and its guarantee of some minimal public assistance to economically needy families, has dramatically increased the need for childcare and foster care; and the market (not surprisingly) is responding. In this sense, the welfare law has recruited children into the market-driven project of making poverty pay.

In the discussion that follows, I comment on the present-day social context of children and families, look at how Public Law 104–193 has affected childcare and foster care, then reflect on the moral and social significance of society's valuation of children in market terms. Although neither privatized childcare nor privatized foster care is new, these practices are newly profitable — childcare because the demand now so far outstrips the supply, and foster care because restrictions on federal funding have been relaxed. Translating children's socially constructed needs into private dollars in this way sends children down a potentially dangerous path. What's good for the market may at times be good for children too, but not necessarily.

Child Poverty and Family Economics

Children's needs are being situated in the market in new ways at a time when many families are struggling economically, despite reports of almost unprecedented prosperity. Although the average income of the wealthiest 5 percent of families increased $96,000 (adjusted for inflation) between 1979 and 1998, the poorest 20 percent of families lost $686 in real annual income during this time (Children's Defense Fund, 2000, p. xiii). Almost one in every five children (13.5 million) is now growing up in poverty, and one in every twelve children is growing up in extreme poverty — that is, in families with incomes of less than half the federal poverty line, or about $6,500 for a family of three (Children's Defense Fund, 2000, pp. xi, xxviii). Poor children increasingly are suffering this level of desperation. More than 5 million children in the United States lived in families with incomes of less than half the federal poverty line in 1998, a 91 percent increase since 1976 (Children's Defense Fund, 2000, p. 2). If present trends continue, one in every three children born in 2000 will spend at least a year in poverty by his or her eighteenth birthday (Children's Defense Fund, 2000, p. 1).

Young children, especially young children of color, have been particularly abandoned in the rising economic tide that has not lifted all boats. Whereas just over 17 percent of all children and youth six to seventeen years old are living in poverty, more than 20 percent of all children younger than six are poor. The rate of poverty for children of color (Black and Hispanic) is almost double the rate for white children (Children's Defense Fund, 2000, p. 6).

These numbers have profound consequences. According to one national study, low-income children are at least 50 percent more likely to die during childhood than other children (Sherman, 1997, p. 5). Poor children also

are nearly 90% more likely than nonpoor children to be born weighing too little and 80% more likely to be born too soon. They are three times more likely to be reported in fair or poor health. More than one million low-income young children have anemia, meaning their red blood cells cannot carry enough oxygen to their bodies. Poor 5- to 7-year-olds have…nearly triple the odds of stunted growth, compared with otherwise similar children from well-to-do homes (Sherman, 1997, p. 5).

Poor children have twice as many cavities and twice as much dental pain as wealthier children, but only half as many visits to dentists (Children's Defense Fund, 2000, p. 14).

Statistics on child poverty can, of course, be read as statistics on family poverty, although they often are not—as if poor children did not live in poor families and as if poor parents could, if they only would, "protect" their children from poverty by getting a job. In fact, 74 percent of all poor children live in families in which one or more of the adults worked all or part of the year in 1998 (Children's Defense Fund, 2000, p. xi). Nevertheless, and despite the general economic prosperity of these times, poor families continue to struggle to secure such basics as food and shelter. Between 1997 and 1998, after a decline the year before, the proportion of children experiencing hunger or worrying about food jumped from 14.6 percent to 19.7 percent (U.S. Department of Agriculture, 1999; cited in Children's Defense Fund, 2000, p. 10). In 1997 only three low-cost housing units existed for every ten renters (including families) with incomes of less than $15,000 a year (U.S. Department of Housing and Urban Development, 1999; cited in Children's Defense Fund, 2000, p. 12). The typical (median) poor household now spends 46 percent of its income on housing (U.S. Department of Housing and Urban Development, 1999; cited in Children's Defense Fund, 2000, p. 11).

Although many people have applauded the sharp drop in welfare caseloads in the wake of the 1996 legislation, what the numbers mean is unclear. Between August 1996 when the law was enacted and June 1999, the Temporary Assistance to Needy Families (TANF) caseload declined by 44 percent nationwide as 5.3 million children and adults lost assistance (Children's Defense Fund, 2000, p. 19). According to a recent study by the Children's Defense Fund and the National Coalition for the Homeless (1998), "Although more families are moving from welfare to work, many of them are faring worse than before. Many former recipients lack food, needed medical care, and stable housing. Among recipients who find jobs, 71% earn below the three-person poverty level." A study conducted by the Urban Institute (and shared with President Clinton before he signed the welfare bill) estimated the law would push 2.6 million more people, including 1.1 million more children, into poverty. A subsequent study showed 10 percent of all families in the United States, including 8 million families with children, will lose income as a result of the legislation (Edelman, 1997, pp. 45–46).

In New York City, welfare caseworkers have been instructed to discourage people from applying for benefits at all and only secondarily to help them find employment. In terms of cutting the welfare rolls, period, the strategy appears to be working well:

> People who push through the smudged glass doors are told to look for jobs, not welfare, and to lean on relatives, not city charity. Those who insist on seeking public assistance must hunt for as many as 20 jobs before getting a formal interview. And two months after workers began delivering the new message in Brooklyn and at another office in Queens, the number of welfare applications there has plummeted (Swarns, 1998, June 22, p. A1).

Perhaps some who are systematically discouraged from assistance are finding decent jobs; more likely, they are simply languishing in poverty (Swarns, 1998, June 22).

As weak as the existing social support structure for children and families is, worrisome signs suggest a harsher future. Despite the booming economy,

> [T]he economic prospects for most young people have been deteriorating for a generation. Entry-level wages for male high school graduates…fell 28% from 1973 to 1997, in real dollars. (College graduates did less badly, but they also lost ground—and it is crucial to remember that traditional four-year college graduates remain a distinct minority of workers.) (Finnegan, 1998, p. A21).

Large-scale social shifts in many ways are being accomplished on the backs of the younger generation. "More and more young people are being shunted into the ranks of the working poor. Demand may be high at the moment for software programmers and management consultants, but it is higher for janitors and cashiers" (Finnegan, 1998, p. A21).

The educational prospects for many young people also are diminishing. The "savage inequalities" in the distribution of educational resources (books, computers, safe buildings, good teachers, dollars per pupil, and so on), which Jonathan Kozol documented in 1991, persist. Dozens of lawsuits challenging inequities in school funding have been filed in states across the nation in recent decades—some lost, some tied up in court for years, and some won. Nevertheless, a large-scale nationwide study found *disparities* in revenues between wealthy and poor districts were virtually the same in 1992 as they had been in 1972 (Evans, Murray, & Schwab, 1997, p. 16). Poor school districts may be getting more state support than they used to, but the funding gap between rich and poor districts has not changed appreciably. "Ghetto schooling" continues to come with the territory of ghettoization, the forces of which are steamrolling ahead (Anyon, 1997; Orfield, 1997). What, if any, educational floor will be guaranteed to all children is unclear in these turbulent times of charter schools, vouchers, various privatization schemes, and, given the enduring disparities in funding, what amounts to publicly subsidized private education for many well-to-do students.

Meanwhile, colleges and universities are moving away from the provision of need-based scholarships and toward more competitive pursuit of the most sought-after students (Bronner, 1998) — with predictable consequences: "These days, almost the entire enrollment rate increase is from the middle income and above. The poor are increasingly restricted to community colleges, even being squeezed out of four-year public institutions" (Morton Schapiro, quoted in Bronner, 1998, p. A1). Harvard University's Dean of Admissions, William Fitzsimmons, offers a different perspective: "I think from the student's point of view, it is a good thing. This is America. This is a market" (quoted in Bronner, 1998, p. A1). True as this may be, it is important to recognize that markets are restrained or unleashed through public policymaking and institutional decision making. What role the ethos of the market plays in shaping the social and educational experience of young people depends entirely on what role it is allowed to play.

Things were different, for example, in the legendary 1950s — a time remembered or imagined (especially by the white middleclass) to have been a golden age of moral coherence when parents parented, children respected their elders, and the society as a whole prospered. Significantly, public policies at that time strongly supported the work of parenting, at least within a traditional middle-class, nuclear family structure. "In that decade, tax policy, education policy, and housing policy worked together in powerful ways to create a society in which families were impressively strong and children flourished" (Hewlett & West, 1998, p. 98). A tax code developed in the late 1940s and early 1950s cut married wage earners' tax liability in half, offered significant exemptions (worth $6,500 in 1996 dollars) for each dependent, and provided sizable deductions for interest paid on home mortgages. Hence, "as the fifties dawned, the United States could legitimately claim a powerful pro-family tax code…. The personal exemption underwrote a sizable portion of the costs of child-rearing, and the tax code worked with other government programs to create a generous supply of low-cost high-quality family housing" (Hewlett & West, 1998, p. 99). Added to this was the GI Bill of Rights, a "de facto family support policy" that provided veterans with unemployment insurance, educational opportunities, medical coverage, and housing subsidies that enabled many young parents to live in a relatively stable social environment (Hewlett & West, 1998, p. 101).

Starting in the 1960s, these pro-family policies were dismantled. Between 1969 and 1983, the income tax rate remained relatively unchanged for single people and married couples without children, but rose an average of 43 percent for married couples with two children, and 223 percent for couples with four children (Hewlett & West, 1998, p. 104). Housing policy in recent decades also has hurt low-income families with children. "As of 1996, the federal government had essentially abandoned the project of making housing affordable for low-income families" (Hewlett & West, 1998, p. 105). New funds subsequently were appropriated. However, in 1997 more than 13 million renters, including families, with incomes of less than $15,000 a year competed for fewer than 4 million subsidized housing units (U.S. Department of Housing and Urban Development, 1999; cited in Children's Defense Fund, 2000, p. 12).

Public policies obviously can help or hurt children and their families. As unacceptably high as the child poverty rate in the United States is, without the Earned Income Tax Credit, 2.3 million more children would have been poor in 1998 (Children's Defense Fund, 2000, p. 17). As often noted, children do not vote and in this sense lack a political voice. Perhaps less often recognized is that although many of their parents do vote (or could), parents as a group lack advocates on either end of the political spectrum. Sylvia Ann Hewlett and Cornel West (1998) make the case well: The Right, with its blanket faith in the market, has ignored the necessary economic foundations of parenting, and the Left, in its often uncritical championing of individual rights and freedoms, has downplayed the need for affirming responsibilities to others, such as children. Whereas conservatives have championed the market as a panacea for any and everything, which hurts children, liberals have championed individual rights over responsibilities, which also hurts children (pp. 92–97).

All this is to say that without the support of public policy, children without financially secure parents are not being groomed for lives in the mainstream of society. Nutritious food in adequate supply, safe homes, good schools, quality health care, hope for the future grounded in realistic prospects — children in poor families cannot count on any of these things. In many ways this looks like the social triage Richard Rubenstein warned about fifteen years ago. However, I think the metaphor of social triage oversimplifies the complexity of our times. Poor children in the United States exemplify what Rubenstein (1983) calls a "surplus population," but they are a population that nevertheless is being integrated back into the society — not as the cliched "future leaders of America," but rather as commodities. This brings me to the 1996 welfare legislation.

Public Law 104-193

The Personal Responsibility and Work Opportunity Reconciliation Act of 1996 marked a fundamental shift in social welfare policy in the United States. The law cut $54 billion of support for programs that provided assistance to low-income families, including AFDC (created in 1935 as part of the Social Security Act), JOBS (a work and training program), and Emergency Assistance (a program providing emergency help to families with children). States now receive fixed block grants, known as TANF (Temporary Assistance to Needy Families), to be distributed on a first-come, first-served basis — in most cases for no more than two consecutive years if the parent does not comply with stringent work requirements. Consequently, being poor no longer automatically qualifies children or families for assistance. Help is limited to five years over the span of a lifetime, and states have the option of setting even stricter limits. In the spring of 2000, families in eighteen states had begun to exhaust time-limited benefits (Children's Defense Fund, 2000, p. 14).

The preamble to the legislation states that it is intended to address the social "crisis" of marital dissolution and births to single mothers. Accordingly, the law makes no provisions for direct support to families in the form of childcare services, parent education programs, or preschools that parents may choose or not choose to use, and no provisions for income supports, unemployment insurance, maternity or paternity leaves, or education allowances (Finkelstein, Mourad, & Doner, 1998, p. 172). The message comes through loud and clear: Mothers unattached to male breadwinners can expect little support in their dual roles as parent and wage earner, despite the consequences for children.

The welfare legislation rests on an interpretation of the social crisis of our time (broken marriages and single motherhood, ostensibly encouraged by the provision of public assistance) that flies in the face of solid research with which Congressional leaders were familiar. The General Accounting Office had released a study in early 1987 reporting "no conclusive evidence to support the prevailing common beliefs that welfare discourages individuals from working, breaks up two-parent families, or affects the childbearing rates of unmarried women, even young unmarried women" (Wilson, 1996, p. 163). As William Julius Wilson (1996) argues, "Although these conclusions should [have] come as no surprise to poverty researchers familiar with the empirical literature, they should have generated a stir among members of Congress" (p. 164). The information was, however, ignored.

Unlike earlier federal legislation affecting children, the 1996 welfare law invokes a rhetoric neither of child protection nor of child rights. Rather, through its language and regulatory provisions, poor children become visible "as the progeny of a morally profligate class of unmarried, undeserving, sexually promiscuous men and women in need of moral reclamation, social reconstruction, publicly administered discipline and paid work" (Finkelstein et al., 1998, p. 172). Portraying children and parents in this way, the welfare law

> disjoins the interests of children from those of their families in quite the same way as traditional child-saving legislative strategies have done—by declaring families to be morally bankrupt and by deploying the disciplinary apparatus of the federal government to impose work requirements, to define who is undeserving and who is not, and to channel public expenditures into services designed to replace families with morally and politically sanctioned substitutes (Finkelstein et al., 1998, p. 172).

The law, in other words, offers a rationale as well as specific provisions for directing the needs of children toward market-generated services. In portraying families "as interdependent economic entities rather than as sites for the rearing and protection of children" and childcare services "as commodities to be purchased and businesses to be regulated rather than as safe havens for children," the law invites us to think in market terms of supply, demand, and profitability (Finkelstein et al., 1998, 173). Focused neither on children's/family's vulnerabilities as human beings nor on their rights as citizens in a democracy, but rather on their needs interpreted in the terms of the market, Public Law 104–193 transforms children into commodities in a broader economy of services.

Childcare: A Multimillion-Dollar Shortfall

The 1996 welfare law imposes work requirements on most recipients of public assistance in the absence of any guarantee that suitable childcare will be available. Recognizing that new work requirements would increase the demand for childcare dramatically, Congress allocated additional monies for subsidized childcare and stipulated that parents with children younger than 6-years-old should not be penalized if they fail to meet work requirements because they cannot find or afford childcare. However, the childcare funds fall far short of the projected need. The Office of Management and Budget predicts a $2.4 billion shortfall if all states meet their "work targets" (Children's Defense Fund, 1996). Furthermore, the promise of understanding if parents of young children cannot find affordable care appears to be empty.

Under the old law, families receiving public assistance were guaranteed the childcare they needed to participate in work or training programs. Former recipients could count on a year of transitional help with childcare costs if they left welfare for a job, and families likely to need public assistance if their childcare costs were not subsidized were eligible for assistance (Children's Defense Fund, 1996). The 1996 law eliminates these programs and provides block grants to states instead. However, states for the most part are not following through. Many are now "sitting on billions of unspent welfare and child health dollars" (Children's Defense Fund, 2000, p. xi). New York, for example,

> in the four years since the overhaul of the nation's welfare laws, has taken at least $1 billion given to it by the federal government for new anti-poverty programs and used it instead to indirectly finance huge tax cuts and other programs that appeal to middle-class voters, according to government and private estimates (Hernandez, 2000, p. A1).

Nationwide, "billions of dollars intended to fund welfare-to-work initiatives remain unspent and available for investment" (Children's Defense Fund, 2000, p. 14).

Nevertheless, the needs are clear. The demand for childcare now far outstrips the supply—with predictable consequences: prohibitive costs, competition for too few subsidized slots, poor quality. Full-day childcare costs $4,000 to $10,000 a year, which makes it at least as expensive as tuition at a public college (Children's Defense Fund, 2000, p. 48). In selected urban areas in forty-nine states, the average cost of childcare for a four-year-old now exceeds the average tuition at a public college. In selected urban areas in fifty states, if both parents in a two-parent family work full-time at minimum wage, they have to spend more than 30 percent of their income to buy childcare at the average price (Children's Defense Fund, 1998b, p. 1). Given the inadequate funding for childcare, parents of only about one in every ten children eligible for assistance under federal law is getting it (U.S. Department of Health and Human Services, 1999; cited in Children's Defense Fund, 2000, p. 48). With too few subsidized slots available, parents below and just above the poverty line are pitted against each other in a competition few can win (Rimer, 1997). Given the overwhelming demand as well as "woefully inadequate" and often poorly enforced health and safety standards, the quality of available childcare varies tremendously. According to a 1996 report by the Carnegie Corporation, childcare and early education services "have so long been neglected that they now constitute some of the worst services for children in Western society" (Children's Defense Fund, 1998a, p. 40).

Although the 1996 welfare law specifies that parents of a child younger than six should not be penalized for failing to meet work requirements if the problem is lack of affordable childcare, incentives to states to reduce their welfare rolls mediate against such flexibility. New York City is a case in point, if also perhaps a worst-case example:

> Two years ago, in the largest program of its kind in the nation, New York City began pushing thousands of single mothers on welfare into workfare jobs with a reassuring promise enshrined in state law: for every woman who needed it, city officials would find two choices of safe, free childcare. Women without someone to watch their children would be excused from work without penalty.
>
> But that promise has gone largely unfulfilled. A severe shortage of childcare for the poor, along with the city's failure to finance more care, has left many caseworkers unable—or unwilling—to help. [P]ressured by city officials to move increasing numbers of women into work, some caseworkers threaten their clients' very livelihood—their welfare checks— bullying some bewildered women into leaving the children in substandard care.
>
> [L]eft with little of the help promised by government, three-quarters of the mothers in workfare rely on unlicensed baby sitters, who are also paid by the city. The lucky ones enlist trusted relatives or close friends. The less fortunate leave their sons and daughters in crowded, dirty apartments with caretakers they barely know (Swarns, 1998, April 14, p. A1).

New York City now lacks childcare spaces for 61 percent of the children whose mothers are required to participate in workfare (Swarns, 14 April 1998, p. A1).

Finally, given the demand, the lack of oversight, and the pressure — passed from states to cities to caseworkers to desperate mothers — to find somewhere, anywhere, to leave the children, the market invites social stratification along familiar lines. Many children of the "well-to-do" experience childcare filled with abundant resources, licensed for safety, and open to educational/care possibilities that increase life opportunities. For many children of the poor and the near-poor, childcare is uncertain, unpredictable, or unavailable. Nevertheless, the need for childcare services is inscribed in public policy, created by the work requirements contained in the 1996 law. Consider also the expanding need and potential profitability of foster care created by these requirements.

Foster Care: "Helter-Skelter" Growth

Shortly before Christmas 1994, Speaker of the House Newt Gingrich provoked a national uproar by championing a bill that would have let states use federal welfare money for orphanages. The critics invoked Charles Dickens. Mr. Gingrich countered with *Boys Town*, the 1938 movie starring Spencer Tracy. Political cartoonists had a field day, and by the time President Clinton denounced the plan as "dead wrong," Mr. Gingrich was protesting that he had been misunderstood. If that was the Great Orphanage Debate, orphanages, it seemed, had lost (Bernstein, 11 May 1997, p. E5).

But the question remained: What about children whose parents, once denied public assistance, would be unable to support them? "Now it turns out that a multibillion-dollar answer lurks in the details of the sweeping welfare law signed [in 1996]: Modern day orphanages, run for profit at Government expense" (Bernstein, 11 May 1997, p. E5).

In all the debate and grandstanding leading up to the legislation that dismantled six decades of social welfare policy, an important change in the rules and regulations governing foster care apparently was overlooked. When the final papers were signed, the word "nonprofit" had been deleted from an old section of child welfare law. This threw the door open for profit-making organizations to compete for the billions of dollars the federal government spends each year to subsidize the care of children removed from homes judged unfit. "Children living with a parent, no matter how poor, can no longer count on government help. But the same children, if placed in an institution or foster home, carry with them an open-ended stream of Federal revenue" (Bernstein, 11 May 1997, p. E5).

A record 547,000 children are now in foster care (Children's Defense Fund, 2000, p. 86), a program that was growing five times faster and costing the federal government eleven times more per child than AFDC when it was abolished (Bernstein, 4 May 1997). The number of children in foster care has increased by 35 percent since 1990, and almost certainly will continue to swell as parents unable to find jobs or childcare lose any public assistance (Children's Defense Fund, 2000, p. 86). So too will the for-profit interest in this population of children almost certainly continue to grow.

> That small alteration [deletion of the qualifying "nonprofit"] is swelling the wave of business interest in the poor that has swept national corporations traded on Wall Street as they move deeper into sectors traditionally left to religious and philanthropic groups, public agencies and mom-and-pop operations. The companies that stand to benefit from the one-word change include managed mental health care giants, like the $1 billion Magellan Health Services, and youth-care chains like the 2,500-bed Youth Services International, started five years ago by the founder of the quick oil-change franchise Jiffy Lube (Bernstein, 4 May 1997, p. A1).

Considerable dollars are at stake because the pool of federal funds for the foster care program, unlike that for other child welfare programs (such as family preservation and support services), is uncapped. "Another example of how the welfare overhaul has opened up opportunities in the business of poverty," says journalist Nina Bernstein (4 May 1997, p. A1). "A profit-making feeding frenzy. These corporations are growing almost helter-skelter, without people who know the field or know kids," says Paul DeMuro, a former commissioner of children in Pennsylvania (quoted in Bernstein, 4 May 1997, p. A1).

Potential conflicts of interest abound. For-profit organizations have a financial obligation to put the interests of shareholders first. Although states are supposed to look out for children and monitor their care, "It's the fox guarding the chicken coop," says Mark Courtney of the Institute for Research on Poverty. "The public agencies don't have their act together well enough to hand over a huge chunk of money to people who have an incentive to maximize profits at the expense of the children in care" (quoted in Bernstein, 4 May 1997, p. A1).

Public agencies, furthermore, have their own stake in a large and growing foster care population: "Each case of child abuse or neglect unlocks significant state and federal funds, not only for the child welfare agency directly concerned but for a satellite ring of substitute caregivers, therapists, and family court lawyers. The more kids in foster care, the greater the revenues of the county" (Hewlett & West, 1998, p. 119). "The funding system gives child welfare bureaucracies incentives to keep even free-to-be-adopted kids in state care," says Conna Craig of the Institute for Children (quoted in Hewlett & West, 1998, p. 119).

Just as foster children lack adequate protection from the market, so, too, in many ways do their parents who may be unable to hide the family poverty often regarded as child neglect (Hewlett & West, 1998; Mack, 1 December 1997; Wexler, 1990). "The broad definitions of neglect used in most state statutes are virtually definitions of poverty. Children are taken away because the family doesn't have a place to live. Children are taken away because the food stamps have run out. Children are taken away because the family can't pay for heat" (Wexler, 1990, p. 18). Scholars estimate that 95 percent or more of the cases labeled as child neglect would be described more accurately as family poverty (Wexler, 1990, p. 53). The Adoption and Safe Families Act, which President Clinton signed in late 1997, was intended to respond to the problem of children remaining in foster care for years. Designed to expedite adoptions, the law makes it easier to sever ties between birth parents and their children—without, however, addressing the problem that "[b]y all accounts, at least half the children in foster care…have been removed from their homes solely because their parents are poor" (Mack, 1 December 1997, p. B5).

Although many foster care providers clearly are concerned and caring people, "others are entrepreneurs who spend most of their time currying favor with social workers to obtain the small human beings who keep the government checks rolling in" (Hewlett & West, 1998, p. 111). Those checks are substantial: an average of $17,500 per child per year, approximately one-third more than a biological parent caring for his or her child would get from AFDC/TANF (Hewlett & West, 1998, pp. 111, 120). Clearly, there are many, many situations in which removing a child from the family home would seem to be the best of all imaginable alternatives. I do not question this, but rather the fundamental assumption on which the institution of foster care seems to rest—namely, that the profit motive can stand in for love. In the words of a sixteen-year-old who has been in foster care for years, "[T]here must be some way of getting money out of the system. Some weeks I feel as though I am just rented out. Even my good foster mom admits that if they didn't pay her, I would be out in the street. That makes me feel bad" (quoted in Hewlett & West, 1998, p. 111). As this girl suggests and as Hewlett and West (1998) argue,

> once we allow the profit motive to replace love, once someone signs on to care for a child because of the money involved, not because he or she is prepared to fall in love with a particular child, we turn the child into a commodity and destroy the heart of the parenting enterprise. Money cannot conjure up devoted long term care (p. 120).

As individuals struggle to parent well with few public supports, children's needs spill into the social arena. In this context, public policies are being enacted that disentangle children's interests from those of their families and define the newly constructed needs in market terms. Writing in 1982, Grubb and Lazerson pointed out the discrepancy between the society's public and private valuation of children: "In contrast to the deep love we feel and express in private, we lack any sense of 'public love' for children." Consequently, they argued, we "are unwilling to make public commitments to [children] except when we believe the commitments will pay off" (p. 52). For example, if early childhood and nutrition programs "do not increase cognitive abilities, and therefore adult success, beyond the shadow of a doubt, they are likely to be considered worthless investments, even if they benefit children in other ways" (p. 44). Notions of public responsibility for, or obligations to, children predicated on a consciousness of investment lead to public policies and programs that offer poor children only the "cheapest possible care" and belie the claim, often heard, that our children are a "priceless resource" (p. 51). This devaluation of poor children has been going on for a long time. What's new, I believe, is defining the newly constructed needs as market "opportunities" in ways that turn children into conduits for channeling public funds into private hands.

Beyond the Market

I wish I could conclude with a blueprint for reducing child poverty and rendering unthinkable the idea that poverty should pay, but I have none to offer. On the contrary, I believe the reigning ideology, manifesting forcefully in

Public Law 104-193, will be extremely difficult to undercut because, on the surface, the law appears to further such putatively desirable aims as public affirmation of the value of work and self-sufficiency (backed by public punishment of those who violate this social ideal) and integration of "children's needs" into the economy of services. The law generates an illusion of a "win-win" scenario: Children receive the care they need and those who provide the care are compensated for their efforts. Work is elevated and given a moral status, "sinners" are punished, and children's needs are transformed into potential sources of profit.

This "reform," however, guarantees more of the same exploitation of the powerless and marginalized and a public discourse that supports and rationalizes, even as it obscures, obscene levels of child and family poverty. Instead, we need new and better public policies (tax laws, housing programs, health programs, ways of financing public education, and so on) aimed centrally at providing the material foundations for safe, equitable environments for as many human beings as possible. We need a politically significant pro-child and truly pro-family movement that does not disempower either as human beings through actions or words and that holds leaders accountable for the consequences of their actions and inactions. Further, we need a public discourse that could support such a movement—which is to say better language for talking about children and families.

This is a fundamentally educational task. Educators (both scholars and practitioners) have an important role to play in educating students and the broader public about the causes and consequences of child and family poverty. More specifically, I believe educators and educational scholars need to engage in a more pointed and publicly prophetic critique. President Clinton knew what the welfare bill would mean for children, and signed it anyway. Congressional delegates knew the legislation lacked a research-based rationale, and gave it their blessing anyway. The problem is not one of information alone but of responsibility. Those of us in the profession of education have a special duty, I believe, to hold political leaders accountable to some degree of truth telling and honesty in matters of child and family welfare.

We need to work to broaden the public discourse on child and family welfare to encompass ways of thinking about children that do not reduce them and their families to the terms of the market. As Valerie Polakow (1993) has argued, we need to speak about children in ways that affirm their existential or spiritual value as well as the claims that value makes on the collective

(p. 173). We need to bring into the public discourse representations of children as human beings with human agency, spirituality, vulnerability, and promise, and language that reconnects the interests of children with those of their parents and families. I am not calling for a naïve faith in the powers of parental love, but rather for a recognition that the market cannot stand in for family ties and experiences. As the market is allowed to wind its way increasingly into the lives of children and adults, we need to monitor, pay attention, and be careful to give to the market only what we collectively choose to give. We also need to recognize that to hand over our children or ourselves, figuratively or literally, is not only to jeopardize human well-being (the protection of which may not be profitable), but also to abdicate the ability to hope for something new, something better, something other than the by-products of a profit-driven market.

Finally, I believe educators and educational scholars need to continue to push against the familiar show-me-the-numbers grain, for educational policies, programs, and practices that nurture the insight and imagination necessary to the work of enriching the public discourse with new language, metaphors, and imagery. This is political work, but also poetic and educational work that requires classrooms, programs, and school climates in which insight and imagination are nurtured and affirmed. Our social imagination has been captured by a market logic that begets only more of the same. Breaking this vicious cycle is, I believe, a fundamental educational challenge of our times. The good news is, this challenge comes with plenty of opportunity for all who want to contribute—journalists, educators, and policymakers; preachers and poets; friends, families, and advocates for children in all walks of life; and, most importantly, the children themselves. The bad news is, the stakes are almost unimaginably high and, therefore, easy to deny, forget, or rationalize away with talk of markets and incentives.

■ References

Anyon, J. (1997). *Ghetto schooling: A political economy of urban educational reform*. New York: Teachers College Press.

Bernstein, N. (4 May 1997). "Deletion of word in welfare bill opens foster care to big business." *The New York Times*, A1.

Bernstein, N. (11 May 1997). "Orphanages, Inc.: The high cost of no intentions." *The New York Times*, E5.

Bronner, E. (30 May 1998). "Bilingual education is facing push toward abandonment." *The New York Times*, A1.

Bronner, E. (21 June 1998). "College efforts to lure the best set others back." *The New York Times*, A1.

Children's Defense Fund (1996). "Summary of the welfare bill" (August 8, 1996). Available from Children's Defense Fund, 25 E. Street, NW, Washington, DC 20001.

Children's Defense Fund (1998a). *The state of America's children: Yearbook 1998*. Washington, DC: Author.

Children's Defense Fund (1998b). *CDF reports* (June). Washington, DC.

Children's Defense Fund (2000). *The state of America's children: Yearbook 2000*. Washington, DC.

Children's Defense Fund and the National Coalition for the Homeless (1998). *Welfare to what? Early findings on family hardship and well-being*. Washington, DC.

Courtney, M. E. (1998). The costs of child protection in the context of welfare reform. *The Future of Children: Protecting Children from Abuse and Neglect*, 8(1): 88–103.

Edelman, P. (1997). The worst thing Bill Clinton has done. *The Atlantic Monthly* (March), 43–58.

Evans, W., Murray, S., and Schwab, R. (1997). Schoolhouses, courthouses, and statehouses after *Serrano*. *Journal of Policy Analysis and Management* 16 (1): 10–31.

Finkelstein, B., Mourad, R., and Doner, E. (1998). "Where have all the children gone? The transformation of children into dollars in Public Law 104–193." In Books, S. (Ed.). *Invisible children in the society and its schools*, (pp. 169–182). Mahwah, N.J.: Erlbaum.

Finnegan, W. (12 June 1998). "Prosperous times, except for the young." *The New York Times*, A21.

Grubb, W. N., and Lazerson, M. (1982). *Broken promises: How Americans fail their children*. New York: Basic Books.

Healy, P. (5 June 1998). "CUNY's four-year colleges ordered to phase out remedial education." *Chronicle of Higher Education*, A27.

Hernandez, R. (23 April 2000). "Federal welfare overhaul allows Albany to shift money elsewhere." *The New York Times*, A1.

Hewlett, S. A., and West, C. (1998). *The war against parents: What we can do for America's beleaguered moms and dads*. Boston: Houghton Mifflin.

Kozol, J. (1991). *Savage inequalities: Children in America's schools*. New York: Crown.

Mack, D. (1 December 1997). "We can't help kids by destroying families." *The Los Angeles Times*, B5.

Orfield, M. (1997). *Metropolitics: A regional agenda for community and stability*. Washington, DC: Brookings Institution Press.

Polakow, V. (1993). *Lives on the edge: Single mothers and their children in the other America*. Chicago: University of Chicago Press.

Polakow, V. (1998). Homeless children and their families: The discards of the postmodern 1990s. In Books, S. (Ed.), *Invisible children in the society and its schools* (pp. 3–22). Mahwah, N.J.: Erlbaum.

Rimer, S. (25 November 1997). "Children of working poor are day care's forgotten." *The New York Times*, A1.

Rubenstein, R. L. (1983). *The age of triage: Fear and hope in an overcrowded world*. Boston: Beacon Press.

Sherman, A. (1997). *Poverty matters: The cost of child poverty in America*. Washington, DC: Children's Defense Fund.

Swarns, R. L. (14 April 1998). "Mothers poised for workfare face acute lack of day care." *The New York Times*, A1.

Swarns, R. L. (22 June 1998). "Stiff rules gut welfare rolls at two offices." *The New York Times*, A1.

Wexler, R. (1990). *Wounded innocents: The real victims of the war against child abuse*. Buffalo, NY: Prometheus.

Wilson, W. J. (1996). *When work disappears: The world of the new urban poor*. New York: Knopf.

■ CHAPTER 3 ■

Constructing Childhood
in a Corporate World: Cultural
Studies, Childhood, and Disney[1]

Sumana Kasturi, Independent Researcher

Children's entertainment is big business. A wide variety of products including movies, books, television shows, toys, amusement parks, and computer programs are created exclusively for children's consumption. The contemporary child is inundated with visual and aural messages that promote the ever-widening choice in products and goods that are specifically designed to appeal to children. Traditional media like television, movies, and magazines have played a vital role in attracting children's attention to such goods. The latest of these media technologies, the Internet, has joined the fray and seems to be doing as well as traditional media in effectively marketing products aimed at children. The ever-increasing number of Web sites specifically targeted at children underscores the advertisers' faith in the persuasive power of the Internet.

Since its entry into the public domain in 1995, the Internet has become an immensely important source of information and a popular medium for entertainment. More importantly, it has become a highly effective marketing tool, as reflected in electronic commerce. In 1998, $7.8 billion worth of business was conducted over the Internet, with products and services aimed at children accounting for a significant proportion. Children have become an increasingly significant consumer group. Another characteristic of the "new" medium is the manner in which the younger segments of the population have taken to it. In general, children are considered to be early adopters of high-tech products. Stories of youngsters spending hours browsing the Net, and of running Web-based businesses, abound and are an indication of the ease with which the Internet has become a part of their lives.

Businesses have recognized that children and young people form an important market for the new interactive media (CME Report, 1996). Given the amount of time that they spend surfing the Web, it would be safe to say that the Internet is a significant source of ideas and images for children.

The Disney company operates popular sites for children on the Internet. The Disney company is worth an estimated $4.7 billion and has grown into a giant media octopus with tentacles in practically every corner of the globe. Through its comics, films, and theme parks, the Disney company has acquired a formidable reputation in the business of children's entertainment. Disney characters have achieved worldwide popularity, and an almost mythic status in the United States. The Disney Web Service is the latest in the long line of Disney's media "products."

Globalization, media concentration, and the ever-increasing access of children all over the world to both traditional and newer forms of the media have resulted in the universalization of a certain model of childhood as "natural" and "ideal" in contemporary urban[2] society. This prevailing model is in large part constructed and propagated by corporations (such as Disney) that have a self-interest in promoting and maintaining such a representation. The content of media messages aimed at children should, therefore, be studied closely to see what pedagogical lessons are being conveyed through the supposedly "harmless" corporate constructed narratives that inundate contemporary children.

This chapter will present a textual analysis of Disney Web sites. The analysis is grounded in a theoretical context provided by critical cultural studies and aims to examine how corporate agendas related to the construction of childhood are manifested. The argument is made that both the content and form of the new media product/text convey specific pedagogical messages: pedagogies of representation and consumption.

Cultural and Childhood Studies:
Contemporary Ties to Corporate Pedagogy

Cultural studies is concerned with how culture (and cultural knowledge) is situated, produced, and consumed within the social, economic, and political systems of a society. What distinguishes cultural studies from other academic approaches is this specific emphasis on the critical and political dimensions of culture and society (Kellner, 1995), focusing on understanding the relationship between "culture, knowledge and power" (Giroux, 1996, p. 42).

Within this paradigm, pedagogy is seen as more than the mere transmission of information, skills, and techniques to students within a neutral environment. Neither the environment, nor the specific skills and blocks of information used with students, are considered to be neutral. Even pedagogical methods are understood as value laden, contextual, and political.

> Cultural studies rejects the notion of pedagogy as a technique or set of neutral skills, arguing instead that pedagogy is a cultural practice understandable only through considerations of *history, politics, power, and culture.*
> (Giroux, 1996, p. 43)

While cultural studies is concerned with how knowledge is created and used, culture can be considered the avenue through which the struggle for dominant narratives occurs. The mass and popular media often disseminate these dominant narratives. However, the process is not always one-sided, since culture also serves as a location for critique and resistance. Within this context, "Pedagogy represents a form of cultural production implicated in and critically attentive to how power and meaning are employed in the construction and organization of knowledge, desires, values and identities" (Giroux, 1996, p. 52). Childhood as a construct and a power-oriented narrative is embedded within this cultural production.

Cultural studies scholars believe that traditional boundaries and distinctions between areas of knowledge and conventional, scientistic modes of understanding and analysis are not adequate to interpret the contemporary, postmodern world. Rejecting the notion of a single, authentic version of knowledge or reality as absolute "truth," scholars interpret reality as socially constructed (Kincheloe and McLaren, 1994). These scholars also believe that the spread of "electronically mediated culture" (Giroux, 1996, p. 45) and the resulting information society have contributed greatly to the postmodern condition. This includes a recognition that audio, visual, and new communication technologies have acted as catalysts in a dramatic shift in the manner in which knowledge is produced and consumed. Society is characterized not by "reality" but by "hyperreality."

> Hyperreality is a term used to describe an information society socially saturated with ever-increasing forms of representation : filmic, photographic, electronic, and so on. These have had a profound effect on constructing the cultural narratives that shape our identities (Kincheloe and McLaren, 1994, p. 142).

Thus, any study of how the dynamics of power and politics work in a society requires an inquiry into the role of media and popular culture in constructing and presenting preferred forms of representation, and in producing and mediating knowledge. A recognition of the *pedagogical* aspect of the media and popular culture is, therefore, integral to the study of contemporary "childhood."

Kincheloe and Steinberg (1997) provide one forceful argument for rethinking the concept of childhood in the postmodern age. They suggest that dramatic socioeconomic changes, as well as a tremendous increase in children's access to information, have significantly changed the nature of childhood. In addition, in the late-capitalist society of the United States, corporations play a significant role in structuring children's lives. Kinderculture, a word coined by the authors in connection with "the corporate construction of childhood" in postmodern America, is an important determinant that needs to be factored into any discussion of childhood, popular culture, and/or pedagogy. The authors point out that by "using fantasy and desire, corporate functionaries have created a perspective on late-twentieth-century culture that melds with business ideologies and free-market values" (p. 4). These megacorporations have produced "educational forms that are wildly successful when judged on the basis of their capitalist content" (p. 4). The ways in which corporations work to create, sustain, and legitimate a type of consumer ethic that has come to dominate the landscape of childhood imagination require thorough, critical examination. Central to such an analysis is a recognition of the workings of power and power blocs, and the "ways power not only represses the production of democratic artifacts but also produces pleasure for children" (Kincheloe & Steinberg, 1997, p. 8). Further, a critical discourse brings about an awareness that learning is not a neutral transmission of static knowledge but in fact consists of the production of social practices which provide students with a sense of place, identity, worth, and value (Giroux, 1989).

A critical view defines pedagogy as the production and construction of knowledge, values, and identity within a context of power relations, and as contributing to the shaping of subjectivities (Kincheloe & Steinberg, 1997). Pedagogy is not viewed as limited to schooling, but as taking place in many social contexts outside of schools. Critical/cultural pedagogy argues for an acknowledgment of learning through popular culture (in this case, as constructed by corporate agendas), contexts within which children receive messages about themselves and the world around them (e.g., toys, magazines, movies, storybooks, television). Popular culture and mass media play a significant role in the way the contemporary child obtains information, forms perceptions, and acquires values. Further, these cultural forms are particularly powerful because of the manner in which they ensure hegemonic power by engaging the desires and loyalties of their consumers, an "explosive cocktail" (Kincheloe & Steinberg, 1997) of power and desire.

Recognizing that the mass media and popular culture lie in the crucial intersection between pedagogy, knowledge production, and childhood, understanding ways in which meaning-making may/can occur becomes important. Equally necessary is the determination of ways in which desire and pleasure are produced and regulated within these cultural contexts. The textual analysis presented in the following pages attempts to address these two issues in the specific context of the Disney Web Service/sites.

Disney as a Pedagogical Site

How does Disney function as a pedagogical site? In the introductory chapter to his book on Walt Disney World, Stephen Fjellman quotes from Orwell and Huxley to introduce the concept of hegemony to his readers. While Orwell's *1984* described a totalitarian society in which control was maintained through constant surveillance, indoctrination, and physical power, Huxley's vision was different. In his *Brave New World*, Huxley envisioned a system of control that was based on the reinforcement of desired behavior through reward. Huxley predicted that we might be tamed by desire and pleasure, and, by extension, our learning would be controlled. This form of covert control is called "colonization of desire" by critical pedagogists (Kincheloe & Steinberg, 1997).

Disney's power lies in this subconscious form of colonization. Further, any analysis or study of the Walt Disney World empire would require an understanding of the context of Disney's place in postmodern, corporate

America; simultaneously the researcher would recognize that the context itself is greatly influenced by the stories Disney tells of America. Disney is among the major producers of idealized visions of "America," and may even be considered a major influence, after the family and formal education, on the perceptions of the world held by many children.

Disney's relationship to education can be described using Gramsci's notion of a "scholastic programme" in which, through schooling and the mass media (among others), people are taught "how the world is and why it ought to be that way" (Fjellman, 1992, p. 9). Hegemonic control requires the production and dissemination of stories that reflect the dominant ideology and the suppression and appropriation of oppositional stories. This cycle of production-dissemination/suppression-appropriation is a significant way in which corporations such as Disney retain control over capital and their audience.

Perhaps nowhere is Disney pedagogy more clear than in the company's theme parks. A favorite topic of discussion and analysis among "Disney scholars," critical attention (see, for instance, Fjellman, 1992; Wilson, 1993, 1994) has resulted in a large body of scholarship on the ways in which corporate pedagogy functions in the Disney parks. The scholarship argues that Disney's geographies appropriate and commodify space, while the histories restructure time for corporate convenience. Disney is viewed as constructing and presenting specific, ideologically loaded stories and lessons for consumers to learn. The following sections offer specific analyses of how Disney pedagogy is manifested in the contemporary technology of the Internet.

Structure and Design

Disney has a significant presence on the Internet, with its many sites, each devoted to a specific venture. Although Disney theme parks, the Disney Channel, Radio Disney, ABC, Buena Vista Movies, etc., all have their own Web pages, this analysis will focus only on those Web pages that have been designed specifically as children's entertainment sites. The Internet is a dynamic medium, with web content changing frequently—every day, or even every few hours. In addition, while the continuous introduction of new technologies and enhanced capabilities results in a vibrancy and efficiency that makes the Web attractive to many, the ephemerality results in a situation in which scholars find it hard to save or store Web content in the same way that films, newspapers, or television programs are generally stored. Over the past two years, Disney sites have changed dramatically—in design, content, and even names. The child-specific sites, located at Disney.com, were initially called "Kids" (free) and "Daily Blast" (paid service) and are presently called "Zeether" (free) and "Club Blast" (paid). The material presented in this chapter has been collected at various stages of the (ongoing) transformation.

Since the conventions ruling the design and structure of web sites are still being formed (and Disney seems to be creating the blueprint for those focusing on "childhood"), analysis using a conventional standard is not possible. However, the sites obviously exhibit Disney's standards of technical and design excellence. Both sites are colorful, cheerful, and attractive. The detailed and sophisticated graphics and the well-integrated audio, video, and music combine to present appealing sensory environments that are attractive to the viewer. The Kids/Zeether and Daily/Club Blast sites are both linked to the Disney.com home page, a site that provides access to many different Disney products—stores, theme parks, and vacations, just to name a few. Both "child-targeted" sites have some combination of stories and articles to read, games to play, coloring and other craft activities, and downloadable images that children can print.

Stories and activities on both sites seem remarkably similar, though those in the paid service seemingly offer better "value." The stories are sometimes longer, and occasionally offer an interactive element not available on the other site. For instance, the paid service offers an interactive story library that requires children to fill in words of their choice and then see how their words are incorporated into a prewritten story. Similarly, the games are slightly more sophisticated and difficult than the ones in "Kids/Zeether." However, the difference between the two is largely cosmetic, with stories and activities at both sites emphasizing passivity, repetition, and occasionally manual dexterity (in using the mouse) rather than attempting to engage the mind of the user. Just as the Disney.com home page contains links to other Disney services, the individual children's sites also provide direct links to these sites—Disney shopping and vacations, in particular.

Pedagogy of Representation

Critical writing on Disney has frequently commented on the unproblematized representations of race, class, and gender in Disney "stories" (e.g., movies, comics, parks). This unproblematized content reappears in the Disney Web sites.

Racism. Charges of racism were leveled at Disney when critics noted the racist underpinnings of early feature films such as *Song of the South* and *Jungle Book* as well as of the health films that were distributed in South America in the 1940s and 1950s (Miller & Rode, 1995; Giroux, 1997a; Smoodin, 1994). The more recent *Aladdin* has been similarly criticized. Scholars and Arab associations in the United States protested its racist portrayal of particular groups of people and cultures.

Study of the Disney Web sites revealed, for example, that the electronic story of *Aladdin* contains many of the racially coded messages that are exhibited in the film. Most prominent are the westernized features of the two main characters, Aladdin and Jasmine, as compared with the other characters. Further, the only woman in the story is Jasmine; all other characters are men. In keeping with other Disney stories, the mothers of the protagonists are generally missing (Haas, 1995), so Aladdin does not have parents and Jasmine has only her father. Also, characters with strong positive roles to play in the plot adopt distinctly American mannerisms (as when Aladdin introduces himself to Jasmine and says "Call me Al," or when the Genie exchanges a high five with the flying carpet). The writers of this story seem to feel that positive characters—be it a boy from another time and culture, or a supernatural being out of a magic lamp—need to display some characteristics of the average young American to be seen as attractive by their young audience. The portrayal of the "other" fluctuates between negative stereotyping and "Americanization." The depiction of nonwhite cultures is further compromised when one notices the portrayal of far-off lands as barbaric and following a feudal way of life; feudalism and autocratic monarchy are depicted as normal and natural.

Critics have also commented on the manner in which Disney offers a nostalgic and whitewashed version of a different time (Fjellman, 1992; Wilson, 1993; Smoodin, 1994). *Beauty and the Beast* is set in eighteenth-century provincial France (Giroux, 1997a), *Aladdin* in an unknown medieval Arab land, *Jungle Book* in the jungles of colonial India. By setting the stories in a far-removed temporal space, Disney is able to portray monarchies, feudal societies, colonization, and undemocratic social structures as natural and unquestionable.

Again, it is possible to see the emergence of these themes in the web sites. *The Lion King* Story Book in "Kids" is such an instance. The "Pride Lands" are ruled by Mufasa, and in the "natural" order of things (according to Disney) his son should succeed him. *"Remember who you are, my son, and the one true king!"*

The usurper to the throne is evil and ugly, and only attains his goal by deceit and betrayal. When the rightful heir returns, the lionesses band together and succeed in putting Simba on the throne. This feudal order in the animal kingdom is again depicted as the natural order of things. Unless one stops to think, it is easy to forget that even in the animal kingdom, the leader of the pack or herd does not so much *inherit* his position as *win* it by displaying his superior strength.

This "naturalness" can be noticed even in Disney's representation of race. The average "American" addressed in the stories and articles on the Web sites is (mostly) white, and (at least) middle class. For instance, when Ariel becomes human, she becomes a white human, not a human of any other race. As mentioned above, both Jasmine and Aladdin have Caucasian features. Only their skin color is dark. (In fact, many Arabs are fair.) Disney's view seems to be based on the simplistic notion that anybody who is not "white" or "yellow" is "brown."

Further, messages about race can be conveyed by more than just stereotypical portrayals, by either inclusion or exclusion of an ethnic group. For instance, apart from the image of Pocahontas at the "trading post" (a location for the downloading of coloring activities), the Native American is completely invisible on the Web site. By making an ethnic group invisible, Disney's worldview renders them nonexistent, or worse, beneath notice.

Finally, critical scholars have revealed two strategies used by Disney that promote racism: the distortion or "sanitization" of history to suit a specific worldview (Giroux, 1997a) and an underlying attempt to promote conformity and cultural homogeneity. All "deviations" from the norm are rendered invisible or perceived as outside the public sphere.

This electronic analysis provided further examples of these ideas. One such instance was on the occasion of Black History Month. An article addressed to parents talked about teaching children black history, offering ideas, activities, and links to useful Web sites. On the surface, the article appears to refute critics' contention that Disney addresses only a homogeneous audience. A closer reading reveals racist assumptions: (a) the belief that only African Americans are interested in, and need to know about, black history, and (b) an unquestioned perspective that schools will never teach black history properly because the goal of education is to prepare "good citizens" (and that curriculum can, therefore, not be changed, especially to reflect color).

The pedagogical messages here are quite unambiguous. Black history is only important to those who are African American. "Good citizenry" does not involve the history/lives of the various racial/ethnic groups that live in one's country. In the name of diversity, Disney teaches racist lessons.

Sexism. Sexist, stereotypic representations of women appear frequently in Disney's narratives. The following example from an animated Web site comic strip indicates that Disney's view of the place of women and their role in society has not changed very much since *Snow White*. For example, echoing Cuomo's (1995) critique of representations of single women as magical (e.g., Mary Poppins), the comic strip on Kids shows Scrooge McDuck being harassed by Magica, the evil witch. She haunts him by appearing in his dreams and demanding that he give her his lucky dime. In desperation, Scrooge goes to Gyro Gearloose, the scientist, for help to stop her from ruining his sleep. After a couple of unsuccessful attempts by Gearloose, the smart triplets Huey, Dewey, and Louie suggest that they use Gyro's "holographic projector" to trick Magica by projecting holographs of Scrooge. At the end of the story, a haggard-looking Magica accepts defeat, admitting she just needs her "beauty sleep." Scrooge calls her a "hag" and the triplets add, "then you'd better sleep for a whole century." This story reiterates many of Disney's favorite themes. The single woman is magical, evil, and ugly. The female is stereotyped as needing her "beauty sleep," even if she is a duck. (Scrooge has lost a lot of sleep too but is never referred to as needing "beauty sleep," nor does the lack of sleep seem to affect his looks.)

Additionally, technology and science (as practiced by men) always triumph over things supernatural (and practiced by women). Within the Disney worldview, magic is most often placed in the hands of the evil character, who is usually female. Even when magic is wielded by the occasional man (e.g., Jafar in *Aladdin*), it is the weapon of the villain; the good rely on science and technology, and triumph in the end. (See Fjellman [1992] and Wilson [1994] for a further discussion of Disney and technology.) Stereotypical notions of gender reappear in the *Aladdin* Story Book. In another example, there is a crisis in the palace of the Sultan. Princess Jasmine has to get married before her birthday (we are not told which one), which is three days away! The wise Sultan tells Jasmine "he wanted her to be taken care of."

The pedagogical lessons here are many. Jasmine's goal in life is to get married. She must have a man to look after her, and therefore must be handed over ceremonially from father to husband. Also, she cannot become the ruler or queen of the kingdom on her own. Only her marriage, preferably to a prince, will ensure that she becomes ruler. The problem is neatly solved when she runs away and falls in love with Aladdin. In fact, the necessity of marriage to ensure succession, or the implication that she cannot take care of herself unless she marries, is not considered to be a problem at all. Her cause for contention is only that she is being forced to marry against her will.

Another instance of stereotyping occurs toward the end of the story, when Jafar imprisons Jasmine, Aladdin, and the Sultan. As Aladdin is trying to overpower the evil Jafar, Jasmine bats her eyelashes and strikes a seductive pose, to distract Jafar. "Jafar," she calls seductively, "I never realized before how...handsome you are."

The pedagogical message is that the only way a woman can contribute in such a situation is by being seductive. She is incapable of either using her mind or her strength to help Aladdin; the only thing she can do is to use her physical charms to distract the villain.

Analysis of the pedagogy of representation in the two web sites reveals many instances of stereotypical representations of race/ethnicity and gender. Further, the representations of history, geography, culture, and lifestyle choices were frequently distorted, biased, or improperly addressed. The examples given above are just a few of the many that my study of the material revealed.

My argument is that all representations, whether they are accurate or not, are pedagogical experiences to the audience (in this case, those who are younger). If stories, games, or articles feature strong, independent, intelligent, and articulate women, children are given opportunities to learn that such women can and do exist, and they may choose to emulate their roles. By the same token, however, stereotypical and distorted representations can result in opposite messages, lessons of women and people of color that are limited and role governed. Finally, agency and resistance must also be considered as a Disney pedagogy of representation is analyzed. Human beings, including children, can and may react to Disney pedagogy in diverse ways — resisting representations and perhaps rejecting Disney, even critiquing biases and taking action against them. A pedagogy of representation is tangible and complex, with very real and multidirectional consequences. My analysis indicates that such a pedagogy of representation does exist on the Disney Web sites, and the multitude of potential lessons must be noted.

Pedagogy of Consumption

Another key feature that this electronic textual analysis reveals is the pedagogy of consumption. I believe that perhaps the single strongest lesson being taught at the Disney Web site is how to consume. The site is organized to lead users along specific paths that lead toward consumption. This can be seen as the predominant structural element of the site—a structure and design geared toward the maximum consumption of Disney products. The limited scope of this chapter does not allow me to lay out the concept in its entirety, but this section will offer an introductory view of what I call a *pedagogy of consumption*, and go on to discuss how this is manifested in the Web sites.

In a society driven by a market economy, the smooth flow of commerce is based on the public's continuous consumption of consumer products. Culture, supported by mass media, is used to foster a commodity perspective and to teach people how to consume, making consumption seem like a natural and necessary part of life. The distinction between fundamental needs and commercially generated needs is blurred, and people find it hard to distinguish between the two. (See Kellner [1989] for a discussion of the raising of public consciousness regarding these issues.)

Fjellman (1992) explains how consumption is offered as the solution to an essentially political problem—"the construction of a just and safe world" (Fjellman, p. 51). Some forms of popular culture promote a consumer ethic and place utilitarianism and individualism as central to the human purpose. "Building on the model of the human being as consumer," corporations and all those who benefit from the prevailing political and economic structure of the market have been so successful that the consumer model "and the personal entitlements attached to it have been accepted as true, beautiful and universal." Thus, personal identity, place in society, and even self-worth are commoditized, with consumption and commodities standing as symbols of this identity. "Our ontological acceptance of the model of consumer as the new human nature leads us to new natural rights of enlightenment and to new evidence of fulfillment" (Fjellman, p. 17). A hegemonic pedagogy of consumption results.

This pedagogy is evident for all demographic groups in the population, including children. The corporate-dominated construction of childhood is also based on these principles, and functions in two ways — (a) by teaching children that they "need" to buy certain products and (b) by teaching adults and parents that an "ideal" or "natural" childhood involves the continuous consumption of these corporate promoted products and services. This two-pronged pedagogy is conveyed in subtle and not-so-subtle ways through media narratives generated by corporations. The Web sites (like other Disney narratives) play a vital role in this larger pedagogical process by teaching children, at a very young age, to fall into this pattern of consumption. For example, the pattern of consumption has been extensively discussed by scholars writing about the theme parks (Fjellman, 1992; Kuenz, 1993; Willis, 1993a and 1993b; Wilson, 1993, 1994). "Conformity with the park's program upholds the Disney value system. Purposeful consumption—while it costs the consumer a great deal—affirms the value of the consumer" (Willis, p. 126). All paths in the theme parks appear to lead to some form of consumption — souvenirs, food, photographs, etc. Similarly, most links on the Disney web sites subtly lead the user toward some form of purchase.

A discussion of consumerism and its relationship to Disney requires more than just a comparison with the theme parks. From the beginning, the company has implemented strategies — both simple and complex — to promote the consumption of its products. While a business would be expected to promote its own products, the power of the Disney enterprise in promoting consumption lies not in the actual messages, but in what DeCordova calls the "sacred bond" that "exists between Mickey Mouse and idealized childhood" (DeCordova, 1994, p. 203). The sanctity and unquestioned acceptance that are accorded to anything bearing the Disney name result in the outright rejection of critique. The privileged status accorded to Disney is as much due to the company's own projection of itself as it is with a public desire to disassociate children's entertainment from political, historical, and ideological meaning.

A historical view of the rise of consumerism in the United States and the role played by Disney provides a clearer understanding of pedagogy. In his article on the connection between Disney and consumerism, DeCordova (1994) calls attention to "two different registers of consumption" that link film and children. First, children are viewed as consumers of the film itself, those who pay money to see the film. Second, children are seen as consumers of the products that are popularized by the films. He notes that "the system of merchandising and promotion employed by Disney and other studios works by creating elaborate networks of mutual reference between these two registers of consumption" (DeCordova, 1994, p. 204).

As with so many other Disney ventures, Disney Online is less a new Disney product and more a platform for advertising other Disney products. This is typical of Disney's marketing strategy. A Disney product advertises all other Disney products as part of its content, achieving a seamless flow of content and commercial that almost completely eliminates the need for exclusive advertising messages. In keeping with this strategy, the Disney web site acts as a vehicle to advertise Disney products (stuffed toys, consumer products, theme parks, etc.), Disney characters (Mickey, Donald, Pooh, Ariel, etc.), and Disney ventures (the Disney Channel, Radio Disney, ABC, television shows, movies, theme vacations, cruises, and movies). In the 1996 Disney annual report, company CEO Michael Eisner mentions with pride the synergistic nature of the Disney company—a nature that is well illustrated and perhaps most fully realized in Disney Online.

The "mutual reference" that DeCordova refers to works strongly in the Disney Online service, with not only two, but *multiple* registers of consumption employed. The Disney Internet service, more than any other Disney venture, seems to utilize this strategy to great advantage. An example of this was a competition advertised on the Disney Web site that required children to listen to Radio Disney and then offered a prize in which the winner was drawn in as a character in an episode of a popular cartoon show on the Disney Channel.

As DeCordova points out, since the beginning, the Disney company was aware of and encouraged the idea that consumption of the films would lead to consumption of the toys and vice versa. This mutual referencing would seem to be working even more efficiently today. Consumption of one Disney product (be it a movie, toy, the Disney Channel, Radio Disney, or Disney Online) would reinforce the desire and the need to consume one or more of the other Disney products.

With the keen awareness of the benefits of "mutual referencing," the Disney company systematically worked toward establishing its reputation as "safe" and "good" for children. The early Mickey Mouse clubs introduced by the company worked successfully to associate the company in the minds of parents with more positive forms of children's activity such as music and painting, dance and sports (since at that time, movie-going was still being debated as an acceptable leisure-time activity for children). The company thus established its reputation as an acceptable provider of entertainment. Membership in Club Blast works in a similar way to the Mickey Mouse clubs, where children can communicate with each other (in cyberspace instead of face-to-face) and participate in contests. However, the participative activities encouraged in the Daily Blast community have very little to do with the artistic, creative, or sporting abilities of its young members. Almost all the competitions involve the children's consumption of other Disney products. Having established its standing in the children's entertainment arena, Disney no longer bothers with promoting the abilities of these children; instead, it concentrates on molding them into ideal consumers, who accept increased consumption as essential to happiness.

Popular press articles in the 1950s likened the membership and popularity of the Mickey Mouse clubs to that of the Girl and Boy Scouts of America. The difference that they failed to mention between the two—relevant as much now as then—was that while one was organized and run mainly as a public service, the Mickey Mouse clubs have private profit rather than public interest as their primary objective.

Like the shopping mall, Disney World represents the "wholesale use of architecture and décor as a means for promoting consumption" (Willis, 1993b, p. 121). Representing the increasing appropriation by private capital of public spaces, scholars have argued that while the Disney theme parks masquerade as public spaces, they are actually "highly developed sites for social control," as well as opportunities for consumption (Willis, 1993b, p. 121). Similarly, corporate Web sites, like the ones under study, represent the corporate take-over of Internet space that has so far been considered democratic and accessible to all. Further, the elaborate audio-video-animated environment that is one of the slickest sites on the Internet is merely "décor" for greater consumption.

Throughout the site, all opportunities for imparting useful, interesting, or educational information are disregarded in favor of providing standardized, simplistic, or stereotypical images and activities to the young users. By depicting consumerism as the ideal and natural way of life, the young audience of these Web sites is taught a definition of the "ideal" and the "natural." Similarly, articles addressed to parents (on other parts of the site) reiterate the dominant theme of consumption: how to have the perfect family vacation (usually at a resort or park), how to celebrate the holidays (with clothes, presents, and decorations emphasized over attitude, relationships, or religion), and so on.

The pedagogical lessons are primarily about what constitutes childhood and parenting—in reality, a corporate construction of what is constituted.

Conclusion

This chapter applies the theoretical concepts of cultural and critical pedagogy to a textual analysis of Disney Web sites. Cultural pedagogy is the recognition that learning occurs not only in school, but also takes place in many other social and cultural sites/contexts (such as the mass media). The chapter argues that for the contemporary child, learning may occur through popular culture and the mass media. From this perspective, two Disney children's Web sites, "Kids/Zeether" and "Daily/Club Blast," were subjected to electronic textual analysis.

Overall, textual analysis of Disney Web sites brings to light many questionable pedagogical messages. Most noticeable are the pedagogies of representation and consumption. The analysis of the pedagogy of representation reveals that there are biases and distortions in the representations of race and gender, biases that have already been noted in other Disney "texts" and "sites," and some that were unique to Disney Online. Further, the Web sites were dominated by a strong pedagogy of consumption that was visible in almost every component of the sites, a pedagogy that would create, legitimate, and sustain a consumer ethic in users.

A social activism is not on Disney's agenda, nor is providing its viewers with accurate narratives of the past and future. Disney executives do not respect the diversities or opinions of consumers. An article about Disney CEO Michael Eisner's interview on CBS's "60 Minutes" illustrates this point well as Eisner is quoted, "When somebody says Pocahontas is anti-Christian or anti-Jewish or anti-black or anti-Native American, I say inside deep down, 'they're nuts.' They really are." Disney is in the business of teaching people to be good consumers by constructing and propagating a worldview compatible with its own corporate interests, one that erases problems of social and economic dimensions, to be replaced by a whitewashed version of homogeneity that is neither true nor democratic. Important social issues and problems are ignored; those few that are addressed are dealt with cursorily and as individual problems rather than as the social issues they really are. Consumerism and economic issues of class are domesticated and resolved in simple, individualized ways. These unproblematized representations of social reality work to validate the status quo and support dominant ideologies. Children, like all of us, are objects and subjects of that corporate interest.

■ Notes

1. A version of this chapter was presented at the AEJMC Conference, Qualitative Studies Division, in August 1999.

2. I use the word "urban" with the acute awareness that large numbers of the world's population are variously referred to as "rural," "tribal," or "native" in different contexts, and that these people live lives that are relatively untouched by the western popular media as we experience it.

■ References

Articles and Books

Bell, E., Haas, L., & Sells, L. (Eds.) (1995). *From mouse to mermaid*. Bloomington, IN: Indiana University Press.

Center for Media Education. (1996). Montgomery, K., & Pasnick, S. Web of deception: threats to children from online markets. Washington, DC: Education.

Cuomo, C. (1995). Spinsters in sensible shoes: Mary Poppins and Bedknobs and Broomsticks. In Bell, E., Hass, L., & Sells, L (Eds.), *From mouse to mermaid* (pp. 212–223). Bloomington: Indiana University Press.

DeCordova, R. (1994). The Mickey in Macy's window: Childhood, consumerism, and Disney animation. In Smoodin, E. (Ed.), *Disney discourse — Producing the Magic Kingdom* (pp. 203–213). New York: Routledge.

Fjellman, S. M. (1992). *Vinyl leaves, Walt Disney World and America*. Boulder, CO: Westview.

Giroux, H. A., & Simon, R. (Eds.) (1989). *Popular culture, schooling, and everyday life*. New York: Bergin and Garvey.

Giroux, H., Lankshear, C., McLaren, P., & Peters, M. (Eds.) (1996). *Counternarratives: Cultural studies and critical pedagogies in postmodern spaces*. New York: Routledge.

Giroux, H. A. (1997a). Are Disney movies good for your kids? In Kincheloe, J. L. & Steinberg, S. R. (Eds.). *Kinderculture — The corporate construction of childhood* (pp. 53–68). Boulder, CO: Westview Press.

Giroux, H. A. (1997b, September). Disney, Southern Baptists, & children's culture. *Z Magazine* (online database).

Haas, L. (1995). Eighty-six the mother: Murder, matricide, and good mothers. In Bell, E., Hass, L., & Sells, L. (Eds.), *From mouse to mermaid* (pp. 193–211). Bloomington, IN: Indiana University Press.

Kellner, D. (1989). *Critical theory, marxism, and modernity*. Baltimore: The Johns Hopkins University Press.

Kellner, D. (1995). Cultural studies, multiculturalism and media culture. In Dines, G., & Humez, D. (Eds.). *Gender, race and class in media* (pp. 5–17). Thousand Oaks, CA: Sage.

Kincheloe, J. L., & McLaren, P. (1994). Rethinking critical theory and qualitative research. In Denzin, N. K. & Lincoln, Y. S. (Eds.), *Handbook of qualitative research* (pp. 138–157). Thousand Oaks, CA: Sage.

Kincheloe, J. L., & Steinberg, S.R. (Eds.), (1997). *Kinderculture — The corporate construction of childhood*. Boulder, CO: Westview Press.

Kuenz, J. (1993). It's a small world after all: Disney and the pleasures of identification. *South Atlantic Quarterly*, 92(1): 63–88.

Miller, S., & Rode, G. (1995). The movie you see, the movie you don't. In Bell, E., Haas, L., & Sells, L. (Eds.), *From mouse to mermaid* (pp. 86–103). Bloomington, IN: Indiana University Press.

Smoodin, E. (Ed.) (1994). *Disney discourse — Producing the Magic Kingdom*. New York: Routledge.

Willis, S. (1993a) Critical vantage points on Disney's world. *South Atlantic Quarterly*, 92(1): 1–6.

Willis, S. (1993b). Disney World: Public use/private space. *South Atlantic Quarterly*, 92(1): 119–37.

Wilson, A. (1993). Technological utopias. *South Atlantic Quarterly*, 92(1): 157–73.

Wilson, A. (1994). The betrayal of the future: Walt Disney's EPCOT Center. In Smoodin (Ed.), *Disney discourse — Producing the Magic Kingdom* (pp. 118–128). New York: Routledge.

Other Sources

The Walt Disney Company 1996 Annual Report.

The Disney Catalog, Winter, 1997.

Disney Online corpreleases/index.html

"Walt Disney is under consideration for reprimand by Arabs Regional, International August 20, 1997. Arabic News.com http://www.arabicnews.com/ansub/daily/day/970820/1997082018.html

CHAPTER 4

What Are Beanie Babies Teaching Our Children?

Dominic Scott, New Mexico State University

From their creation in 1992, Beanie Babies have captured the imaginations of millions of children worldwide. These soft, cuddly bears and other animals are about eight inches long and sell for an affordable recommended retail price of $5. Aimed at the eight- to eleven-year-old preteen market, these cute little creatures have insinuated themselves into many areas of our cultural consciousness. That Ty Warner, the owner of Ty Inc., which produces Beanie Babies, could attain such a commanding position in the creation of children's *lebenswelt* (Husserl, 1973) is a tribute to the power of cultural creationism in a globalized, consumer society.

Americana, Beanies, and Globalization

Unlike the previous wave of popular collectibles, the electronic life forms known collectively as giga pets, Beanie Babies are extremely traditional and fall within the cuddly toy and teddy bear categories of playthings. Indeed, the first major chain to carry them was Cracker Barrel, a down-home, all-American eatery chain with a country crafts store attached. So, early on, Beanies staked their claim within the Americana nostalgia industry. Beanies capitalized on the perennial appeal of stuffed animals, especially teddy bears, to the American consciousness. As Guber and Berry (1993), in rationalizing the adoption of bears by Nabisco as the icon for Teddy Graham crackers, point out:

> It is easy to understand the bears' appeal. Virtually every child (and many adults) has a teddy bear he or she can snuggle. From the original teddy bear — a stuffed animal manufactured on the heels of a famous story about Teddy Roosevelt's sparing a young bear's life — through A.A. Milne's *Winnie the Pooh* stories, through "The Teddy Bear Picnic," Smokey the Bear, and the Care Bears, the animal has had a special place in the popular culture. Moreover, teddy bears have been trendy of late. Upscale teddy bears, with price tags of more than $100, have been popping up in department stores" (p. 204).

Within a few short years, resale values of Beanie Babies would dwarf even this figure, with some "rare" editions fetching $3,000 on the "secondary market."

Beanies symbolize a rejection of the encroaching power of technology over young lives in the form of Nintendo, Sega Dreamcast, and Sony Playstations, and release children from the thralldom of preprogrammed playthings such as Tamagouchis, Furbies, and Star Wars Translators. Beanies represent more traditional toys like dolls, teddy bears, and bean bags, the comfort of the way things never were (Coontz, 1992).

Kids and Marketing

Initially seen as an entree to their parents' pocketbooks, children are increasingly viewed as a marketing sector in their own right. McNeal (1992) outlines three markets that constitute the marketing power of children. First, children are a primary market influenced by their own money, needs, wants, and desires on which "they have well over $8 billion of their own to spend, spend around $6 billion on toys, sweets, clothing, and many other items, and save the rest" (p. 15). Second, there is the influence market, in which children "directly influence over $130 billion in household purchases and indirectly influence that much again" (p.15). Finally, there is the future market, in which children are seen as consumers for life who will respond readily to brand loyalty. "If they [marketers] can woo and win the child, they're likely to enjoy that loyalty for 70 years" (Reese, 1997, p. 50).

The rise of the consumer kid saved many manufacturers from economic oblivion. "Apparel retailers, stung by a slowdown in sales to adults, saw kids age 4 to 12 increase their spending on clothing from less than $750 million to about $2.5 billion just from 1992 to 1995" (Reese, 1997, p. 50). A major factor in this growth was the increase in targeted advertising. As Reese reports, "more than $2 billion is spent on advertising directed at kids, 20 times the amount that was spent a decade ago" (1998, p. 37). Drawing from marketing professor James McNeal (1992) in his textbook on how to market to children, Reese (1997) quotes, "There's not a consumer goods marketer out there that doesn't address children as either a current or potential market" (p. 37). McNeal's marketing team describes the hypothetical ideal child consumer as "a confident 9-year-old [girl] with a cute little nose and arms full of shopping bags, emerging from a department store. This combination of characteristics — confident, a big spender, able to cope in the marketplace — seems to summarize well this new economic force" (McNeal, 1992, p.18). This description could also be a profile of the typical Beanie Baby collector.

Beanies: Marketing With a Difference

Given the growing share of marketing budgets spent on advertising to children, it must seem counterintuitive to discover that Beanie Babies are not marketed in the traditional sense of mass advertising or consistently through major retail store distribution. Beanie sales have grown from an estimated $1.7 million in 1995 to $674 million in the United States in 1998 (Goldman, 1999, p. 10). Ty Inc., as a privately held company, is not required to publish its sales figures, but was quick to correct the 1998 estimates above as being too low. "Our net income for 1998 exceeded $700,000,000" ("Beanie baby sales," 10 October 1999).

How has this been achieved? Ty Inc. has been careful to "under-market" their bears in down-home, mom-and-pop type stores, combining global distribution with local signification. Volunteer-staffed gift stores in hospitals are a favorite venue, as are local gift shops. Hallmark stores and Cracker Barrel, while not strictly fitting this model, nevertheless adhere to the down-home, local (albeit synthetic) image. This apparent missed opportunity for mass distribution has made good sense. David Siegel, general manager of Small Talk, which helps marketers reach kids, is reported by Reese (1998) as emphasizing, "With kids, word of mouth is very powerful. If they don't like the way they've been treated...it kills [the product] immediately" (p. 38).

Ty Inc. has carefully cultivated a kids' network for their products by controlled releases of new Beanies and staccato-like supplies of existing ones so that kids need to network, search the Internet, and check regularly with stores to stay abreast of the latest news in the Beanie market. Skill at tracking down the latest releases can result in feelings of power, one-upmanship, and superiority that imbue the actual Beanie with additional significance. It produces a form of "cultural capital" and "distinction" (Bourdieu, 1988, 1984) that allows kids to see themselves apart from their parents and adults, possessing secret powers conferred by market prowess. Kids identify with the irony of their role in navigating an uncertain world of supply and availability, willing accomplices in their own self-marketing, in a process unknown to, or only dimly perceived by, the significant adults in their lives. Beanies have succeeded in creating a secret space within the world of marketing by providing a pseudo counter-hegemonic product that is in scarce supply and whose sporadic availability demands extensive networking, research, and vigilance to find out where and when the latest consignment will be available.

Unlike the usurpation of public and personal space that advertising propagates, and the inevitable reactions to it, Beanie marketing is immune from such accusations. Beanies are, consequently, shielded from the recent wave of radical activism in which advertisements are altered to critique and circumvent the intended messages of the advertisers. This campaign of adbusting and culture jamming (Klein, 1999) has produced parody in which "Joe Camel turns into Joe Chemo, hooked up to an IV machine...and Apple Computer's 'Think Different' campaign [contains] a photograph of Joe Stalin...with the altered slogan 'Think Really Different'" (Klein, 1999, p. 282). By eschewing advertising altogether, Ty Inc. has circumvented any such criticism of its invasion of young minds.

It would be wrong, however, to conclude that there is no marketing strategy whatsoever. Since February 1998, Cyrk Inc., a "promotional marketing company specializing in the design and development of innovative, high-impact promotional products and programs" ("Cyrk reports," 10 February 2000), has handled the promotion of Beanie Babies via the Beanie Babies Official Club. "For a retail price of $10," business director Steve Murphy waxed to Mary Beth Sobolewski (editor-in-chief of *Beanie World Magazine*), "a collector gets the entire kit including the membership card, checklist, newsletter, membership certificate, Beanie Baby stickers..." (Sobolewski, 1998, p. 19). Cyrk has recently been rewarded with a growth in net sales of 30 percent for 1999 ("Cyrk reports," 2000).

The Beanie marketing strategy of selective venues, avoiding advertising, and word-of-mouth guerrilla marketing has resulted in Beanies being less intrusive, less invasive, and less coercive than most of the other products marketed to children which have also become modern cultural artifacts (e.g., Barbie, GI Joe, Ninja Turtles, and Teletubbies). However, it is precisely because they are less intrusive, invasive, and coercive that they command power to mold young minds in ways that only appear to be spontaneous, self-directed, and volitional. Undermarketing induces a high level of commitment by kids to the Beanie market, since their knowledge of Beanies allows them to feel invested in, and dependent on, everything that Beanies represent. Beanies grant kids a level of autonomy and freedom that is both appealing and powerful, allow them to define themselves in unique ways that defy adult notions of childhood innocence, and encourage them to take bolder steps into the magical world of marketing and consumption. Kincheloe et al. (2000) point out that

> The contemporary child's access to commercial kinderculture and popular culture both motivates the child to become a hedonistic consumer and undermines the innocence, the protracted status from the tribulations of adult existence children have experienced since roughly the 1850s (p. 392).

Kids as Global Consumers

Beanie Babies are available globally and so convey their messages as American models and icons to a growing international clientele of preteens eager to emulate their American counterparts. In the world's "27 most industrialized countries (including the United States)...there are almost three-quarters of a billion children...representing around 23 percent of their total population" (McNeal, 1992, p. 232). Riches undreamed of await the savvy marketer who can penetrate the "90 percent of the world's population of families and 75 percent of family personal income...[that lie] beyond the borders of the United States" (McNeal, p. 230). After studying North Atlantic and Pacific Rim children's minimum average weekly incomes, McNeal estimated that "the industrialized world's children have around $117 billion to spend" (McNeal, p. 249). Furthermore, overseas markets for kid's products offer more upside potential due to a lack of saturation and satiation.

Mass goods represent culture, not because they are merely there as the environment within which we operate, but because they are an integral part of that process of objectification by which we create ourselves as an industrial society: our identities, our social affiliations, our lived everyday practices (p. 215).

As human beings, many of us in capitalist societies have learned to revel in the freedom to both create and be created by the products we choose to have in our lives. We may even deny that artifacts such as "dolls and books encode the cultural values of their creators" (Brady, 1997, p. 219), even when those values are to create products that are cute, cheap, and will sell to both children and adults. However, even more significant are the messages conveyed by the knowledge that is omitted in the production and marketing of the products. As an example, most Beanies are manufactured in Asian factories; no debate or even mention of this fact ever emerges. Additionally, the world of Beanie Babies is a carefully controlled environment (e.g., collector pricing books, controlled availability), a marketing biosphere in which only certain, preselected species of ideas are allowed to flourish. Yet, within these confines, children are free to elaborate and fantasize around major generative themes. For many, this is a powerful act of self-creation.

Consumption as Self-Creation

Global kids, rather than being seen as mere pawns in the "McDonaldization of society," to use Ritzer's (1996) ominous phrase, are actively creating their own identities that are beyond the reach of adults. "Consuming…becomes a process of 'bricolage' in which the self is actively constructed by particular individuals in specific situations but within the constraints of particular sociohistorical circumstance" (Alfino, Caputo, & Wynyard, 1998, p. 7). This "self-creation" is a mixture of resistance to traditional power relationships of family and traditional cultures, and a more affirmative cultural creation that grants kids a privileged position in the modernity project that is invading and overwhelming their world. Consequently, Beanie Babies provide world-wise kids the opportunity to acquire the "street smarts" of globalized markets and to be interpreters of the new terrain of commodities for their parents and peers. While their parents struggle with the alienating effects of laboring in the capitalist economy, children enjoy the ultimate privilege of experiencing the creative pleasure of the consumptive act. The pleasure comes, not only from the enjoyment of the multifarious varieties of Beanies, but also from the skill demonstrated in commodity interpretation.

Mediating the Global Village

Beanies are an important mediational tool, in the Vygotskyan sense of the word, that helps children learn about the world that marketers would wish to exist—a world of make-believe in the veracity of the market and the supremacy of consumption. "What needs to be stressed here is his [Vygotsky's] position that it is not the tools or signs, in and of themselves, which are important for thought development but the meaning encoded in them" (Knox & Stevens, 1993, p. 15). Through indulgence in Beanie marketing and loyalty to the Beanie logo, children are introduced to

> the euphoric marketing rhetoric of the global village, an incredible place where tribes people in remote rain forests tap away at laptop computers, Sicilian grandmothers conduct E-business, and "global teens" share, to borrow a phrase from Levi's Web site, a "world-wide style culture" (Klein, 1999, p. xvii).

Global kids quickly grasp the encoded meanings in Beanie Babies as a passport to the global village.

Beanie Babies and Learning

Focusing on the collection of large numbers of Beanie Babies potentially contributes to the construction of capitalist beliefs and assumptions about what is important for human beings. Whether unintended, conscious behavior, or openly recognized as problematic, Beanies (like other products) can contribute to a capitalist desire. Children may learn, for example, that there are different categories of classification (ordinary bears and the more collectible, and hence more desirable, Beanie Bears), a distinction necessary for understanding the relative importance of different types of products based around brand loyalty and imaging. Accepting distinctions between ordinary people and rich people, undesirable people and mainstream people, between us and the "other" is a natural extension of this newly acquired faculty of differentiation.

The sheer volume of Beanies (there are over 200 varieties) reassures children that Beanies, like the world of products and things in which they are active players, are ubiquitous and pervasive. People, relationships, jobs, communities, and cultures may come and go, but there are always plenty of things to compensate.

To ensure the totality of the Beanie universe, Beanie siblings, known as Teenie Beanie Babies, have been given away with McDonald's Happy

Meals intermittently since 1997. The stir that this great giveaway created became a media spectacle, with parents and children ordering and then dumping McDonald's Happy Meals just to get the "free" Teenie Beanie Babies. In 1998, not to be caught short on supplies as on previous occasions, McDonald's worldwide increased its order of Teenie Beanie Babies from 84 million to 150 million items (Gibson, 1998). This strategic alliance with McDonald's was more than mere happenstance. McDonald's has aligned itself with the all-American image to become the "ultimate icon of Americana" (Kincheloe, 1997, p. 252), and Beanie Babies fit neatly into this nostalgia in a way in which both cultural icons reinforce each other in their common quest for legitimation as America's flagships. Corporate synergy creates "cross-promotional brand-based experiences that combine buying with elements of media, entertainment and professional sports to create an integrated branded loop" (Klein, 1999, p. 146). The influence of each is multiplied.

Beanies: Economics 101

Beanies teach about price, value, scarcity, and product differentiation within a microcosm of Ty products. However, with this learning comes much that is undesirable: as examples, the supersaturation of young lives with material things, and the sheer waste of food to obtain Beanies (as in the case of McDonald's Happy Meals). Beanies work at a deeper level as well, since a retired Beanie can be traded for a price considerably higher than its initial selling price (its initial public offering?); Beanies have taken on some of the qualities of stocks. The mere hope of increased future value drives prices relentlessly upward, without any consideration for their real valuation. The "secondary market," as it is known to all Beanie aficionados, plays a vital role in socializing children into the magical world of the global marketplace, in which derivatives and other paper forms of value are traded, legitimated, and reified. This free trade in Beanie currency creates the illusion of both consumer sovereignty and perfect markets, since for a few dollars any kid can rent a table at the multiplicity of Beanie shows around the country and sell or buy Beanies at whatever price the market will bear (no pun intended). Here, even the free McDonald's Teenie Beanie Babies can sell for as much as $150 for a complete set. Children can dream of becoming Beanie moguls by testing the limits of consumer greed for free goods. In the world of Beanies, the cultural message is clear—anyone can become a Bill Gates (or a Ty Warner) through the blessings of the globalized marketplace. As with many of us in capitalist societies, children may become active participants in the desire for colonization (Steinberg & Kincheloe, 1997). This is more than an "affective moment of [power] evasion" (Fiske, 1993, p. 255). By providing the temporary elation of quasi-agency, it inculcates a false consciousness of economic and cultural efficacy. Thus, it succeeds in "depositing myths indispensable to the preservation of the status quo" (Freire, 1997, p. 120).

Beanienation.com, a major source of information and a secondary marketing site, has had almost 3 billion hits since its inception (Beanienation.com). Ty.com, the official Beanie site, has had more than 4 billion hits (Ty.com). The rapid incorporation of Beanies into the Internet commerce of collectibles adds a further modernist dimension to Beanie trafficking. Information about new releases and retirements is instantly available, while current prices and demand and supply factors allow for continuous reevaluation of the value of a Beanie portfolio. Now kids can be like their parents (or the parents they think they should have) and buy and sell their investments at a whim with a phone call or the click of a mouse. Technology with a purpose becomes easy to navigate as children learn how to access the world through the pursuit of Beanie knowledge. "The 8-through-12-year-old is expanding his knowledge of and appreciation for different places and peoples, so the Earth and indeed the entire solar system are now fair game" (Acuff, 1997, p. 105).

Multicultural Lite

Beanies also teach about a synthetic multicultural world in which Britannia bear and Erin bear coexist in market harmony, devoid of any historical contextualization. Similarly, Maple, Libearty, and Osito bears can be traded with NAFTA-like ease on Beanienation.com., without any reference to the tragedy created by free trade in goods and capital when free movement of people is denied (and enshrined in the North American Free Trade Agreement).

Ty has been careful not to make a black Beanie that in any way conjures up images of golliwogs. Indeed, with Erin, Britannia, and Germania Bears, Ty has created Eurocentric icons that are culturally relevant for over 75 percent of Americans and provide support for supremacist notions of cultural dominance that could be construed as a form of "imperialistic nostalgia" (Rosaldo, 1989). The European colonization of North America is reproduced, symbolically, by the inclusion of these Euro-Beanies and the exclusion of Black and Native American ones. Great care has gone into creating a clean-cut image of Beanies that confirms accepted notions of

Eurocentric racial purity and harmony. As a result of this careful sanitization, Beanies, unlike Tinky Winky (the Teletubby from England), are not subject to Jerry Falwell's wrath as examples of homosexuality ("Falwell's paper claims," 6 June 1999). Nor are they plagued by product recalls such as Mattel's Tarzan figure, whose arm becomes erect when you press his lower abdomen ("Mattel stifles Tarzan's hand," 10 June 1999), or Homies, the tiny Chicano-like figures created by David Gonzales, which have been criticized for supposedly creating negative stereotypes of Latinos ("Toys anger anti-gang forces," 29 May 1999). Beanies are politically correct and teach precisely what Rousseau recommended for Sophie — "to guard her reputation and do what convention prescribed" (Noddings, 1998, p.18).

Beanies represent a variety of dualistic and perhaps oversimplified images of the world. As examples, the political complexity of modern American political life is simplified with childlike ease through Lefty (the Democratic donkey) and Righty (the Republican elephant). Children can learn other aspects of social studies by being introduced to the sixties' Grateful Dead through the psychedelic colors of the Garcia bear, while world peace is acknowledged through the Peace bear. They can celebrate the holiday season with Santa or Snowball, Valentine's Day with Valentina or Valentino (images of Latin lovers?), and St. Patrick's Day with Erin. Easter brings a plethora of bunnies — Hippity, Hoppity, Floppity, Hippie, Nibbler, Nibbly, and Ears, and Eggbert, the Easter chick. Spring is the season of Chops, Fleece, and Ewey, while the Fourth of July brings Liberty, Glory, and Spangles. Thanksgiving is represented by Gobbles, while a tribute to Halloween is marked by Spooky, Pumpkin, Batty, Radar, Spinner, Web, and Tie-dyed Batty (a production mistake that pushed up its value). For the more conservative, there is a collection of traditional teddy bears known as Teddies, in six different colors. Notably absent are a Labor Day bear (Rosie the Riveter need not apply), a Cinco de Mayo bear, or even a Teacher bear.

Conservative Messages

Conservative values are emphasized throughout, especially those of delayed gratification, as children wait, sometimes for months, to see if the latest releases have arrived in their local official Beanie dealer store. Shakti Gawain (1985) would be gratified to learn that the official Beanie Web site provides space for a new positive affirmation each day. Some recent affirmations were: "I know my beanies will always be my best friend," "A beanie a day makes the sun come and stay," and "When you feel down and blue, give a beanie a hug, and they'll forever love you!" Since Beanies only hold their value if their tush tags remain attached and the Beanie is unblemished, deep moral messages of sexual abstinence are subtly suggested. Just as teenagers have appropriated words and transformed them into their opposites, ("bad" now means good, "ghetto" is desirable), so the Beanie brigade have labeled Beanies that have been played with (and consequently soiled) as "loved," meaning of little or no (market) value.

Beanie moral messages extend to the marketplace as well. Brand purity is assiduously guarded when imitations appear. *Beanie World Magazine* offers tips on how to spot a Beanie fake, and an independent Beanie verification Web site (BeaniePhenomenon.com) offers a Beanie authentication service. Fake Beanies have been seized regularly by U.S. Customs officials at ports and airports (Dunne, 1998, p. 33). Ty Inc. sues anyone caught imitating its Beanie Babies. In 1999, a trademark infringement suit was filed against HolyBears, a Houston-based company launched in January 1999 to help churches and schools raise funds for charitable purposes. If upheld, the courts would "impound and destroy all HolyBears...includ[ing] fuzzy critters with names like Forgiveness, Purity and God Bless Texas. Each HolyBear features a Bible-shaped tag attached to its paw" (Hassell, 1999). HolyBears founder Rob LeClair's reported affirmation carries a transcendental message: "Our bears are little messengers of God's word, and we will fight to protect them from destruction, even as we pray for their aggressors" (Hassell, 1999).

Beanies as Good and Evil

Beanies, viewed as wholesome and good, have opened the door to an oppositional dark side, an excellent illustration of Cartesian dualism. A rival strain of Beanies is known as Meanies and are marketed by the Idea Factory, Inc. Meanies, by contrast to the mortal Beanies, are nonterminating, meaning that they are always current and thus are unlikely to go away. This dark and permanent side of the psyche is embodied in such characters as Boris the Mucosaurus, Splat the Road Kill Kat, Hurly the Pukin' Toucan, Lucky the (one-footed) Rabbit, and Peter Gotta PeeGull, etc. Meanies, "an edgy alternative to Ty Inc.'s cuddly Beanie Babies, aimed at boys 6-12" (Stanley, 1998, p. 49), offer an additional dimension to the credibility of Beanies in their attempts to include the full range of emotional possibilities in a self-created cosmos. Beanies, by contrast with Meanies, perform a dialectic function of highlighting the goodness of the world.

Beanies embody a transcendental message of hope and redemption. Death is not final after all, since terminated Beanie Babies are resurrected as Beanie Buddies, bigger (and more expensive) reincarnations of your favorite bears. In fact, the Beanie pantheon now includes six generations—Teenie Beanie Babies, Beanie Babies, Beanie Buddies, Large Buddies, Extra Large Buddies, and Jumbo Buddies (the latter sell for about $100). Imaginary play-mates are redundant when the market can provide you with a steady flow of your favorite, once lost, friends. Thus, children are initiated, via Beanie cul-ture, into a "consumption theology that in effect promises redemption and happiness via the consumptive act" (Steinberg & Kincheloe, 1997, p. 11).

Beanie Science

Beanies also teach children science through a collection of life forms from dogs (21 varieties), birds (23 types), raccoons, elephants, buffaloes, puffins, kangaroos, hedgehogs, lobsters, flamingos, a panda (Peking), a squirrel (Nuts), a platypus (Patti), and a monkey (Nana), to a spider monkey (Mooch). Conservation is taught by including Manny the Manatee, Freckles the Leopard, Flash and Echo, the Dolphins, Congo the Gorilla, Chilly the Polar Bear, Canyon the Cougar, Splash the Whale, Velvet the Panther, and Peking the Panda.

Beanies go further than mere instruction. They prepare children for the world of academia, certification, and licensing through the Beanie swing tag, the only way to tell if a Beanie is genuine or not. But just as a primary degree is not sufficient to guarantee a good job, the tags have been supplemented with a tush tag (a more advanced form of certification similar to a master's degree?) that is sewn onto the Beanie's bottom. Since professionalism requires regular accreditation to demonstrate continuing competence, Beanie tush tags are changed each year and now incorporate holograms to avoid imitation. A beanie with a missing tag commands only 50 percent of the price of a complete one. Let this be a lesson to all who fail to get their diplomas!

Beanie Merchandising

Beanie Babies have revolutionized the rules of merchandising by breaking many of the laws of marketing. Consumer sovereignty, if it ever existed, is as dead as Nietzsche's God in Beanie promotion. There are no refunds on Beanies, and stocks are usually limited and scarce. Some stores hold raffles just for the privilege of buying Beanies, while others phone customers to inform them of their limited opportunities to complete their purchases.

The Secondary Market

Frequent Beanie retirements have also generated a vibrant secondary market that has spawned a whole industry of Beanie shows, Beanie collectors guides, and Beanie Web auctions. Indeed, the presence of such a large contingent of Beanie traders is credited by *USA Today* as possibly contributing to the meteoric rise of eBay's stock price from $18 to $73 in only a month (Henry, 1998). Clearly, Beanies are also good for the stock market. Beanies have brought economic liberation to the masses by creating a burgeoning secondary market where any eight-year-old can outbid or outwit a seasoned collector of Beanie retirees, teaching both the democratic nature of free markets. In this context, Beanies and Beanie knowledge are shared equally by young and old.

Conclusion

Beanie Babies provide a microsociety that interweaves market forces and imagination to create a seamless fabric that binds minds to the dominant paradigm of the global marketplace. This world is complete even to the Beanie pledge:

> We pledge allegiance to the Ty Corporation
> and to all those who love it so
> and to the tag, for which it stands
> one kingdom of happy animals
> cute and cuddly, big and tiny
> with miles of smiles and
> happy collecting for all (http://www.Ty.com).

Beanies are also a symbol of the disillusionment with technological dependency, and a hearken back to a romanticized age, to "the way we wish we were" (Coontz, 1992, p. 8). Beanie Babies can best be viewed as a Trojan horse designed to gain entry into the subconscious. In global terms, Beanies can inculcate notions of consumption, markets, freedom, and inclusiveness that are actually materialistic, exclusive, and controlling. Further, a false sense of international camaraderie may be created based on possession of brand products, on an idealized playground of marketing and exchange.

Through Beanie Babies (especially the collection of multiple forms), the global child (and also the adult consumer) is constructed as both naive and worldly, a creator of, and created by, the global marketplace, as an indweller of traditional spaces as well as a competent manipulator of technology and power. Beanies are products (along with many others) that have lubricated the wheels of materialist globalization, a complex site of both agency and control. Beanies join with many other Euro-American artifacts in the construction of a global capitalist hegemony, in the creation of a human desire for material objects and financial control.

■ References

Acuff, D. S. (1997). *What kids buy and why: The psychology of marketing to kids*. New York: The New Press.

Alfino, M., Caputo, J., & Wynyard, R. (1998). Nostalgia and mass culture: McDonaldization and cultural elitism (pp. 1–18). In Alfino, Mark, Caputo, John S., and Wynyard, Robin (eds.), *McDonaldization revisited: Critical essays on consumer culture*. Westport, CT: Praeger.

Beanie baby sales figures misstated. (10 October 1999). *Los Angeles Times*, C4.

Bourdieu, P. (1984). *Distinction*. New York: Routledge.

Bourdieu. P. (1988). *Homo Academicus*. Stanford, CA: Stanford Academic Press.

Brady, J. (1997). Multiculturalism and the American dream. In Steinberg, S. & Kincheloe, J. (Eds.), *Kinderculture* (pp. 219–226). Boulder, CO: Westview Press.

Cannella, G. S. (1997). *Deconstructing early childhood education: Social justice and revolution*. New York: Peter Lang.

Coontz, S. (1992). *The way we never were: American families and the nostalgia trap*. New York: Basic Books.

Cyrk reports record 1999 revenues, and stronger than expected fourth quarter and year end results: Company announces plans for new e-business subsidiary. (10 February 2000). *Business Wire Inc*. Press release.

Dunne, C. (1998). News flash! More counterfeit beanies seized. *Beanie World Magazine*, (1) 5:33.

Falwell's paper claims "demonic legend" behind festival name. (6 June 1999). *The Sun News*, A10.

Fiske, J. (1993). *Power play, power works*. New York: Verso.

Freire, P. (1997). *Pedagogy of the oppressed* (20th ed). New York: Continuum.

Gawain, S. (1985). *Creative visualization*. New York: Bantam Books.

Gibson, R. (22 May 1998). Teenie beanie babies make reappearance at fast food chain— McDonald's adds inventory and changes promotion to avoid snags. *The Wall Street Journal*, C24.

Goldman, A. (1999). End of the line for beanie babies? *Sun News Business*, 10.

Guber, S. S. & Berry, J. (1993). *Marketing to and through kids*. New York: McGraw Hill Inc.

Hassell, G. (22 September 1999). Ty raises cain over HolyBears, *The Houston Chronicle*, Business, 1.

Henry, D. (27 October 1998). Itching for cyber flea market eBay. *USA Today*. http://www.usatoday.com/life/cyber/tech/ctd722.htm.

Husserl, E. (1973). *Cartesian meditations*. (Trans. Cairns, D.). The Hague, Netherlands: Martinus Nijhoff.

Kincheloe, J. L., Slattery, P., & Steinberg, S.R. (2000). Introduction: Contextualizing teaching. *Education and educational foundations*. New York: Longman.

Kincheloe, J. L. (1997). McDonald's, power and children: Ronald McDonald (aka Ray Croc) does it all for you. In Steinberg, S. R. & Kincheloe, J. L (Eds.), *Kinderculture* (pp. 249–266). Boulder, CO: Westview Press.

Klein, N. (1999). *No logo*. New York: Picador.

Knox, J. E., & Stevens, C. (1993). Vygotsky and Soviet Russian defectology: An introduction to Vygotsky. *The collected works of L. S. Vygotsky, Vol. 2. Problems of abnormal psychology and learning disabilities*. New York: Plenium.

Mattel stifles Tarzan's hand action. (10 June 1999). *The Sun News*, A10.

McNeal, J. U. (1992). *Kids as customers: A handbook of marketing to children*. New York: Lexington Books.

Miller, D. (1987). *Material culture and mass consumption*. Oxford, UK: Basil Blackwell, Ltd.

Noddings, N. (1998). *Philosophy of education*. Boulder CO: Westview Press.

Reese. S. (1997). Kids as big busine$$. *Education Digest*, 62 (Mar. 97): 49–53.

Reese, S. (1998). Kidmoney: Children as big business. *Arts Education Policy Review. v 99* (Jan/Feb. 98):37–40.

Ritzer, G. (1996). *The McDonaldization of society: An investigation into the changing character of contemporary social life*. Thousand Oaks, CA: Pine Forge Press.

Rosaldo, R (1989). *Culture and truth: The remaking of social analysis*. Boston: Beacon.

Sobolewski, M. B. (June 1998). The official beanie babies club. *Beanie World Magazine*, 5, 19.

Stanley, T. L. (1998). Quaker buoys cap'n crunch with anti-beanie babies, meanies. (10 August 1998). *Brandweek*, 49.

Steinberg, S. R, & Kincheloe, J.L. (1997). Introduction: No more secrets-kinderculture, information saturation, and the postmodern childhood. In Steinberg, S. R. & Kincheloe, J. L (Eds), *Kinderculture* (pp. 1–30). Boulder, CO: Westview Press.

Toys anger anti-gang forces. (29 May 1999). *The Sun News*, A1/A3.

Viruru, R. (2001). *Early childhood education: Postcolonial perspectives from India*. New Delhi: Sage.

CHAPTER 5

The Complex Politics of McDonald's and the New Childhood: Colonizing Kidworld

Joe L. Kincheloe, City University of New York
Brooklyn College and Graduate Center

Childhood as we know it, of course, has not existed very long in historical time. Such an understanding is central to this book, as Gaile Cannella and I as editors and the various authors analyze the forces that shape and reshape childhood in the early twenty-first century. As several analysts have argued, childhood does not float in some timeless and placeless space, above and beyond the influence of historical and social forces. Like any other human dynamic, childhood is shaped by macro-social forces such as ideology. While individual response to such forces may be unique and self-directed, it is not simply free to operate outside of the boundaries drawn by such social influences.

Thus, the editors and authors here agree that childhood is a social construction, and based on this assertion set out to examine the forces that are presently constructing it. This chapter originates in that effort, as it examines the representative role that McDonald's plays in this process. McDonald's is representative of the many multinational corporations that devote great resources to marketing to children. The childhood issues that are raised by the activities of McDonald's elicit many questions about both the nature of childhood in the first decade of the twenty-first century and the ways present socioeconomic, political, and educational institutions contribute to its construction and reconstruction.

As Gaile Cannella has referenced in her work, this quest is still rather unique in the research and knowledge production that informs the literature of professionals who work with children. Much too often such literature has been content to leave the definition of childhood uncontested and separate from larger social forces. Thus, over the last few decades childhood has been viewed as "nonsocial" or "pre-social," more the province of developmental psychologists with their universalizing descriptions of its "normal" phases. Such academic approaches, while pursued with good intentions, have not served the interests of children and those who seek to help them. By undermining an appreciation of the diversity and complexity of childhood, such viewpoints have often equated difference with deficiency and sociocultural construction with "the natural." The complicated nature of childhood, childhood study, child psychology, social work for children, and childhood education demands more rigorous forms of analysis (du Bois-Reymond, Sünker, & Krüger, 2001; Cannella, 1997; Steinberg & Kincheloe, 1997; Jenkins, 1998).

The New Childhood

As Shirley Steinberg and I argued in *Kinderculture: The Corporate Construction of Childhood*, a new era of childhood has been emerging over the last several decades with relatively few people who make their living studying or caring for children noticing it. Since we made that observation in 1997 more and more individuals have recognized this paradigm shift, yet it is still not part of the mainstream discourse of most child-related fields of study and practice. This shift has been shaped in part by the development of new information technologies and the so-called information explosion resulting from them. While information technologies are not the only factors reshaping childhood, they are very significant in this process. Because of this significance, Steinberg and I argued that those with the financial resources to deploy such technologies have played an exaggerated role in reconstructing childhood. This, of course, is why I chose to study the McDonald's corporation.

Because of the profound changes initiated by a variety of social, economic, political, and cultural forces, many analysts maintain we can no longer make sense of childhood using traditional assumptions about its nature. While childhood differs profoundly around the world, we can begin to discern some common trends in industrialized and to some degree in industrializing societies. With increasing numbers of one-parent families, the neoliberal withdrawal of government from social responsibility for the welfare of children, the transformation of the role of women in society, and increased access to information via new information technologies, the world of children has profoundly changed over the last couple of generations.

In respect to changes in access to information it can be argued that children now in the era of the new (postmodern?) childhood possess huge amounts of information about topics traditionally viewed as the province of adults. Some scholars have argued that children often have more information than adults in these domains because of the time many have to access television, radio, the Internet, CDs, etc. One of the traditional ways suggested to differentiate between children and adults has involved knowledge of the world (Postman, 1994). In light of recent changes in information access, it is safe to conclude that traditional distinctions between childhood and adulthood may no longer be relevant (Casas, 1998).

Such factors not only change the way we categorize childhood and adulthood but change the nature of the relationship between them. Such changes hold profound consequences for parenting, teaching, social service case work, child psychological counseling, etc. In the context of parenting, evidence indicates that many children have gained more influence in the life of the family. In such families negotiation, engagement, and more open and egalitarian forms of interaction have replaced authoritarian, hierarchical parent-child relationships. One can identify this loss of traditional forms of parental control in families operating in a variety of social and cultural contexts. To illustrate the confusion and conflict about perceptions of childhood and how we should address children, it is important to note that right at the time traditional assumptions about, and categorizations of, children have been crumbling, the mobilization of the iconography of "the innocent child" has become omnipresent.

One cannot separate this innocent iconography from a larger right-wing reeducation project that began to take shape in the mid-1970s in relation to the reforms and liberation movements of the 1960s and early 1970s. What children need—especially those that have been "spoiled" by liberal forms of permissive parenting—the argument went, was a dose of old-fashioned parental authority and discipline. As children gained new forms of empowerment in the environment of the new childhood, their adult-like self-assurance and affect induced many individuals to intensify their attempt to assert childhood innocence and the need for a new adult authority.

The harder it became to answer questions about the duration of childhood, the demarcation between childhood and adolescenthood, the universality of developmental stages, or the cognitive capacities of children, the more frequently we have witnessed the raising of the flag of childhood innocence. In the confusion brought on by the advent of the new childhood, many nations in the industrialized world have witnessed profound disagreements in efforts to establish the age of competence. In this context numerous legal advocates have called for a reconceptualization of the very notion of competence that accounts for recent social changes in the nature of childhood. Driven by information technologies and media, these social changes have helped provide children with new degrees of control over the information they encounter. New technologies have allowed them to engage this information on their own time schedules in isolation from adult supervision (du Bois-Reymond, Sünker, & Krüger, 2001; Hengst, 2001; Jenkins, 1998).

In this new private space children use their access to information and media productions to negotiate their own culture, albeit within the ideological confines of the productions to which they are privy. Acting on this prerogative, children find it increasingly difficult to return to the status of passive and dependent entities that the iconography of innocence demands. This conflict between the empowerment and new agency that many children sense in the context of the new childhood versus the confinement and call for higher degrees of parental, educational, and social authority of the ideology of innocence has placed many children in confusing and conflicting social situations. The types of efficacy and self-direction they experience, for example, outside of school creates personal styles and modes of deportment that directly clash with the expectations of them possessed by numerous educators. The outcome of such interactions is not surprising, as the self-assured, adult-like countenance of particular children is perceived by educators as insolent and disrespectful behavior.

In my conversations with such children and educators, the recipe for conflict is apparent. Concurrently, this same recipe for conflict is present in the interactions of parents and children in the social context created by the new childhood. When this social context is juxtaposed with the tendency of Western societies, U.S. society in particular, to view children as economically useless, we begin to understand the sense of confusion and frustration felt by many children. While the labor market demands that they delay their entry into the workforce to a later and later age, children are seduced by the material desires of a consumption-based view of selfhood and educated by an information environment that opens the secret knowledge of adulthood to them far earlier in their lives than previously considered appropriate.

Thus, children in this new social context receive conflicting signals about their role in society, about what it means to be children. In the literature on childhood in the early twenty-first century, we are beginning to observe debates about the future economic role of children. Those who embrace the innocence paradigm advocate the protection of children from economic participation, while those who celebrate the changes leading to the empowerment of children discuss the reemergence of the "useful child." Do not confuse this latter position with a lack of concern for the abuse of children through the horrors of child labor. With both parents working outside the home, many argue, new domestic responsibilities may fall to children that will further change their social role in the family. Recognizing this shift, advertisers are already beginning to advertise home appliances and food in children's magazines.

In the new childhood the distinction between the lived worlds of adults and children begins to blur. While certainly childhood and adulthood are not one in the same, the experiences of adults and children are more similar now than they were before. Even the materials and artifacts of children's play in the last years of the twentieth and first years of the twenty-first centuries come from the same informational networks that adults use in their vocational lives. Corporate producers, marketers, and advertisers, recognizing these dynamics before other social agents, have reduced prior target market segmentations based on chronological age to only two: (a) very young children and (b) all other youth. Abandoning divisions suggested by developmental psychology, such business operatives realize how blurred age categorization has become (Hengst, 2001).

As Lynn Spigel (1998) argues, television producers who had traditionally attempted to produce separate programs for children and adults quickly came to realize that adults liked children's shows, and that children loved to watch "the very things that adults deemed inappropriate juvenile entertainment" (p. 122). Anyone who spends much time with contemporary children knows that they enjoy television shows, movies, musical groups, video games, Web sites, and modes of consumption produced for much older audiences. Recognizing this blurring of age distinctions, marketers for Disney have in recent years targeted children, adults, and elderly people in their advertisements. No age restrictions need be placed on the type of entertainment found in Disneyland, Disney World, and Euro Disney.

It is important to note that despite this blurring of the lines that separate childhood and adulthood, childhood has not simply collapsed into adulthood. Indeed, the new childhood seems to distinguish itself from adulthood on the basis of an affective oppositional stance in relation to it. In this essay this concept of oppositionality provides a central insight into the ways McDonald's utilizes its corporate power to speak directly to children. Children, many argue, like many ethnic groups, seek to distinguish themselves from those with whom they are frequently in contact—adults. In this cultural context many researchers have noted that ironically the more similar different ethnic groups become, the more emphasis is placed on maintaining a specific group's uniqueness. In this context it is interesting to observe how children—especially those from middle-class and above backgrounds—are drawn to cultural productions and even food (e.g., McDonald's) that transgress parental boundaries of propriety, good taste, and healthfulness. Children's consumption in this context can be viewed many times as an act of resistance to the impositions of child-centeredness and middle-class norms.

Along with their new self-assured demeanors and egalitarian styles of interacting with adults, this resistance to dominant cultural assumptions adds to the negative perception of children held by many adults. When adults ask why contemporary children seem so defiant and hard to discipline and control, it is important to understand the social factors relating to our notion of the new childhood. In response to such queries I often maintain that children simply don't see themselves in the same way many adults do. In the contemporary information environment, "new children" resist innocent representations of themselves as little tikes who need adult permission to operate. Of course, not all children react to the new childhood and their access to popular culture and other forms of adult information in the same manner; diverse children in different social situations relating to race, class, gender, sexuality, religion, geographical place, and other dynamics will respond differently.

The fact remains, however, that adults have lost the authority they once held because they knew things that purportedly sheltered kids did not. Adult knowledge in an electronic information society is uncontainable; children now see the world from more adult perspectives—or at least how reality is filtered by corporate information producers. Television in the last half of the twentieth century, for example, created a world where parents had less power over the types of things children would want to consume. And few realized the ideological consequences of children possessing the desires and fantasies that television advertisers and corporate marketers encouraged. McDonald's enters this story, as it used television advertising to insert itself into the consciousness of children (and, of course, adults). Early in its corporate history the company recognized the family politics and ideologies that were developing around the nature of childhood. It quickly became a player in the public conversation about these matters, as it concurrently directed huge amounts of money to its marketing to children (Spigel, 1998; Hengst, 2001).

McDonald's, Family Values, and the Ideology of Childhood Innocence

McDonald's founder Ray Kroc was obsessed with positioning his chain of restaurants in opposition to the social changes he saw occurring around him in the 1960s. He perceived such changes as tearing down the very values on which America had been founded, especially the value of the traditional family with dad working and mom staying home to take care of the children. Kroc and his corporate leaders understood their most important marketing priority was to tap into this protection of traditional values and to portray McDonald's as a "family kind of place." As an outward symbol of this commitment, McDonald's management in the late 1960s modified the spaceship-like red and white ceramic look of McDonald's restaurants to look more like the suburban homes that were built in the era. Ad campaigns proclaimed that McDonald's was home and that anywhere Ronald McDonald goes "he is at home." Indeed, home in the traditional everyone-knows-his-or-her-role Krocian articulation is where the burger is.

McDonald's ads of the era deployed home and family as paleosymbols—signifiers of our oldest and most basic belief structures. Such symbols positioned McDonald's as the defender of the traditional roles of men, women, and children and connected them to "the American way of life." Kroc (1977) would not have used the word "paleosymbol," but he understood that McDonald's should promote an image that in his words was a "combination YMCA, Girl Scouts, and Sunday School." Devised to tap into the right-wing depiction of the traditional family under attack from anti-family feminists, homosexuals, and other "screwballs," McDonald's so-called "corporate legitimation ads" didn't sell hamburgers directly, they sold social relations and ideology. In the midst of social upheaval and instability, McDonald's was presented as a rock of ages, a refuge in a society gone mad. McDonald's brings us together and provides a safe haven for our innocent children who are being exposed to all the filth of larger society.

After its unprecedented growth in the 1960s, McDonald's by the early 1970s began to realize it was no longer the "cute little company of the 1950s." Watching what he considered the horrors of the antiwar, civil rights, women's, and other social movements of the late 1960s, Kroc realized that connecting McDonald's to the traditional home and family would not only provide the nation with ideological service but would paint a happy and moral face on McDonald's, the big corporation. In the zeitgeist of the late 1960s and early 1970s, corporate leaders felt the sting of public criticism and sensed the need for legitimation ads touting that the social benefits and good citizenship of corporations was high. The corporate use of legitimation ads was successful, as public opinion came to view big business in a more positive light. McDonald's use of the theme of family values as a source of legitimation was one of the most successful campaigns in advertising history (Goldman, 1992; Love, 1986).

Popular Culture and the New Childhood

It is obvious in the first decade of the twenty-first century that childhood has changed. While many factors have contributed to this dynamic, this chapter will focus on popular culture, in particular the role McDonald's plays as a corporate knowledge producer in a media culture. Whenever one studies the relationship between cultural change and popular culture, attention must be given to the complexity of cultural production and reception. Simply put, researchers must understand that all audiences of popular and media texts make their own meanings of them. Just because McDonald's advertisers, for example, produce ads inscribed with particular ideological meanings, it does not mean that all receivers of such ads derive the set of meanings intended by the producers. Nevertheless, analysts of popular culture and popular culture for children (kinderculture) cannot discount the ideological intentions of corporations such as McDonald's. The relationship between producer and receiver is always complex and contradictory.

Since parents no longer possess the same amount of control of the cultural experiences of their children, they have lost a degree of influence they once played in shaping their children's values and worldviews. In the 1920s, for example, with the protected childhood firmly established, children had limited experiences that fell outside parental supervision or child-produced activities shared with other children. Since the 1950s more and more of our children's experiences are produced by corporations—not as much by parents or even children themselves. Popular and media culture are now the private domain of the child, even replete with earphones. At this point a key theme of *Kidworld* emerges: traditional notions of childhood as a time of innocence and adult-dependency have been challenged by children's access to corporate-produced popular culture.

As this change has occurred, parents and concerned citizens have typically ignored the corporate-controlled nature of television. Dissent toward television and the popular culture it transmits has been structured around the image of child as victim of the medium—little interest is generated concerning the power dynamics surrounding access to the dominant mode of communication in contemporary U.S. society. Within the paradigm of the innocent child, a belief persists that adults can roll back the social, cultural, and economic changes that have shaped childhood over the last few decades, that we can simply plug up the holes through which adult secrets reach children in an electronic hyperreality. Such an undertaking would demand a form of child sequestration tantamount to incarceration.

The task that faces childhood professionals and parents is intimidating but essential. We must develop education, parenting skills, and social institutions that will address this cultural revolution in a way that both nurtures and respects our children. Childhood professionals need to teach our children about particular scholarly knowledge work skills, while concurrently learning from them specific processing abilities that young people have developed in relation to the chaos of information in the electronic hyperreality. In this transformed context school becomes not as much an institution of mere information delivery as a hermeneutical site, that is, a place where meaning is made, where understanding and interpretation are engendered. Of course, this runs directly contrary to the standards-driven educational reforms of contemporary political leaders that focus on the memorization of isolated data for standardized tests, with little interest in the sophisticated cognitive abilities or potentialities of our children.

Children have learned much from popular culture's "cultural pedagogy." Cultural pedagogy refers to the idea that education takes place in a variety of social sites, including but not limited to schooling. Pedagogical sites are those places where power is organized and deployed, including libraries, television, movies, newspapers, magazines, toys, advertisements, web sites, video games, virtual realities, books, sports, etc. Our work as childhood educators demands that we study both in-school and cultural pedagogy if we are to make sense of the educational process in the first decade of the twenty-first century (Spigel, 1998; Steinberg & Kincheloe, 1997; Hinchey, 1998; McLaren, 2000; Kincheloe, 2001; Grossberg, 1995). Operating on the assumption that profound learning changes one's identity, we see the pedagogical process as one that engages our desire. The process of engaging our desire involves our yearning for something beyond ourselves shaped by the social context in which we operate, our affective investment in that which surrounds us. In this way cultural productions can capture our imagination and in the process shape our consciousness.

The organizations that create this cultural curriculum are not educational agencies but rather commercial concerns that operate not for the social good but for individual gain. Cultural pedagogy is structured by commercial dynamics, forces that impose themselves into all aspects of our own and our children's private lives. Patterns of consumption shaped by corporate advertising empower commercial institutions as the teachers of the new millennium. Corporate cultural pedagogy has "done its homework"—it has produced educational forms that are wildly successful when judged on the basis of their capitalist intent. For example, McDonald's market analysts understood the emerging concerns with "family values" after the social upheavals of the 1960s. It was not merely accidental that their expensive marketing campaigns connecting McDonald's with family values emerged at a time where such concerns were fermenting within the U.S. population.

As Steinberg and I argued in *Kinderculture*, this corporate pedagogy has replaced traditional classroom lectures and seatwork with dolls with a history, magic kingdoms, animated fantasies, interactive videos, virtual realities, kickboxing television heroes, spine-tingling horror books, Happy Meals, and an entire array of entertainment forms produced ostensibly for adults but eagerly consumed by children. Such teachers have revolutionized childhood. Such a revolution has not taken place in some crass manner with Leninesque corporate wizards checking off a list of institutions they have captured. Instead, the revolution (contrary to the 1960s idiom) *has been tele-vised*, brought to you and your children in vivid Technicolor. Using fantasy and desire, corporate functionaries have created a perspective on culture that melds with business ideologies and free-market values. The worldviews produced by corporate advertisers to some degree always let children know that the most exciting things life can provide are produced by your friends in corporate America. The economics lesson is powerful when it is repeated hundreds of thousands of times.

Situating the New Childhood in a Global Context

One cannot study the nature of childhood or McDonald's without situating both in the context of globalization. In short, globalization involves the expansion of corporations across national borders and the development of a group of cross-border economic relationships. Globalization is an ideology dedicated to promoting the value of the privatization process and its supposed inevitable triumph around the world. One of the disturbing aspects of globalization involves the fact that it was never approved democratically by peoples around the planet. Corporations have consistently called the shots and shaped the process of globalization in a manner that serves the interests of business. Governments controlled by corporate influence have played their part, typically issuing policy decrees that were arrived at without democratic deliberation.

With corporate ownership of media outlets, the public has been subjected to huge propaganda campaigns by international knowledge producers and their elite allies. Such a process has consistently weakened democracy, as it contains the power of labor, scales down the welfare state, produces a corporate-friendly body of public information, and undermines public education as it champions a privatized, neoliberal, and even more regulatory model in its place, and constructs new forms of cultural pedagogy to promote market values, consumerism, and good business climates. In this cultural pedagogical context multinational corporations have put together an ideological campaign to make their ways of seeing socioeconomic and political reality the "commonsense" of everybody everywhere.

The neoliberal corporate ideology of globalization touts the superiority of market economics, the ineffectiveness of government in the promotion of economic and political progress, the benefits of deregulation and privatization, a form of individualism and personal responsibility that benefits corporations by discouraging the formation of groups of citizens to challenge corporate power, the silliness of concerns with ecological destruction of unregulated corporate growth, and many other notions beneficial to corporate profits. These dynamics shape not only the grander economic and political spheres of life but also the intimate and personal aspects of individuals' lived worlds in the first decade of the twenty-first century.

The changes in childhood and the discourse about family values taking place in more and more societies can no longer be viewed outside the influences of globalization. Traditional conceptions of family and modes of childrearing are changing in response to such influences. As women, for example, have entered the workforce and renegotiated their social roles, the impact of these changes on children and family life has become apparent. Globalization must be understood as a central force in the study of contemporary childhood (Herman, 1999; Giddens, 1999). Indeed, *Kidworld* is a globalized phenomenon and this chapter is dedicated to an effort to confront the antidemocratic child-unfriendliness of the process. McDonald's, of course, is a key player in the ideological goals of globalization.

Corporate power without social responsibility opens tremendous opportunity for profit making and cultural damage. In so many contexts we can see the micropolitics of how this macro-feature of globalization plays out. Just one example of McDonald's power that we see play out again and again in many nations involves an ad sponsored by the health-conscious National Heart Savers Association (NHSA). As newspapers prepared to run the ad documenting the fat content of McDonald's burgers, McDonald's threatened to sue for libel. Arguing that the well-documented charges of the NHSA were "outrageous lies that no responsible newspaper should publish," lawyers for McDonald's induced five major newspapers to not run the ad (*Editor and Publisher*, 26 May 1990). Thus, corporate power operated to control knowledge production in a way that maintained its positive corporate image: "our burgers are good for you." In England, McDonald's was willing to spend tens of millions of dollars and many years in court fighting two unemployed activists who passed out a one-page leaflet entitled, "What's Wrong with McDonald's," in the much-publicized McLibel case (Vidal, 1997).

In the first decade of the twenty-first century everything about McDonald's is connected to globalization. As a multinational corporation McDonald's is hard at work restructuring world markets to support the maximum accumulation of profit. In order to hide its corporate agenda, its lack of social responsibility, and its identification as an *American* company, McDonald's disguises itself in other countries as a local operation. Thus, while McDonald's has globalized its production and marketing operations, it has attempted to present itself in a way that engages local cultural appeal. In the midst of its globalizing activities McDonald's, not unlike other transnational corporations, filters its cultural pedagogies through the cultural lenses of the local. The so-called globalized McWorld is mediated through local situations and local perceptions. A successful hegemonic power wielder attempting to win popular consent to its legitimacy would operate in no other way (Kellner, 1998; Goldman & Papson, 1996).

This localization within globalization is consciously promoted by McMarketers via a personalization motif. "You deserve a break today" has transmogrified into *"My* McDonald's." These restaurants claim the ultimate local status—they're *yours*, whether you are from Beijing, Fiji, Tel Aviv, or Peoria. And this, curiously, is what many analysts don't get: McDonald's customers are induced to produce idiosyncratic meanings of the Big Mac. When their customers "customize" the meanings of their consumption, McDonald's marketers have succeeded. Analysts unfamiliar with the complex workings of power wielders read this marketing/hegemonic success as an indication that concerns about corporate domination are overblown. Those social analysts and educators concerned with McDonald's and other corporate power wielders effects on children, the argument goes, are guilty of the same type of moral panic as the Christian Right (Buckingham, 1998). I believe this is a serious misreading of the relationship between globalized power wielder's and the best interests of children.

So concerned is McDonald's about implanting this perception of localization/personalization in the mind of the public that the company actually employs a vice-president for individuality. The stated function of this officer is to make "the company feel small" despite the reality of globalization. In Beijing, McDonald's markets itself to the Chinese people not as an American but as a Chinese company. Executives invest time and much money to let the Chinese people know the local features of the restaurants, including the local production of the beef and potatoes. The vast majority of the staff members, they are quick to assert, are Chinese. Despite omnipresent and fierce debates about Americanization and transnational corporate exploitation in Korea, many observers miss the power dynamics at work. Sangmee Bak (1997), for example, argues that Korean customers of McDonald's use creative consumption to transmutate the restaurants into Korean institutions. When researchers focus simply on the process of consumption, omitting any reference to production, in this case the marketing strategies of McDonald's, it is not surprising that power is erased. Hence, a complex power-driven global/local process is magically transformed into a happy individualized game of creative consumption. Concerns about corporate construction of childhood experience are irrelevant in this framework.

In such representations McDonald's is released from complicity in relation to, for example, East Asian environmental problems, economic exploitation, labor abuse, gender inequality, childhood obesity, and ideological conditioning of both children and adults. Many observers noting the culturally specific forms of marketing, advertising, and localization impulses that companies such as McDonald's employ, make the argument that transnational capitalism is *not* promoting cultural homogenization. In earlier decades the dominant model of assessing McDonald's global impact employed a crude cultural homogenization model. Such a perspective assumed that transnational corporations were homogenizing the world, that Beijing would soon look like Nashville and that the Chinese and the Tennesseans would think and act alike. If companies such as McDonald's were operating as global/local franchises and working their way into local cultures, then such crass homogenization was not taking place. In the absence of homogenization many analysts concluded that corporations were exerting little cultural, social, political, or economic effect (Salva-Ramirez, 1995-1996; Yan, 1997; Collins, 1998; Bak, 1997).

No Homogenization, but a Powerful Impact: McDonald's and the Ideology of Modernization

I became fascinated with the impact of McDonald's early in my life. In *The Sign of the Burger: McDonald's and the Culture of Power* (2001), I write of my personal relationship with McDonald's as a child growing up in the rural mountains of Tennessee. The company's signification of modern, up-to-date "with-it-ness" was a key feature of McDonald's appeal to me. As a siren of modernity calling me away from my premodern southern Appalachian upbringing, McDonalds' played a significant role in helping shape my evolving identity and eventual entrance into the modern, if not postmodern, America of the middle and late 1960s. To understand McDonald's for me and millions of other children and young people around the world was to move from the backwoods to the cultural center.

In *The Sign of the Burger* I chronicled numerous interviews with individuals from India, Burma, Egypt, Nigeria, Indonesia, Turkey, and other nations who had learned the same modernization lessons I had derived from the cultural pedagogy of McDonald's. This ability of McDonald's to connect its corporate image to the modern, to "what's happening," is a central theme in the way McDonald's influences the lives of children. Vandana Shiva (1997) taps right into this modernist dimension and its effect on children's consciousness when she refers to McDonald's attempt to invade India:

> There is a small middle-class and a tiny elite section that I believe feels inferior about what they are, that has been so subjected to the pressures of Westernization that they feel like second-rate Westerners, and people would go in [McDonald's] for the experience not because of what the experience is, but what it symbolizes.

As with modernity and "things modern" in general, McDonald's makes an Indian or a rural Southerner feel that he or she is getting something better than anything experienced before. McDonald's way of life involves something that is superior to *your* food, *your* culture, *your* family, and *your* perceptions of the way you presently conduct your daily affairs. Such elicitations don't homogenize the Indian and the Southerner but they do shape new ways of being that are accompanied by different life goals and different aspirations. Such influences represent the normalizing power of the Golden Arches in our lives. To "be somebody," my multinational interviewees and I understood in our own cultural and childlike ways that a modification of identity was necessary.

Of course, McDonald's marketers clearly appreciate this process and promote the corporation "as an exemplar of modernity" (Yan, 1997, p. 44). Indeed, hundreds of millions of people around the world in the first decade of the twenty-first century associate McDonald's with not only America but with the glorious benefits of Western modernization. McMarketers in this context have connected the sign of modernization to the company's devotion to scientific management with its standardized procedures of product generation, organization, and labor control. In China, for example, a central aspect of McDonald's advertising involves the assertion that the restaurant's food is carefully produced by modern scientific procedures and is thus much safer and "better for you than traditional Chinese foods." In a starkly misleading manner the company ties the modernist signifier to its operations by declaring the nutritional value of its *scientifically* constituted cuisine, even to the point of asserting the positive presence of fat in its burgers and fries. An important motivation for Chinese parents taking their children to McDonald's involves preparing children to succeed in a modern form of living. Learning about America, acquiring English, and observing how "moderns" live are believed to be central to the social advancement of young people.

McDonald's restaurants in China employ Aunt and Uncle McDonalds to extend the connection to this modernist Western signifier. Their role is represented as more than mere social directors—they are better described as facilitators of learning. Teaching children about topics such as geography, the West, and dancing, Aunt and Uncle McDonald come to embody the modernity and its closely associated ethic of success so valued by many Chinese people at the end of the century (Yan, 1997). Much like my own intuitions in Tennessee, many Chinese view McDonald's as a vehicle for escape from the blinders of traditionalism.

A similar modernist dynamic is occurring in Korea and Japan, where traditional eating rituals involved the communal sharing of rice from the same cooking pot. At McDonald's the meal is removed from this traditional, premodern communal style and individualized. This individualization is viewed by Koreans and Japanese, especially children, as a marker of modernity in its promotion of individual choice and uniqueness (Bak, 1997). In my traditional rural southern Appalachian background, my extended family's love of sharing brown beans and cornbread from the same cooking pot and iron skillet was viewed by many young people as another sign of our premodern status—or as we might have termed it, being "hicks" or "rednecks." No one ate beans by themselves in isolation from the group.

The hegemony of the call of modernity induced my peers and me and increasingly young people around the world to forsake the cohesiveness (and claustrophobia) of traditional communities for the material mobility of modernity. Much to its marketers' credit in the value system of the corporate cosmos, McDonald's has successfully provided customers with a "modern experience." In a sociopolitical and pedagogical context this experience of "eating modernity" is part of a larger privatized hegemonic process of changing the world and modifying the identity of its people one by one.

In China, totalitarian governmental leaders have grown increasingly aware of this modernization pedagogy. After embracing McDonald's in the previous decade, Chinese state policy has begun to issue concerns about McDonald's as agents of cultural imperialism. In this construct McDonald's takes its place alongside popular music, television, movies, videos, comics, fashion, and home design. Emerging from the crass conception of cultural imperialism as cultural homogenization, Chinese leaders are starting to understand the subtlety of the globalizing hegemonic process. McDonald's in my life in the southern United States forty years ago and in the lives of people in countries around the world in subsequent decades operated to desacralize premodern cultural experience. Holding out the view of a better life, the company subverted premodern alliances, networks, and affiliations. Social relationships are torn asunder as the private, abstract individual is constructed—an individual whose advertising-produced material desires necessitate his or her rejection of "old-fashioned" group membership.

Obviously, it is difficult to discern the specific impact of McDonald's marketing strategies, the way childhood is shaped, what is attended to, and what is ignored. The process is complex, involving the production of meanings and signifiers and their reception by individuals standing at different points in the sociocultural web of reality. But complexity does not imply that power is not influencing those with whom it comes into contact. Scholars of childhood must become rigorous ethnographers and semioticians examining in detail what children make of and do with the products they purchase. The analysis of such consumptive acts is inseparable from concurrent analysis of the act of production. While children may not directly receive the ideological meanings from McDonald's advertisements that Ray Kroc intended, ignoring the ideological dimension of McDonald's various forms of cultural production will produce misleading child research (Watson, 1997b; Best & Kellner, 1991; Goldman & Papson, 1996; du Gay et al., 1997).

Ideology, Consciousness, and Power: Colonizing Children's Desires

In a neoconservative/neoliberal era the attribution of ideological influence to corporate behavior elicits charges of deterministic modes of analysis. In reviewing Steinberg's and my analysis of corporate influence on childhood in *Kinderculture*, David Buckingham (1998) charged that power analysis reflects an old form of politics that promotes a technological determinism. Such a way of seeing views technological change producing absolute and inevitable social and psychological consequences for children. Such approaches are dangerous in their concern with validating the "democratic choices" and interpretive freedom of the consumer, and they ignore the influence of cultural producers. A more complex and balanced approach appreciates the complicated nature of power's effect on childhood and seeks to explore the construction of both consciousness and the unconscious. Many analysts have maintained that ideology is best transmitted in an unconscious manner and that resistance to such domination is always possible.

The process, for example, in which McDonald's engaged my interviewees and myself concerning the ideology of modernization is a terrifically complex unconscious process. My interviewees, for example, spoke at length about their perceptions of how they associated themselves with McDonald's modernity. All of them understood this dynamic in an idiosyncratic but conscious manner. As far as the ideological effects of such a process, none of them entered our conversations with such realizations. Interestingly, however, many of them began to consider such ideological effects as they answered questions about the influence of the modernization dynamic on their life paths. In these contexts the macro-aspects of the ideological interact with the micro-aspects of individual consciousness—and both must be examined by the scholar of childhood. The corporate producers of children's culture, kinder-culture, have developed increasingly sophisticated ways to colonize children's desires, both conscious and unconscious. They understand better, unfortunately, than many academic scholars of childhood the ways meaning can be manipulated by dominant forms of power (Gottdiener, 1995; Spigel, 1998).

In our naiveté about this complex process many scholars of childhood completely miss the hegemonic and ideological dynamics of McDonald's colonization of childhood and the profound effects this has when combined with thousands of other producers of kinderculture. After interviewing McDonald's customers in Seoul, South Korea, anthropologist Sanjee Bak (1997) wrote the following:

> Most customers I interviewed told me that their food choices do not simply reflect government guidelines or the agendas of interest groups that play on patriotic themes. Nor do they think that they are blindly influenced by the sophisticated marketing strategies of multinational restaurant chains. The young people who use the pleasant environment of McDonald's to socialize and study are fully aware that the management's intended use of this space is at odds with their own. Many customers even feel that they are taking advantage of the company by not spending enough money to compensate for the service received (p. 160).

The analytical failure here involves the need to look beyond the face value of an interviewee's words, a task of research discussed throughout the history of ethnographic research. How is subjectivity produced? How is consciousness constructed? Researchers asking these questions have often referenced the recursive nature of this process: Neither the human agent nor the macro-social power wielder operates independently of each other. Each is shaped via the recursive interaction with the other (Giddens, 1986). Bak has excluded the macro-social in his interpretation of the meaning of these comments. As Anthony Giddens (1986) argues, it is a basic interpretive mistake to equate an individual's knowledge of a topic with what he or she holds in his or her conscious mind about it. The actions, social practices, and ideological observances one engages in can best be described as a form of tacit knowledge to which a researcher can never gain *direct* access.

Bak's mistake mirrors that of many educational and sociological researchers who interview individuals about, say, racism. Most interviewees in this period of history will tell such inquirers that they are not racist. Upon, however, further indirect questioning and observation, one may be confronted with a variety of comments and behaviors that indicate otherwise. Contrary to the pronouncements of previous researchers of power who focused only on the production of ideology by social, political, economic, and cultural institutions, people are not cultural dupes. But a complex, measured analysis of the interaction of power producer and individual receiver indicates that in situations such as the consumption of McDonald's products and self-representations, individuals are influenced in ways that they themselves don't consciously recognize. If they consciously recognized such ideological influences, McDonald's advertising and marketing wouldn't work as well as they do.

With these dynamics in mind the power of McDonald's and other producers of kinderculture rests on the fact that it employs a pedagogy of pleasure. The power of McDonald's or Disney, Mattel, Hasbro, Warner Brothers, Pizza Hut, etc., is never greater than when it produces pleasure among children. In this manner consumption is linked unconsciously to identity formation (Warde, 1994), meaning in some degree that individual subjectivity cannot be separated from consumptive practices. Status in one's subculture, individual creations of style, knowledge of cultural texts, role in the community of consumers, emulation of fictional characters, internalization of values, affective deportment, perception of one's role in an institution (the family, for example) promoted by popular cultural texts/products—all contribute to the personal identities of children. Corporate-produced popular culture provides children with intense emotional experiences often unmatched in any other phase of their lives. It is not surprising that such energy exerts powerful influences on self-definition, on the ways children organize their lives, and on the very nature of childhood, without children ever recognizing it. Often they are too caught up in the pleasure of it all to reflect on the impact.

The New Epistemology of Childhood

Thus, children's relation to McDonald's and other forms of popular culture is complex: it is not always oppressive; it is not always empowering. All phases of the relationship must be analyzed in their specificity and uniqueness. In the same manner every aspect of McDonald's does not signal a macro-social dynamic at work; on the other hand, however, many do. Researching the impact of McDonald's on children's attention to the testimonies and actions of specific child customers of McDonald's is certainly necessary, but it is not sufficient in the inquiry needed to tell this story. When one conducts interviews and observations of children in relation to their connection to McDonald's, such inquiry may yield little insight if not accompanied by the researcher's understanding of cultural knowledges and social formations (Grossberg, 1992, 1995).

For example, it was interesting to observe and record the following interaction between mother and child in a doctor's office. As to its larger insight into McDonald's and childhood, it necessitates analysis against the backdrop of cultural knowledges and social formations. The mother is struggling to contain a restless and frightened six-year-old boy waiting to see the doctor:

> MOTHER: Would you please sit still and stop crying. Stop it! Now! I'm not going to take you to McDonald's if you don't stop it.
> CHILD: (screaming) I want to go to McDonald's. Let's go, Mommy. Please...let's go now. (crying) I want to go to McDonald's.
> MOTHER: I'm going to brain you. Now you just stop it.
> CHILD: I want a coke and a cheeseburger. Please (screaming) McDonald's, McDonald's, McDonald's! Cheeseburger!
> MOTHER: (slapping child across face) You're not going to McDonald's, young man.
> CHILD: (louder screams and hysterical crying) McDonald's! McDonald's! McDonald's!

A level of this child's desire had been tapped into by McDonald's marketers that transcends rational understanding. In his time of stress in the doctor's office the child seeks the comfort of his provider of pleasure. He doesn't want to go home; he wants to visit the Golden Arches. Reading her child's reactions, the mother appeals to the most severe threat she can formulate in the situation — the threat of not going to McDonald's. As the child breaks free from the mother's restraint, he runs around the waiting room screaming, crying, and flailing his arms. She chases him for several moments, finding it difficult to corral the child. Finally catching him, she carries him back screaming, crying, and flailing to her seat. She reassesses her strategy in her attempt to diffuse the situation:

> M O T H E R : I'm gonna buy you two cheeseburgers and one of them hot apple pies.
> C H I L D : (immediately calmed by the prospect of consumption at McDonald's) You are?
> M O T H E R : Yes, and I'm going to get you some of those animal cookies you like. Hippo-hippo-hippopotamus.
> C H I L D : I love those cookies. I LOVE THEM! Cheeseburgers and cheeseburgers.

The two continue to talk fondly of various McDonald's offerings. The child grows calmer and happier with every reference to McDonald's products — burgers as pacifiers. Consumption in this child's cosmos is the pathway to salvation. An important and profound lesson about the nature of life in contemporary America has already been learned: the centrality of consumption in everyday life. A second lesson may involve the position of McDonald's as a primary provider of pleasure in the child's world. I cannot help but contrast my own notions of pleasure and where it might be obtained in the premodern, "before McDonald's" rural Appalachia I had experienced at the age of six. What is important about the doctor's office vignette? Is it the factual account of the incident or a multitextual interaction connecting my own subjectivity, social theoretical backdrops, and issues of McDonald's capacity as a contemporary power wielder to colonize childhood desire? The intersection of the micro and the macro thickens the interpretive possibilities of the ethnographic account (Fontana, 1994).

There is, of course, no final meaning to "trouble in the doctor's office"; the interpretations I offer are dependent on the social structures and the ideological constructs in which I have invested. Though meaning here is loose and slippery, it does not mean that my readings are irrelevant. I stand ready to argue their contribution to the effort to understand McDonald's social power and resulting impact on contemporary childhood. It can be maintained that the vignette is a micropolitical reflection of a new childhood that positions children at the vortex of the new information environment, that decenters parents' roles as the primary providers of aid and comfort to their children. If childhood is an unstable historical category, then a new set of material realities, ideological assumptions, and configurations of power have made an impact on its arrangement. The child in the doctor's office possessed a detailed, if not expert, knowledge of McDonald's product line that he had learned via television. This knowledge was no longer regulated and the impact of this new condition was immediately recognizable (Manning & Cullum-Swan, 1998; Jenkins, 1998).

The new childhood, thus, is enabled by a new epistemology of childhood. One of the many historical factors that shapes childhood involves children's access to knowledge. In the electronic information environment of the late twentieth and early twenty-first centuries, children gain access to previously forbidden knowledges without parents knowing where or how they were obtained. Satellite and cable television systems carry 400 or more stations, Internet web sites multiply every year, and children have far more time to study and analyze these sources than adults. I have spoken to many children from the ages of five-years-old and older who tell me that "TV is their life." In the new information environment and the new childhood that accompanies it, attention to television, Internet, video games, music CDs, videos, and other productions is the *vocation* of children. They are the experts in this domain and their knowledge surpasses almost every adult. How can they respect those individuals (most adults) who have so little knowledge about such an important dimension of life?

The epistemological construction of the new childhood is not the only factor shaping the historical watershed of the late twentieth and early twenty-first centuries, but it is very important. Through their new access to information children know that there exists an esoteric knowledge of adulthood and that adults are hiding information from them. And this information, they often reason, like McDonald's hamburgers, is something that can bring them pleasure. The traditional educational curriculum was based on the assumption that children were devoid of information. In this context the role of the curriculum was to provide them with a sequential set of facts about the world that would fill their epistemological void.

In the electronic information environment of the twenty-first century, such curriculum assumptions are naive. Children now have huge volumes of information at a very early age (Spigel, 1998; Casas, 1998). Information-delivery pedagogies serve to replicate a larger social process, only in a much slower and, in the perception of children, boring manner. In light of the new childhood the primary role of formal education may need to consider moving away from the monolithic role of information delivery to more of a meaning making, interpretive orientation. As children gain access to more and more information, they need help conceptually connecting and making sense of the data they have already absorbed. The new childhood demands new forms of social analysis, new understandings on the part of childhood professionals, and new modes of education (Spigel, 1998; Casas, 1998).

Seducing the Child: Teaching the Curriculum of Consumption

With the advent of television in the years following World War II, the age boundaries of consumption began to shift. The power of television undermined the capacity of parents to control what would become the objects of children's desire, what they wanted to consume. Businesses saw the potential of television; they could directly and often in isolation from parents provide consumer education for children (Spigel, 1998). With no one to monitor the process they could immerse children in the corporate curriculum of consumption. Television had produced a new form of domination in American society using an emerging form of techno-power. I borrow this term from Doug Kellner (1989) to describe the expansion of corporate influence via the use of technological innovation. Using techno-power derived from television and other technologies, McDonald's has increased its ability to maximize capital accumulation, influence social, cultural, and political life, and influence children's consciousness.

McDonald's is devoted to bringing out the kid in all of us, corporate executives proclaim. With their firm grip of unprecedented forms of techno-power, McDonald's entire operation works to seduce children with its kid-friendliness. Its name evokes the warm associations of Old McDonald and his farm. The safety of McDonald's provides asylum, if not utopian refuge, from the kid-*unfriendly* contemporary world of child abuse, broken homes, and childnapping. Offering something better to escape into, the company's television depiction of itself to children as a happy place where "what you want is what you get" is very appealing (Garfield, 1992). Thus, by the time children reach elementary school they are often zealous devotees of McDonald's who insist on McDonaldland birthday celebrations and surprise dinners. Obviously, McDonald's advertisers are doing something right, as they induce phenomenal numbers of kids to pester their parents for Big Macs and fries.

McDonald's and other fast-food advertisers early on discovered an enormous and previously overlooked children's market. Children aged five to twelve annually spend about $9 to $11 billion dollars of their own money, according to what research study you believe. They influence household spending of an additional $160 billion each year, and research indicates all of these numbers are increasing (Sengheu, 2000). Every month nineteen out of every twenty children aged six to eleven visit a fast-food restaurant. In a typical McDonald's promotion where toys like Hot Wheels or Barbies accompany kids' meals, company officials can expect to sell 30 million to child customers. By the time a child reaches the age of three, more than four out of five know that McDonald's sells hamburgers. As if this level of child-consciousness colonization were not enough, McDonald's, along with scores of other companies, has targeted public schools as a new venue for child marketing and consumption. In addition to hamburgers for A's programs and advertising-based learning packets for science, foreign language, and other subjects, McDonald's and other fast-food firms have attempted to operate school cafeterias (Hume, 1993; Ritzer, 1993).

Make no mistake about it: McDonald's and its advertisers want to transform children into consumers—indeed, they see children as consumers in training (Fischer et al., 1991). Ellen Seiter (1993), however, warns against drawing simplistic conclusions about the relationship between advertisers and children, as have, she says, many well-intentioned liberal children's advocacy groups. ACT (Action for Children's Television), the leading voice against corporate advertising for children, fails to capture the subtle aspects of techno-power and its colonization of childhood. Viewing children in the culture of innocence who should watch only "good" television, meaning educational programs that portray middle-class values, ACT has little appreciation of the complexity of children's television watching. Children in the twenty-first century are not passive and naive television viewers. As advertising professionals have learned, children are active, analytical viewers who often make their own meanings of both commercials and the products they sell.

Whatever meanings they make, however, children definitely receive many of the messages that the advertisers want to insert into their minds. Over 81 percent of children aged three to six recognize the McDonald's logo and can match the Golden Arches to hamburgers. Successful consumer training is taking place here. Indeed, it doesn't take a great researcher to quickly discern that the basis of McDonald's operation involves the colonization of children's consciousness. In the phenomenal McLibel trial in England in the mid-1990s — England's largest civil trial — McDonald's marketers presented lengthy defenses of their focus on this seduction of children. To accomplish such captivation, McDonald's bombards them with songs, jingles, toys, gifts, collectibles, "lovable characters," and a clown. As a McDonald's ad running in the Chicago market in February 2001 self-consciously put it: "Resistance is futile!"

Brand loyalty is best created in children around the age of two, McDonald's spokespeople told the British court. If we can create an image of McDonald's in their mind at this age, we can induce them to get their parents to bring them to McDonald's. Using this connection with children, spokespeople continued, the corporation directs its efforts into new countries. When McDonald's first enters a country its advertisements are all aimed at kids — as one spokesperson put it at the trial: McDonald's "reaches families through children" (Vidal, 1997, p. 140). In the move to foreign markets spokespeople revealed that much money was delegated to the effort to connect McDonald's to soccer and other sports so children and parents will view McDonald's as a supporter of fitness and vigor. Such a connection will make people think, they maintained, that the company's food is healthy. In China, Hong Kong, Japan, Taiwan, and South Korea, observers watch these child-marketing dynamics play out like clockwork. Children are the vanguard of McDonald's new East Asian customers. The same changes in childhood occurring in the United States now seem to be affecting East Asia, as the independent consumption power of children is rising while their voice in the family is strengthening (Kovel, 1997; McSpotlight, 1997; Mintz, 1997).

Focused on the child as the center of its advertising universe, McDonald's turns all of its guns on teaching the curriculum of consumption. Promoting a McKids clothing line with embroidered McDonald's logos, Happy Meals for kids flying United Airlines, deals with TV networks for a dedicated in-store McTV channel for children, and a string of different magazines for children with an annual distribution of about 28 million copies, the company wants children to feel that they will be ridiculed and laughed at if they don't go to McDonald's (Synder & Waldstein, 8 February 1988; Kovel, 1997; Densten, 1992; Hume, 1987; McSpotlight, 1997). For these and numerous other tactics targeted at children, many governments around the world, including Sweden, Finland, Denmark, Germany, and Japan, have banned a variety of McDonald's marketing tools on the grounds that they exploit children.

Kroc knew immediately as he observed Mac and Dick McDonald's restaurant in the San Bernadino desert in 1954 that children were the key— the key to the heart of adult patronage of the Golden Arches. As he viewed the new medium of television emerging around him, he was particularly impressed with its lessons to children in the art of persuasion. Kroc was inspired by television's ability to coach kids on how to pester their parents for all the consumable goodies portrayed on the shows. This inspiration became the grounding concept for McDonald's Operations Manual—the so-called McBible. Encourage children, it implored McMarketers, to demand a greater voice in the family's decision on where to go to eat. In the McLibel trial one McDonald's executive testified that the company teaches children songs about the restaurant "to keep the memory of McDonald's at the forefront of their minds so they can again ask their parents if they can come to McDonald's" (McSpotlight, 1997). Amazingly, McDonald's official legal position during the trial was that their marketing never encouraged children to ask parents to take them to McDonald's.

Selling the System: McDonaldland

McDonaldland, I must admit, fascinates me as a site where the kidworld is colonized. In *Kinderculture* I presented a detailed deconstruction of the ideological inscriptions of the characters (Kincheloe, 1997). McDonaldland is a kid's text fused with Kroc's psyche that emerges as an effort to sell the system, to justify consumption as a way of life. As central figure in McDonaldland, Ronald McDonald emerges as a multidimensional clown deity, virgin-born son of Adam Smith, press secretary for free-enterprise capitalism. He is also Ray Kroc's projection of himself, his ego creation of the most loved prophet of utopian consumption in the McWorld.

All of the other characters in McDonaldland, the company's promotional literature reports, revere Ronald. He is "intelligent and sensitive…he can do nearly anything…. Ronald McDonald is the *star*." If children are sick, the promos contend, Ronald is there. Even though he has become "an international hero and celebrity," Ronald is still the same friend of children he was in 1963 when he was "born." According to the promotional literature designed for elementary schools, Ronald "became a citizen of [the McDonald's] International Division" in 1969 and soon began to appear on television around the world. Kroc was propelled to a new level of celebrity as the corporation "penetrated" the global market. Now known everywhere on earth, Kroc/Ronald became the Grand Salesman, the successful postindustrial Willy Loman—they love me in Moscow, Belgrade, Beijing, and New York.

The Operations Manual describes Ronald McDonald as a "strong marketing tool who loves McDonald's and McDonald's food. And so do children, because they love Ronald. Remember, children exert a phenomenal influence when it comes to restaurant selection. This means that you should do everything you can to appeal to children's love for Ronald and McDonald's" (McSpotlight, 1997).

Ronald and the McDonaldland characters were specifically created, McDonald's records indicate, for two to eight-year-olds. Advertising for this group was not designed to promote food but to highlight the "McDonald's experience." Such an experience involves more the entertainment value of McDonald's as a fun and colorful place to go. Such McDonaldland productions have worked better than the Dr. Frankensteins who created Ronald McDonald would have ever imagined. The success of Ronald's "world citizenship" is illustrated by children's love of him in Beijing. He is universally known in the city and merely the mention of his name produces great excitement.

Chinese children testify that their love for Ronald is based on his humor, kindness, and his understanding of the hearts of children. Interestingly, in light of the efforts of McDonald's to obscure its American origins, about two-thirds of children in Beijing think Ronald came from McDonald's headquarters in the city while one-third know of his origins in the United States Children in Beijing speak enthusiastically about their experiences in the restaurant. They tell stories about birthday parties, about the characters Aunt and Uncle McDonald created by the company for marketing purposes in China. As prime citizens of the Chinese McDonaldland, Aunt and Uncle McDonald recite poems, sing songs, and play games with young customers. Particular children describe the excitement of having "Happy Birthday" sung to them over the restaurant's loud speaker. One cannot come away from these accounts without an understanding of the profound power McDonald's exercises in the lives of Chinese children.

In the context of the nutrition of McDonald's products, the company spares no expense in the promotion of the illusion of the healthiness of its food in every country in which it operates. In addition to the distribution of misleading school materials about McDonald's promotion of children's health, the company has positioned Ronald McDonald in a rock band called Ronald and the Nutrients. Dressed in vitamin and mineral costumes, the band sings and plays songs designed to semiotically connect the company to good nutrition and the practice of eating food from fundamental nutrient categories on a daily basis (Yan, 1997; Vidal, 1997). One former Ronald McDonald, Geoffrey Giuliano, issued a public apology for his collaboration in these types of McDonaldland activities. Revealing that he was not sufficiently McDonaldized to continue, Giuliano said that he could no longer participate in crass efforts to use the Ronald charter to hook children on food that is bad for them and the world (*Toward Freedom*, 1999). "I brainwashed youngsters," he said, "into doing wrong" (quoted in Kovel, 1997, p. 30).

In an interview for a television documentary, Giuliano spoke of children's love of the Ronald character:

> I once went to a town called Bellevue, Ontario and they had let school out for the day and there were literally 15-20 thousand kids, my road manager called in Ronaldstock. I had one little microphone and did corny little "needle through a balloon" magic tricks and stuff. Nobody could see or hear anything but, I mean, it was like a national hall, it was as if the President had come to town. For Ronald McDonald. That's the kind of hero worship that takes good money to buy, you have pay for that, it's called brainwashing, and you gotta start young (McSpotlight, 1997).

And the McDonaldland characters:

> The McDonaldland characters, I've forgotten all their names, it was so stupid, but we were told that if they asked where the food came from that the hamburgers grow in a patch with the French fries next to them, it was just wacky, it was really whacked, and the McDonaldland characters were as close as we were allowed to get to the facts. In fact the only grain of truth in those characters was the one called the hamburglar—he was a criminal who used to steal all the hamburgers. Maybe that was some sort of perverse reflection of the corporate McDonald's mentality, I don't know. They were all subservient in the court to Ronald, the king, the monarch, myself. I was the only one allowed to talk—you had to be highly trained to talk (McSpotlight, 1997).

The Right-Wing Contradiction:
Free Market Values vs. Childhood Innocence

McDonald's stands squarely at the crossroads where one group of right-wing advocates of the market run into another right-wing group proclaiming the innocence of childhood. Though both of these tenets are parts of the conservative faith, something has to give when the interests of one intersect with the other. Advocates of the free market want nothing to interfere with the right of corporations to operate in a way that will best enhance profits. Of course, advocates of childhood innocence argue that nothing takes precedence over the protection of children. On this issue the right-wing advocates of family values find themselves between the political rock and the hard place with little wiggle room. This is one of many areas where the inherent contradictions of the unencumbered market exert an adverse effect on people in general and children in particular.

Parents have realized that children's enthusiasm for kinderculture, with its enthusiasm for particular television shows, toys, and foods, often isolates them from adults in their lives. What many parents and childhood professionals don't realize is that kids' exposure to market-produced popular culture has profound effects on children's consciousness and the adult conception of childhood innocence. Drawing on this technology-enhanced isolation, children turn it into a form of power. They know things that mom and dad don't. How many parents understand the relationship between Mayor McCheese and the French Fry Guys in McDonaldland? In this context battle lines begin to be drawn between children and parents, as kids want to purchase McDonald's hamburgers and toy promotions.

Strife between parent and child in working- and lower/lower-middle-class homes may revolve around money; tension in upper-middle-class homes may concern aesthetic or ideological issues. Questions of taste, cultural capital, and self-improvement permeate child-adult interaction in such families. In the ethnographic interviews I've conducted in relation to McDonald's as a cultural dynamic, I found numerous expressions of these conflicts. One upper-middle-class parent put it this way:

> What I resent the most about McDonald's is the way they cultivate such bad taste in my children. Those awful hamburgers! My god, after those hamburgers children can't appreciate the difference between good and bad cuisine. They have to be deprogrammed. I don't know what to do

sometimes; the more I try to deprogram them the angrier they get, the more they want to go back to McDonald's. I wish I could just shut McDonald's down.

What interesting cultural interactions between children and adults are set up by McDonald's! The child's ability to negotiate the restrictions of adult values is central to the development of an independent self. In the course of this struggle for independence and the experience of contradiction with the adult world, children of middle/upper-middle class, upwardly mobile parents may find negotiation of these dynamics quite difficult. Because of the parents' strict views of the inappropriateness of McDonald's and other forms of popular and television-based children's culture, the potential for parent-child alienation is great. At the heart of this familial conflict, ironically, is the knowledge production of the free market.

Again irony emerges in that it is the free market—that icon of the Right—that has recognized that children of the contemporary electronic era feel oppressed by ideology of childhood innocence. By drawing on the child's discomfort with middle-class protectionism and the accompanying attempt to "adjust" children to a "developmentally appropriate" norm, advertisers hit on a marketing bonanza. If we address kids as kids—with a dash of anarchism and a pinch of hyperactivity—they will love our commercials even though parents (especially from the middle/upper-middleclass) will hate them. By the end of the 1960s, commercial children's television and advertising were grounded on this assumption. Such productions throw off restraint, discipline, and views that children should be innocent, humble, and reticent. Everything, for example, that educational television embraces—earnestness, child as incompetent, unknowledgeable adult, child in need of discipline—market-driven commercial television rejects. In this market context, commercial television and the productions that colonize it such as McDonald's exacerbate children's oppositional culture.

Colonizing Positionality: The New Covert Kinderculture

Clearly understanding the contradiction between innocence and free marketing, McDonald's early on set its sights on the colonization of the covert and oppositional culture of kids. A covert children's culture has existed for a couple of centuries in schools and on playgrounds. The covert children's culture of the past, however, was produced by children and propagated via child-to-child interaction. Twenty-first century children's culture is created by adults and dispersed via television and other electronic sources for the purpose of inducing children to consume. As they carefully subvert middle-class parents' obsession with achievement, play as a serious enterprise, and self-improvement-oriented "quality time"—a subversion with several social benefits—advertisers connect children's culture to their products. McDonald's has done an excellent job of inconspicuously promoting these dynamics.

In the globalized kidworld we can see these dynamics at work. McDonald's and other forms of fast food constitute a central topic of conversation for Hong Kong school children. Parents and adults for the most part know little about this subject (Watson, 1997c). The changes in kinderculture in Asia have come remarkably quickly, as children get more and more of their information from corporate sources and less and less from their family. The fodder for the covert children's culture is provided by McDonald's, and its consequences in diverse places is profound. McDonald's, of course, is aware of the tightrope it is walking between tapping the kinetic power of children's subversive culture and the possibility of offending guardians of propriety. In this context McMarketers are always attempting to strike the right balance (Deetz, 1993; Mintz, 1997).

In their so-called "slice-of-life" children's ads, advertisers depict a group of preteens engaged in "authentic" conversations around a McDonald's table covered with burgers, fries, and shakes. Using children's slang ("radical," "dude," "we're into Barbie") to describe toys in various McDonald's promotions, children discuss the travails of childhood with one another. In many commercials children make adults the butt of their jokes or share jokes that adults don't get (Seiter, 1993; Goldman, 1992). Subtle though it may be, McDonald's attempts to draw some of the power of children's subversive culture to their products without anyone but the kids knowing. Such slice-of-life ads are opaque to the degree that adults watching them don't get it—they don't see the advertiser's effort to connect McDonald's with the subversive kinderculture.

This oppositional aesthetic is a key aspect of contemporary kinderculture. Henry Jenkins (1998) defines it as a phenomenon that "challenges or reverses adult categories and carves out a kids-only culture" (p. 29). Products such as fast food that kids can buy with their own money are often more liberated from the "good taste" of middle-class adulthood than more expensive commodities family members might buy as gifts for children. Because of this oppositional aesthetic, advertisers now know that the marketability of a child product can be predicted by the degree of negative reaction it elicits from a parent. The popularity of Ugly Stickers, Wacky Packs, Garbage Pail Kids, Toxic High stickers, "Beavis and Butthead" and "South Park," and McDonald's food over the last few decades reveals the power of this childhood oppositionality and the ways it can be colonized by marketers (Spigel, 1998).

When this oppositional aesthetic is combined with the fast pace of market change, even adults in their late twenties find their consumptive cultural cosmos quite alienated from teens and children. And this is exactly part of the appeal: The children's consumption community grants them a particular and unique identity separate from those even close to them in chronological age. This kindercultural oppositional identity can be found not only in the United States but all around the McDonaldized world. For example, many children in Hong Kong refuse to eat with their parents and grandparents in traditional Chinese restaurants or in dim sums, demanding that family members take them to McDonald's. The same is true in Taiwan where children make a qualitative distinction between the modernity of McDonald's and the old-fashionedness of local modes of dining—they choose, of course, McDonald's modernity as an oppositional rejection of cultural tradition (Martin & Schumann, 1997; Bell & Valentine, 1997; Watson, 1997c; Kellner, 1998).

Knowing the proper behaviors that dining in McDonald's mandates is another factor that sets children apart from their parents and extended families. Children in Beijing reported that understanding the expected behaviors in the restaurant made them feel more civilized (Yan, 1997). Such an observation reminded me of my cultural experiences with McDonald's in Sullivan County, Tennessee. My parents, raised in the rural Tennessee of the early twentieth century, were profoundly intimidated by the process of ordering at McDonald's. They quickly relegated this job to me. The couple of times my parents tried to order, they became confused and embarrassed by the fast-paced questions and expectations. At the age of eleven I felt a sense of being more civilized than they were, more of a modern than a hillbilly with my ability to negotiate the ordering and other expected behavioral processes. Such feelings set up a cultural chasm between my parents and myself at this point of my life. They were not the adult models I wanted to emulate in my quest for the modern identity. My oppositionality grew.

I was embarrassed by my parents' lack of modernity. One child in Hong Kong who had carefully watched McDonald's TV commercials to learn the McProtocols spoke of his own embarrassment, thirty years after my own, about his grandfather's inability to eat properly at McDonald's. In one of my interviews in a McDonald's outlet in Johnson City, Tennessee, I spoke to an elderly East Tennessee farmer waiting in line with his nine-year-old grandson:

> J L K: You taking your grandson to McDonald's?
>
> G R A N D F A T H E R: Yep, he loves this stuff.
>
> J L K: You like it?
>
> G R A N D F A T H E R: (laughing) Not particularly. I'm not much for it.
>
> J L K: You enjoy bringing him here?
>
> G R A N D F A T H E R: (laughing uncomfortably) Not much. I've never quite understood how all this works. He tries to tell me but I'm just too old to get it. He thinks I should be sent out to pasture. I don't know. Maybe he's right.

Even in the specificity and uniqueness of the local situations, these larger themes of oppositionality, modernity, alienation, and embarrassment continue to play out.

McDonald's continuously attempts to colonize oppositional characters. After the movie *Bill and Ted's Excellent Adventure* was released, the company designed an excellence campaign featuring a stoned, long-haired, countercultural kid who was used to inscribing his countercultural oppositionality on the Golden Arches. As surfer-valley dude tells the viewers:

> In the past, when ancient old dudes cruised, they used the stars to lead their way. This was not a very excellent system because they were lost all day and ended up living in bogus caves. But luckily we dudes of today have a most excellent number of highways and very many busy streets, and even more excellent than that—they've all been built right next to a McDonald's (Goldman & Papson, 1996, p. 11).

When advertisers engage in this type of subcultural appropriation, they have to get it totally correct. If the look or the words are even slightly off target, children and young people will retreat from a positive identification with the product. The company must understand the oppositional ideology that drove the formation of the subculture in the first place. Some advertisers call this practice "lifestyling for children" (du Gay et al., 1997).

All of these dynamics encourage a sense of independence on the part of children. We have our own kinderculture that no one else understands, our own peer group that resists penetration by adults, our own ideology of oppositionality that unites us, our own identity that is even recognized by television executives and advertisers, and our own products that we understand in a way no one else does, so let us have our independence, they demand. We are no longer children in any traditional sense; we are a new younger and mutant age category. We are not adults, but we are "adultified." McDonald's savvy sociologists of childhood recognized these social changes early and treated children as adult-like self-determining agents who call for more familial shots than generally assumed.

The adultified child is better coiffured, wears more jewelry and clothing, demands more and better quality entertainment, possesses more economic resources, and is more oppositional to adults than previous generations of children. These changes in childhood have taken place amazingly quickly in the United States and around the world. In Hong Kong, for example, children hardly ever ate outside the home. In a little over two decades they not only eat out often but make decisions about when and what to eat (frequently McDonald's) without adult interference. The same fast change has taken place in Japan, as children in this country have gained new eating and consumption habits with all the accompanying cultural modifications. The new childhood is a reality that demands new ways of thinking about teaching, counseling, helping, providing social services, and relating to children. Childhood ain't never gonna be the same (Mintz, 1997; Watson, 1997c; Ohnuki-Tierney, 1997).

Power Relations, Children and Adults, and Food

In Western societies over the last five centuries, the process of eating and behavior at the dining table have undergone great changes. In the sixteenth century bodily functions such as spitting, urinating, and gluttonous eating were performed without embarrassment in public. In the seventeenth and eighteenth centuries these practices began to change, as self-control, eating in moderation, and bodily management during eating came to gain social value. The concept of manners developed in this context, and the eating table came to be seen as an important venue for social regulation in general and social training for children in particular. McDonald's, of course, changes this process by colonizing not only what but where and how children eat.

This post-sixteenth century change in eating habits served to make the dinner table a primary pedagogical site for young children. Parents, especially middle, upper-middle, and upper-class parents, not only taught their child to consume "good" food but to connect eating to important aspects of identity and personhood. Many elements of socioeconomic class and cultural capital were negotiated at the dining table: "Young ladies don't eat that way"; "a gentleman holds his knife and fork this way and sits up straight." In these ways children learned to control their bodies and assume expected social locations. Of course, in these dinnertime cultural rituals particular modes of deportment were negotiated and contested. Dinner was often a power struggle between parents and children, as battles were fought over body management and what types and "quality" of food were to be eaten. With the advent of the new childhood these battles became more frequent and more intense.

McDonald's marketing campaigns directed toward children induced young people to resist the parental pedagogy of the dining table. In the power struggles that ensued, children, buoyed by their desire for "the McDonald's experience," challenged parents' delineation of "good food" and proper dining deportment. Thus, McDonald's and countless other corporate knowledge producers once again came to replace parents' perspectives on the education of children. The pedagogy of dining is merely one more example of the ways the corporate construction of kinderculture imposes a wedge between parents and children and often under the flag of family values exacerbates familial conflicts. Scholars of childhood attempting to make sense of the experience of the new childhood in the twenty-first century must take into account the complex process by which children vis-à-vis various forms of knowledge production reject, oppose, or negotiate parental, teacher, and other adult manifestations of authority. Presently, in the discourses of the various child professions, these complex dynamics are not well understood (Bell & Valentine, 1997; Jenkins, 1998).

The Politics of the New Childhood

Children, adults, parents, and childhood professionals are caught in a zeitgeist of cultural transition in the meaning of childhood. In various countries around the world these parties are struggling to deal with the lived implications of these complex changes. Many people in these diverse locations have wondered how conceptions of childhood innocence intersect with the specific realities of children's everyday lives in the emerging new childhood. In this complex context we begin to contemplate the politics of the new childhood and its implications for the childhood professions. Entering into this deliberation we must take into account not only the power dynamics raised by McDonald's and other corporate influences but the way issues of childhood are positioned in the public discourse.

Traditionally viewed as a "soft" and feminine issue compared with "hard" masculine political topics such as taxes and national defense, the politics of childhood reflected the traditional gender divide of the feminine domestic space and the masculine public space. Recently with the right-wing trumpeting of family values, childhood politics has taken a more central role. In the United States the Democratic party in the 1990s began to challenge the Republican domination of family values issues. Democrats such as Hillary Clinton challenged the Republican role as the protector of our children with a call for public "it takes a village" support for programs that helped children. Regardless of political party, however, both views of childhood politics were grounded firmly on the ideology of the innocent child.

In twenty-first century U.S. politics no one steps outside the discursive universe of innocence ideology and the fetishization of children. This fixation on childhood innocence is typically accompanied by a universalization of childhood, a belief in the similarity of childhood across historical and cultural boundaries. This produces a misleading image of children standing outside of culture, a view of childhood that confuses mythology with reality. In this context the profound differences in children's experience may be overlooked, problems children face may be dismissed, and children's abilities may be discounted. Make no mistake, there are differences between the mainstream U.S. political parties as far as a politics of childhood is concerned. Republicans want to dismantle the public sphere as they focus on the individual experiences of children. The Democrats' vision places the child back in the public sphere, evoking a middle ground between state and private responsibilities (Jenkins, 1998).

Nevertheless, neither party seems interested in reconceptualizing childhood politics in light of the changes in childhood over the past several decades. Children exist perpetually in a "protected space," a realm where the major responsibility of adults involves shielding the innocent child from the corruptions of adult culture. Such viewpoints also support a recovery of patriarchy and the effort to police women who were perceived to be gaining too much power and influence via feminism and the women's movement (see Kincheloe, 2001). With the advent of the discourse of family values, women who worked outside the home for purposes of economic necessity or for personal reasons were placed "under suspicion" for failing to meet maternal responsibilities.

In such a neopatriarchal context women working outside the home were deemed by right-wing observers to be responsible for the decline of family values and the vulnerability of unsupervised children. As the rhetoric of family values re-sentimentalized the bond of devoted mother-innocent child, pressures intensified on women to stay home with children or if they couldn't, to at least feel guilty about their work-time away from them. The innocent child needs constant maternal supervision, the argument goes, and it is not the man's job to provide it. In this context we begin to see the ideological demands of the innocent child: We must return to a traditional society where women understood that care for the domestic space was their central and exclusive concern. A regressive politics of childhood begins to emerge.

In this regressive context an ambivalence toward children becomes more apparent. Adults long for children but are often subconsciously aware that their actual proximity can be annoying, time consuming, and even dangerous (Spigel, 1998). As adults look around them, especially with the ideological support of the right-wing representation of neglectful mothers and adult-like, threatening children, they are frightened by what they perceive as adults in the bodies of children. This ambivalence toward and fear of the "new child" was a central theme of Shirley Steinberg's and my *Kinderculture*. The regressive politics of childhood, with its image of the innocent child intact, views the new child as an aberration—a worldly smart-ass who is simply too big for his or her britches. Such undesirable children in this ideological context are often easy to hate.

This ambivalence/fear of the worldly child manifests itself more at the subliminal level than in overt public conversation—although in my research it is signaled clearly in many private conversations. As one mother told me:

> Children today have no respect for adults. They don't care about anything and would just as soon rob you as look at you. It's the fault of the parents. It's all about families and mothers who don't have time for children. Those women are going to reap what they sow. We're going to have to discipline them kids, show 'em who's boss. They don't get that at home. The world's going to hell.

Children with power seem especially threatening to adults. In *Kinderculture* we argued that one of the best ways to trace this social theme was to examine the cultural unconscious as manifested in movies and other forms of popular culture. In that context Steinberg and I explored numerous movies produced as the new childhood was taking shape that represented children as maniacal killers and monsters. The sheer number of such representations indicated to us that something was happening at the subconscious level that reflected adult reactions to the changes taking place in childhood.

The precocious child is a threat to what Valerie Polakow (1992) labels the right-wing order paradigm: a way of seeing that demands pedagogical adherence to the established developmental sequence and reward for the docile and obedient child (Cannella, 1997). In the ideology of the innocent child there is something quite disconcerting to the conservative order about a child-savant who learns about life "out of sequence" from television, the Internet, and other electronic media. Independent and self-sufficient children with an "inappropriate" insight into the adult world constitute the monsters in the evil-children movies. An important theme of this regressive politics of childhood rears its head in this context: Despite their "natural innocence," there is something to be feared about the latent monster in all children.

The conservative concern with order and equilibrium is reasserted in light of these repressed parental fears. The precocious child must be rendered obedient; the body must be regulated in the it's-for-your-own-good discourse of justification. Parental fears find legal expression in new laws defining new classes of juvenile crime, making juvenile records public, establishing boot camps for young criminals, outlawing the sale of spray paint to curb graffiti, and eliminating age guidelines in treatment of youth offenders (Vogel, 1994).

Recently published children's books attempt to frighten precocious children who become too adult into not only obedience but a new form of dependency. Written to counteract too much child identification with Macauley Culkin's precocious, independent, and successful Kevin character in *Home Alone*, Francine Pascal's *Ellen Is Home Alone* (1993) paints a gruesome picture for children who want to stay home alone. Her message is simple and straightforward: Staying home alone is scary; as a child you are incompetent; if you try to act like an adult you will be severely punished; if you resist parental control you may *die*. Pascal's infantiphobia and the "hellfire pedagogy" she uses to enforce discipline is not unlike Jonathan Edward's imagery of children in the hands of an angry God. The message is clear: The wages of adul-tification of children in the innocence paradigm and its regressive politics of childhood is death.

Constructing a Progressive Politics of Childhood and Childhood Education

The purpose of this analysis of the complex politics of McDonald's and the new childhood is not only to understand some of the sociocultural dynam-ics shaping contemporary childhood but to begin the process of developing a progressive response to these new realities. Without a progressive childhood politics and pedagogy, we are left to the mercy of the patriarchal, authoritarian, misogynistic, and child-fearing regressive politics of the Right. Our pro-gressive politics not only critiques traditional patriarchal family arrange-ments and unregulated corporate influences but sets into motion a process of developing new ways that families, educators, psychologists, and social workers might help nurture and raise children. Such new strategies must be connected to conceptions of democratic participation, social justice, and polit-ical transformation.

In this context a progressive politics of childhood and childhood education works to create situations that contribute to the empowerment of children. Our vision of a desirable politics of childhood helps children artic-ulate their own agendas and construct their own cultural experiences and facil-itates their understanding of the complex dynamics that shape their relationships and interactions with adults and the adult world. Here we sup-port work with children that helps them make sense of and critique their place in the web of reality, while at the same time developing a more mature picture of the society that produces the knowledge that bombards them. The ideology of childhood innocence undermines such an effort to help children make more sense of their lives. The innocent child is passive and can oper-ate in a domain of protection. He or she is objectified by adult fetishization and is denied the right of self-direction. When such innocent children encounter the lived world of the twenty-first century childhood, negative consequences often emerge.

Central to our childhood politics and the pedagogy that accompanies it is the development of a media and power literacy for both adults and chil-dren. Since the advent of an electronic hyperreality has revolutionized the ways knowledge is produced in the world and the ways children come to learn about the world, an understanding of this process is a necessity in the twenty-first century. The cultural pedagogy of McDonald's is an informal form of learning that oftentimes is not even consciously viewed as a pedagogical moment by children or adults even as it takes place in front of them. This is why a power literacy is so important to a progressive childhood politics and pedagogy: Much of the knowledge children learn in a curriculum of hyper-reality is produced by dominant power wielders in a manner that serves their political and economic interests. This point is central in any reconceptualized curriculum of childhood.

In such a curriculum children and adults learn that free-market needs set the agenda of corporate information producers. As the market frees children from the protective encapsulation of the ideology of childhood innocence, it ensnares them in the corporate ideology of consumption and market values. With an understanding of the corporate/market curriculum, the phenomenal power it wields, and the profound influence it exerts on children, we can approach issues of children's resistance to adult authority from a very different vantage point. Instead of viewing such actions simply as "misbehavior" or a psychologized "testing of limits and boundaries," we might see the situation in a sociopolitical context. Such a perspective could help us view the event as the adultified child perceives it: "I am not being given the respect I deserve as a knowledgeable agent." In most other situations in the child's life he or she is treated as a self-directed agent. The resistance displayed in this circumstance might be conceptualized as a manifestation of frustration engendered by living in a world with such divergent conceptions of the social role of children (Jenkins, 1998; Hengst, 2001).

When we view contemporary children in this manner, we begin to open new levels of understanding that lead to new avenues of adult-child interaction, new forms of trust and communication. The objective is not to simply conflate childhood and adulthood—there are obviously differences that require adults at times to exercise authority and to protect children. The effort that a progressive politics and pedagogy describes is one that engages both adults and children in the pursuit of a more complex portrait of kinderculture. With this knowledge adults and children can work together for democratic, just, and cognitively sophisticated cultural and educational change. In this manner children's quality of life can be improved in a manner that makes childhood a more happy and beneficial time for both children and adults (Casas, 1998).

Smarter Kids Deserve a Smarter Education

A simple but profound aspect of the new childhood that demands inclusion in a progressive politics involves new and more complex understandings of the cognitive abilities of children. While children are almost as vulnerable as adults to the hegemonic and ideological seductions of corporate knowledge producers, their abilities to discern unique meanings from the information saturation of hyperreality is quite remarkable. Like other individuals who differ from those whose identities help place them near the centers of race, class, and gender power, developmental/cognitive psychology underestimates their abilities (Kincheloe, Steinberg, & Hinchey, 1999; Kincheloe, Steinberg, & Villaverde, 1999; Kincheloe, 2001). Many argue that because of the new childhood and the sophisticated cognitive abilities that develop within it, the argument that childhood is a preliminary and preparatory stage of development prior to a substantially different, higher phase of adulthood is no longer valid (Hengst, 2001).

In the first decade of the twenty-first century we must accustom ourselves to the argument that kids are much more capable than generally assumed. The smarter our questions to children become and the more we take time to listen to them, the better we understand the sophistication of their efforts to seek self-direction and construct a unique identity. In light of the complexity of the contemporary information environment, children's ability to process it with such speed is remarkable. I am amazed when I watch an eight-year-old surf the Internet, watch television, listen to a music CD, and talk on the telephone while doing her homework—and fully attend to all tasks. One of the goals of a progressive politics and a progressive pedagogy of childhood involves helping adults understand these phenomenal abilities. Not only will adults understand and appreciate children more, but they may learn some valuable lessons (Hengst, 2001; Casas, 1998).

In this social and cognitive context of the new childhood we begin to reassess childhood education. How can schools stay the same when the large percentage of women and men in the workforce combined with the adultifying experiences children encounter have combined to profoundly change the everyday life of children in the new childhood? Such realities have operated to shift household chores and responsibilities, inducing some scholars to argue that mothers and children have switched roles in many contemporary homes (Hengst, 2001). These social, cultural, and economic alterations have set traditional expectations on their head. For example, the comfortable notion that one goes to school and then goes to work after educational preparation is beginning to fall apart. The old ways of thinking about and implementing education are being pressured by changing families, knowledge access, patterns of consumption, sexual knowledge and activity, views of adults, and self-perceptions.

One would be hard-pressed to discover public discussion of these issues or educational policies based on a recognition of them in contemporary U.S. education. The nature and the spirit of standards-based educational reform has so obsessed schooling in the United States that little time can be granted to anything outside the short-term improvement of standardized test scores. What is remarkable in this era of school reform is few people have noticed that schooling plays a decreasing role in the education of children. An increasing quantity of what children know comes from sources other than school. Indeed, the very importance of education-based, academic knowledge is becoming less important to children who see it as rather quaint in the expanding universe of knowledges.

Obviously, corporate-produced kinderculture is a primary source of knowledge in the new childhood. The traditional knowledge of school is viewed as less prestigious, less necessary in the commerce of everyday life. The contention that school knowledge is more important than the practical knowledge of the workaday world is no longer accepted by children and increasing numbers of adults. Such changes portend not only a new childhood but a new era of education where the form it takes will be difficult to predict. Where we can document changes in the everyday lives of children and even some changes in styles of parenting, we see far fewer changes in schooling. Schools cling to the concept of the innocent child who is more dependent and less self-directed than the image of children constructed in the new childhood.

Thus, the work of childhood educators, psychologists, and social workers remains entrenched in prior ways of conceptualizing children. As my coeditor Gaile Cannella has argued in diverse contexts, developmental psychology, humanistic childhood education, and child-centered pedagogies — as well-intentioned as their practitioners may be — do not always serve the best interests of children. Thus, the point of this analysis of McDonald's and the new childhood and of *Kidworld* in general is not simply to describe the changes in childhood and some of the forces that shape them, but it is to contribute to the process of rethinking the world of childhood professionals in ways that better serve the needs of contemporary children (du Bois-Reymond, Sünker, & Krüger, 2001; Hengst, 2001; Jenkins, 1998).

A progressive politics and a progressive pedagogy transcend reductionistic modes of education that simply transfer an unproblematized body of academic knowledge to children. At the same time such orientations completely ignore cultural pedagogies such as McDonald's and the increasingly important role they play in the life of children in the first decade of the twenty-first century. In this context childhood professionals devote more attention to truly listening to children, taking into account their perceptions of the world, considering their concerns and desires, and respecting their goals and aims. Of course, a neoprogressive politics and pedagogy will protect children when they need protecting, nurture them when they need nurturing, create new spaces where they can develop exciting new abilities and modes of empowerment, and love them in smarter ways.

■ References

Bak, S. (1997). McDonald's in Seoul: Food choices, identity, and nationalism. In J. Watson (Ed.), *Golden Arches East: McDonald's in East Asia*. Stanford, CA: Stanford University Press.

Bell, D., & Valentine, G. (1997). *Consuming geographies: We are where we eat*. New York: Routledge.

Best, S., & Kellner, D. (1991). *Postmodern theory: Critical interrogations*. New York: The Guilford Press.

Buckingham, D. (1998). Review essay: Children of the electronic age? Digital media and the new generational rhetoric. *European Journal of Communication, 13* (4):557–565.

Cannella, G. (1997). *Deconstructing early childhood education: Social justice and revolution*. Peter Lang: New York.

Casas, F. (1998). *Children, media, and the relational planet: Some reflections from the European context*. <http://www.childresearch.net/cybrary/mabm/cmrp/comments.htm>.

Collins, S. (1998). Review of James Watson (Ed.), *Golden Arches East: McDonald's in East Asia*. <http://www.mcs.net/~zupko/cs_book.htm>.

Deetz, S. (1993) *Corporations, the media industry, and society: Ethical imperatives and responsibilities*. Paper presented to the International Communications Association. Washington, DC.

Densten, S. (25 March 1992). McDonald's adds publishing to menu. *Advertising Age, 63* (12): 1, 45.

du Bois-Reymond, M., Sünker, H., & Krüger, H. (Eds.). (2001). *Childhood in Europe*. New York: Peter Lang.

du Gay, P., Hall, S., Janes, L., MacKay, H., & Negus, K. (1997). *Doing cultural studies: The story of the Sony Walkman*. London: Sage Publishers.

Editor and Publisher (26 May 1990). Anti-McDonald's advertiser defends ads. 123 (21), 11.

Fisher, P., et al. (1991). Brand logo recognition by children aged 3 to 6 years. *Journal of the American Medical Association, 266* (22):3145–3148.

Fontana, A. (1994). Ethnographic trends in the postmodern era. In D. Dickens and A. Fontana (Eds.), *Postmodernism and social inquiry*. New York: Guilford Press.

Garfield, B. (24 February 1992). Nice ads, McDonald's, but that theme is not what you want. *Advertising Age, 6* (8):53.

Giddens, A. (1986). *Central problems in social theory: Action, structure, and contradictions in social analysis*. Berkeley: University of California Press.

Giddens, A. (1999). *Globalization: An irresistible force.* <http://www.globalpolicy.org/globalize/define/irresfrc.htm>.

Goldman, R. (1992). *Reading ads socially.* New York: Routledge.

Goldman, R., & Papson, S. (1996). *Sign wars: The cluttered landscape of advertising.* New York: Guilford.

Gottdiener, M. (1995). *Postmodern semiotics: Material culture and the forms of postmodern life.* Cambridge, MA: Blackwell.

Grossberg, L. (1992). *We gotta get out of this place.* New York: Routledge.

Grossberg, L. (1995). What's in a name (one more time)? *Taboo: The Journal of Culture and Education,* 1:1–37.

Hengst, H. (2001). Rethinking the liquidation of childhood. In du Bois-Reymond, M., Sünker, H. and Krüger, H. (Eds.), *Childhood in Europe.* New York: Peter Lang.

Herman, E. (1999). *The threat of globalization.* <http://www.globalpolicy.org/globaliz/define/hermantk.htm>.

Hinchey, P. (1998). *Finding freedom in the classroom: A practical introduction to critical theory.* New York: Peter Lang.

Hume, S. (1987). McDonald's tests in-store kid video. *Advertising Age, 58* (51):1, 94.

Hume, S. (1993). Fast-food caught in the middle. *Advertising Age, 64* (6):12–15.

Jenkins, H. (1998). Introduction: Childhood innocence and other modern myths. In Jenkins, H. (Ed.), *The children's culture reader.* New York: NYU Press.

Kellner, D. (1989). *Critical theory, Marxism, and modernity.* Baltimore: Johns Hopkins University Press.

Kellner, D. (1998). Foreword: McDonaldization and its discontents. In Alfino, M., Caputo, J., and Wynyard, R. (Eds.), *McDonaldization revisited: Critical essays on consumer culture.* Westport, CT: Praeger.

Kincheloe, J. (1997). McDonald's, power, and children: Ronald McDonald (a.k.a. Ray Kroc) does it all for you. In Steinberg, S. and Kincheloe, J. (Eds.), *Kinderculture: The corporate construction of childhood.* Boulder, CO: Westview Press.

Kincheloe, J. (2001). *Getting beyond the facts: Teaching social studies in the twenty-first century.* New York: Peter Lang.

Kincheloe, J. (2001). *The sign of the burger: McDonald's and the culture of power.* Philadelphia: Temple University Press.

Kincheloe, J., Steinberg, S., & Hinchey, P. (Eds.) (1999). *The post-formal reader: Cognition and education.* New York: Falmer.

Kincheloe, J., Steinberg, S., & Villaverde, L. (Eds.) (1999). *Rethinking intelligence: Confronting psychological assumptions about teaching and learning*. New York: Routledge.

Kovel, J. (1997). Bad news for fast food: What's wrong with McDonald's? *Z Magazine*, 26–31.

Kroc, R. (1977). *Grinding it out: The making of McDonald's*. New York: St. Martin's Paperbacks.

Love, J. (1986). *McDonald's: Behind the arches*. New York: Bantam.

Manning, P., & Cullum-Swan, B. (1994). Narrative, content, and semiotic analysis. In Denzin, N. and Lincoln, Y. (Eds.), *Handbook of qualitative research*. Thousand Oaks, CA: Sage.

Martin, H., & Schumann, H. (1997). *The global trap: Globalization and the assault on democracy and prosperity*. New York: Zed Books.

McLaren, P. (2000). *Che Guevara, Paulo Freire, and the pedagogy of revolution*. Lanham, MD: Rowman and Littlefield.

McSpotlight. (1997). <http://www.mcspotlight.org>.

Mintz, S. (1997). Afterward: Swallowing modernity. In J. Watson (Ed.), *Golden Arches East: McDonald's in East Asia*. Stanford, CA: Stanford University Press.

Ohnuki-Tierney, E. (1997). McDonald's in Japan: Changing manners and etiquette. In J. Watson (Ed.), *Golden Arches East: McDonald's in East Asia*. Stanford, CA: Stanford University Press.

Polakow, V. (1992). *The erosion of childhood*. Chicago: University of Chicago Press.

Postman, N. (1994). *The disappearance of childhood*. New York: Vintage Books.

Ritzer, G. (1993). *The McDonaldization of society*. Thousand Oaks, CA: Pine Forge Press.

Salva-Ramirez, M. (1995–1996). McDonald's: A prime example of a corporate culture. *Public Relations Quarterly, 40* (4):30–32.

Seiter, E. (1993). *Sold separately: Parents and children in consumer culture*. New Brunswick, NJ: Rutgers University Press.

Sengheu, R. (2000). *Children's consumerism*. <http://www.mcom.ttu.edu./mc5378/rsengheu>.

Shiva, V. (1997). *Vandana Shiva on McDonald's exploitation and the global economy*. <http://www.mcspotlight.org/people/interviews/vandana_transcript.html>.

Snyder, D., & Waldstein, P. (8 February 1988). Big Mac opens in Sears stores. *Advertising Age, 59* (6):1, 70.

Spigel, L. (1998). Seducing the innocent: Childhood and television in postwar America. In Jenkins, H. (Ed.), *The children's culture reader*. New York: NYU Press.

Steinberg, S., & Kincheloe, J. (1997). *Kinderculture: Corporate constructions of childhood*. Boulder, CO: Westview Press.

Toward freedom. (1999). Clown conversion. <http://www.towardfreedom.com/dec99/ notebook.htm>.

Vidal, J. (1997). *McLibel: Burger culture on trial.* London: Macmillan.

Vogel, J. (1994). Throw away the key. *Utne Reader, 64* (July/August): 56–60

Warde, A. (1994). Consumers, identity, and belonging: Reflecting on some theses of Zygmunt Bauman. In Keat, R., N. Whiteley, and N. Abercrombie (Eds.), *The authority of the consumer.* New York: Routledge.

Watson, J. (1997b). Introduction: Transnationalism, localization, and fast foods in East Asia. In J. Watson (Ed.), *Golden Arches East: McDonald's in East Asia.* Stanford, CA: Stanford University Press.

Watson, J. (1997c). McDonald's in Hong Kong: Consumerism, dietary change, and the rise of a children's culture. In Watson, J. (Ed.), *Golden Arches East: McDonald's in East Asia.* Stanford, CA: Stanford University Press.

Yan, Y. (1997). McDonald's in Beijing: The localization of Americana. In Watson, J. (Ed.), *Golden Arches East: McDonald's in East Asia.* Stanford, CA: Stanford University Press.

CHAPTER 6

A Toy Story: The Object(s) of American Childhood[1]

Janice A. Jipson, National Louis University
Nicholas Paley, George Washington University

(1) Think about how toys help organize those behaviors we ascribe to boys and girls as gender

while maintaining and continuing to produce a history of contradictory and unequal social relations.

(2) Apply a materialist feminist mode of inquiry to toys and childhood by examining various texts such as *Time* magazine, the Wal-Mart sales brochure, and Fisher-Price advertisements on television for their foundational assumptions.

Sale! Furby Babies. They learn to speak English faster and have their own baby Furbish phrases (Kmart, 1999).

Star Wars Droid Developer Kit (Target Store).

Draw some more blobs of tubby custard and finish coloring the picture (*Teletubbies*, 1998).

Lovable Woody plays his guitar, sings songs and whistles. If Woody hits a bad note you can help him tune his guitar too! Batteries included (Wal-Mart, 1999).

(3) Determine what is concealed, or excluded, in relation to what is presumed or presented.

How can there be two Devils?

(Erik, 1999)

Barbie is walking out of a store. A store is a place. Look at the pictures and words below. Draw a line to connect each picture to the correct word (*Barbie*, 1999, 10).

(4) Try making visible those meanings that the culture allows us to say through inquiry into the power relations organizing allowed as well as disallowed meanings.

Choose from the McDonaldland Happy Meal Girl or Birthday Girl. Each comes with "magical" working accessories (Toys "R" Us, 1999).

You are my last hope, Captain Kangaroo.

(5) Demystify the ways in which dominant or ruling-class beliefs are authorized and inscribed in our subjectivities,

> What does it mean
> To be a girl, a boy,
> A preschooler, a teen?

Pretend to shop without leaving the house! Features electronic sounds, built-in scanner, credit cards, built-in microphone, catalog, pretend Money and scannable price cards (Wal-Mart, 1999).

Our institutional arrangements,

> Like childcare, Toy-saurus,
> Birthday parties?

And our various cultural narratives

> That would be magazines,
> Comic books, television!

Water bubbles on the stove top, sizzles on the grill. Plus a faucet really works (ShopKo, 1999).

Use the power of the Lego force to build your own Star Wars droids (*Star Wars Insider*, 36).

(6) Explore taken-for-granted beliefs, values, and assumptions encoded as power relations within the social texts and practices of playthings.

(7) View toys as central to the reproduction of the social order.

It's About the Toy Industry!

(8) Examine how toys help produce that which is allowed to count as reality.

(9) Question how they constitute a material force and at the same time are continually being shaped by economic and political forces.

(10) Deconstruct practice to expose textual boundaries and the ideologies they manage, revealing the taken-for-granted order they perpetuate and opening up possibilities for change.

(11) Ask how the toy-industrial complex connects major institutions involved or invested in the production of toys and toy ideology and how the

Laa-Laa's plate is empty.
What can you see that is
Full of tubby toast?
(*Teletubbies*, 1998).

Room for Barbie and her entire family. Includes furniture and sound effects (Wal-Mart, 1999).

What does Obi-Wan say to QuiGon while they wait for the Viceroy? (Knudsen, 1999, 13).

Wow! Pokémon has evolved
Which one is Weepinbell?
Which one is Bellsprout?
Which one is Victreebel?
(Pokémon, 1999).

I've dusted the fastest racers in the known universe—and you're next! (*Disney*, 1999, 21).

Includes 10 bone crunchin' WWF favorites—plus a bonus championship belt (Toys "R" Us, 1999).

Bruce Moose on the Loose.
Bruce Moose dances to the music as you try to get the loops on his antlers (Toys "R" Us, 1999).

Look at Barbie's pretty blouse and skirt! Color each picture that shows a piece of clothing. (*Barbie*, 1999, 12).

significance of the toy complex makes visible the commodification, accumulation, and labor issues underlying the consumption of toys — and also in the secondary and tertiary markets.

One of the essentials is missing (Paley & Jipson, 1999).

(12) Resist.

The imaginary world made possible by toys allows for an imagined relationship between the individual and the world — a system that relies on romantic notions to create and maintain the illusion of well-being. This romantic view prevents us from seeing how institutionalized childhood actually works to organize children while preserving racial, class, and sexual hierarchies — the effect of this illusory depiction of reality is that childhood is taken for granted and unquestioned while gender is understood as something people are socialized into or learn.

The rapture of Pokémon (Poké-mania, 1999, E-1).

(13) Reconstruct taken-for-granted social arrangements and expose economic, political, and ideological conditions upon which they depend.

When summer came, the Walker family raised vegetables to earn extra money so Poppa could go south to look for Sam and Esther (*Pleasant*, 1999, 29).

Tinky Winky, Dipsy and Laa-Laa are sitting on their tubby seats. Who is missing? (*Teletubbies*, 1998).

Charges forward and files missiles remotely. Includes a Megazord Transmorpher. Choose Deluxe Stratoforce Megazord or Deluxe Centaurus Megazord to battle evil space aliens. Each Zord is comprised of 5 smaller vehicles (Wal-Mart, 1999).

Ticket to tomorrow! 60 exciting activities with extra cartridges included. Helps to improve foreign language and typing skills while having fun. Every day/also VTECH Ultra Girl PC. Lots of fun learning activities — just for girls! (Target, 1999).

Includes secret pouch to store miniature Teletubbies toys (Kmart, 1999).

Elmo & Ernie — rock sensations! Each plays 2 cool songs and shake to the rhythm. Ages 1 & ½ and up (Toys "R" Us, 1999).

With toys like these -
It really is better to GIVE.
(Barry, 1999, 1G)

(14) Expose materialism, the division of labor, and the distribution of wealth (private property) in the context of historically prevailing local, national, and state interests and ideological struggles over meaning and value.

Video games represent social and cultural "texts" that can be read and interpreted on a number of different levels (Provenzo, 1991, p. 99).

(accumulation)

Certain rare cards are viewed as so valuable that kids are getting into fights over them at school. Lawsuits are being filed. It's only a matter of time before Al Gore proposes some

Samantha wears a flowing white gown trimmed with lace and pink ribbons. Fine lace forms the wide shoulder ruffles and edges the neck, $18.00 (*Pleasant*, 1999, 40).

Make'n Shake Nail Polish Maker. Create any color in the rainbow (Target, 1999).

Darth Sidious's apprentice is
a. Darth Vader
b. Darth Maul
c. Darth Evil
(Knudsen, 1999, 54).

For the American Girl who needs her own wheels, this wheelchair is just right. It comes with adjustable footrests, $28.00 (*Pleasant*, 1999, 64).

Connect the dots to see who this fearsome Pokemon is (*Pokémon*, 1999).

Along came the Noo-noo to tidy up the tubby toast mess (*Teletubbies*, 1998).

When you purchase awesome DK Star Wars books, you can also get your very own paper-engineered, posable, 3-D droid! (*Star Wars Insider*, 99).

The more you play with Pickachu the more he warms up to you. Squeeze his paw or give him a hug and his ears and mouth wiggle and cheeks light up (Wal-Mart, 1999).

kind of massive federal Pokemon program (Barry, 1999, G-1).

Take what you find along the way and in your way and put it there, too (Jipson & Paley, in press).

Thousands of local children chanting "gotta catch em all, gotta catch em all!" each morning as they troop to their schools (Poké-mania, 1999, 1E).

(15) Reconsider materialist feminist arguments that the nexus of social arrangements and institutions form the social totalities of patriarchy and capitalism and thereby regulate our everyday lives by distributing cultural power and economic resources unevenly according to gender, race, class, and sexuality.

(profit)

Monsters make for disquieting playmates (Chua-Egan & Larimer, 1999, 81)/Know this Pokemoniacs: your world is alien and barren to me (Corliss, 1999, 82)/Show me the Pokemoney (*Time*, 1999, 91).

Barbie really "walks" and pushes the stroller.

She magically eats cereal again and again—right before your eyes (Toys "R" Us, 1999).

Catch Pokemon at great prices—Link to both red and blue versions to catch all 150 monsters (Target, 1999).

Imagine the Possibilities!
(Fisher-Price, 1999).

Jar Jar is banished from his home (Knudsen, 1999, 8).

Flight Control Buzz Light Year understands and reacts to your comments and actions! He has 3 modes of play, pop-out wings, moveable head and joints and much more! (Wal-Mart, 1999).

Squeeze her hand, she coughs or cries and her cheeks glow red. Make her well with medicine. She says 3 phrases, and comes with accessories (Toys "R" Us, 1999).

Woody accidentally winds up with the other for-sale junk and gets stolen by Al, the sleaziest toystore owner there is (*Disney*, 1999, 28).

Some toys are weird, some are appealing, and some are both (Techno-gadgets, 1999, 3).

(16) Acknowledge that the materialist feminist analytic examines capitalism as a regime for the production of surplus value; the securing of private property; the exploitation and alienation of life and labor; the division and distribution of labor and wealth; and the exploration of meaning-making systems that reproduce capitalism and patriarchy.

The fantasy of children's innocence transcending adult racism (Goldin, 1998, 138).

(17) Interpret how patriarchy organizes difference by positioning men in hierarchical opposition to women and differentially in relation to class.

Trash is central to consumer culture (Twitchell, 1999, 3).

Buzz and Woody ride in their car for bath time fun (Wal-Mart, 1999).

Choose from Hidden Majesty, Ultimate Hair and Royal Elegance Queen Amidala (Toys "R" Us, 1999).

The Menace of Darth Maul expansion set has 30 rare, 40 uncommon, and 60 common cards (*Star Wars*, 1999, 8).

Jessie the doll was once owned by a little girl called Emily. But Emily grew up and gave Jessie away. Jessie now has a fear of being abandoned (*Disney*, 1999, 33).

Cool infrared technology remotely activates warning lights, alarms and exploding panels on the Royal Flagship. Ages 4 & up (Toys "R" Us, 1999).

Make up your own rock Pokémon. Give it a name, and draw it below. What special race powers does it have? (Pokémon, 1999).

Barbie is exercising (Barbie, 1999, 23).

Screech around hairpin turns and get ready for an awesome crash! With intersections, 4 hairpin turns and 3 Hot Wheels cars. Batteries sold separately (Toys "R" Us, 1999).

Your American Girl's got spirit to spare and a cheer to share! Dress her

The specific search for lower prices based on systematic comparison shopping (Miller, 1999, 49).

(18) Reveal how the unmediated contact a child has with his/her connections with toys allows the child to experience not a complicated, conflictual, and contradictory world but the illusion of tranquillity, plentitude, and fullness.[2]

Once consumption is separated from concerns of class and oppression/exploitation and made part of a lifelong attempt at creating meaning, we can finally appreciate why mall-condo culture is so powerful (Twitchell, 1999, 47).

Children's entertainment, like other social spheres, is a contested public space where different social, economic, and political interests compete for control (Steinberg & Kincheloe, 1997, 7).

(19) Consider how capitalism's continued success depends on the main-

in a classic pleated skirt, pullover, ankle socks, white tennies, and a red ponytail wrap. She's wearing red briefs (*Pleasant*, 1999, 56).

Go to infinity and beyond (Target, 1999).

Zur's main weapon of choice is his Zurgotronic ion blaster. When primed and ready, this evil weapon dispatches ion bolts with deadly accuracy—for extra Buzz-destroying power! (*Disney*, 1999, 30).

A mole laughs at you, then you bash him with your mallet! You're playing electronic Whac-A-Mole right at home! (*Disney*, 1999, 18).

Five lions transform into a giant robot with light-up eyes, sword, shield, and firing missiles! Action figures fit in cockpits (Toys "R" Us, 1999, 3).

Barbie is dressed as a bride. A declarative sentence always starts with a capital letter (*Barbie*, 1999, 41).

Draw lines between the droids that match (Knudsen, 1999, 16).

Dress like your doll (*Pleasant*, 1999, 66).

tenance of regimes of difference as well as on a range of material forces across ethnic, racial, and class boundaries.

(20) (Know that) forms of children's cultural expression are therefore intimately bound up with the changing alignments that define a community's social beliefs and practices of cultural transmissions (Kline, 1993, 44).

It is evident that the subjective significance of such objects implies the reduction or relief from anxiety, hence their function (Muensterberger, 1994, 27).

The child is now to be constituted as a projection or image that enables adult consciousness to range through possible views of selfhood (James, 1999, 57).

Jedi have good memories. How good is yours? (Knudsen, 1999, 67).

Choose Coastwatch, Simulation Station, Ninja Fire Fortress, Chrome Crusher or Construction Site (Wal-Mart, 1999).

Barbie is pretty. Barbie is pretty and beautiful. Pretty and beautiful are synonyms. Trace the synonym for each word (*Barbie*, 1999, p. 60).

Give someone a big hug. Color the picture (*Teletubbies*, 1998).

■ Notes

1.   This paper was constructed from an environmental scan conducted in Janesville, Wisconsin, during Thanksgiving vacation, 1999.
2.   We borrowed Althusser's idea, which was borrowed from Lacan's notion of the imaginary, "the imaginary relationship of individuals to their real conditions of existence" (1971, p. 52).

■ References

Althusser, L. (1971). *Essays in self-criticism*. Atlantic Highlands, NJ: Humanities Press.

Barbie first grade workbook: Hands on english. (1999). New York: Modern Publishing.

Barry, D. (28 November 1999). Dave Barry's holiday gift guide. *Wisconsin State Journal*. 1G.

Chua-Egan, H., & Larimer, T. (22 November 1999). Poke'-mania. *Time*, 81.

Corliss, R. (22 November 1999). The man who just doesn't get it. *Time*, 82.

Disney Adventures. (December 1999). New York: Disney Publishing Worldwide.

Fisher-Price television advertisement. (23 November 1999).

Goldin, S. (1999). Unlearning black and white: Race, media and the classroom. In H. Jenkins (Ed.), *The children's culture reader*. New York: New York University.

James, A., Jenks, C. & Prout, A. (1995). *Theorizing childhood*. New York: Teachers College Press.

Jipson, J., & Paley, N. (2000) *Questions of you and the struggle of collaborative life*. New York: Peter Lang.

Kline, S. *Out of the garden: toys and children's culture in the age of TV marketing*. New York: Verso Books.

Kmart mailer. (24 November 1999).

Knudsen, M. (1999). *Star Wars Episode 1: Galactic Puzzles and Games*. New York: Random House.

Miller, D. *A theory of shopping*. Ithaca, NY: Cornell University Press.

Muensterberger, W. (1994). *Collecting: An unruly passion*. New York: Harcourt Brace.

Paley, N., & Jipson, J. (1999). Standards. *The International Journal of Leadership in Education*. 2, 377.

Pleasant Company for American girls! (Spring 1998). Middleton, WI: Pleasant Company.

Poké-mania. (21 November 1999). *The Janesville Gazette*, 1E.

Pokémon Sticker Series #3. (1999). New York: Golden Book.

Provenzo, E. (1991). *Video kids: Making sense of nintendo* (p. 99). Cambridge, MA: Harvard University Press.

ShopKo mailer. (25 November 1999).

Show me the Poke'money. (22 November 1999). *Time*, 91

Star Wars Insider. (Oct.–Nov. 1999). Aurora, CO: The Fan Club.

Steinberg, S. & Kincheloe. J. (1997). *Kinder-culture: The corporate construction of childhood.* Boulder, CO: Westview Press.

Techno-gadgets, traditional toy choices. (25 November 1999). *Wisconsin State Journal,* 3.

Teletubbies: A funny day color-the-leader-book. (1998). New York: Modern Publishing.

Toys "R" Us mailer. (25 November 1999).

Twitchell, J. (1999). *Lead us into temptation: The triumph of American materialism.* New York: Columbia University Press.

Wal-Mart in-store advertisement. (26 November 1999).

■ PART II ■

Childhood Studies and Diverse Postmodernisms

CHAPTER 7

Korean Early Childhood Education: Colonization and Resistance

Mee-Ryoung Shon, Morehead State University

Maintaining historical beliefs in education grounded in Confucianism, Koreans accepted Christian kindergartens as a form of resistance to Japanese oppression, as a place in which the Korean language, names, songs, and beliefs could survive. A Korean Early Childhood Education emerged that has the appearance of modernist, Euro-American schooling, yet maintains elements of Confucianism and is occasionally labeled Buddhist education. The purpose of this historical chapter is to share this story of early education as both colonization and resistance, an education that both oppresses and denounces the oppressor.

Korean History

Korea, one of the most Confucian of all countries, has over 4,300 years of history. With a philosophical influence from Central Asia and China, Koreans shaped elaborate cultural, political, social, and religious codes. The early growth and development of the Korean people was not uniform, but was generally characterized by active contact, and sometimes struggle, with the Chinese people. From the time the Koreans developed an agricultural society, centering on the cultivation of rice, their culture gradually became identified with that of China. Korea produced iron tools and weapons and developed politically, economically, culturally, and philosophically under a strong Chinese influence (Nahm, 1989).

Koreans have used Chinese characters for writing since around the second or third century A.D., although Korean language uses an entirely different system. Even after the invention of the Korean alphabet *Hangul* in 1446, Chinese continued to be used as the official script until the late nineteenth century. As calligraphy was closely connected with the culture and values of China, Korea was under the strong influence of Chinese culture, philosophy, and politics. For example, the early rulers of the *Koryo* Dynasty (A.D. 918–1392) adopted the Chinese example of employing a civil service examination to recruit officials, which required applicants to compose verses on given topics. Handwriting was naturally included in the criteria for judgment. Such a system gave impetus to the interest in improving handwriting among the upper classes. Chinese calligraphy practices among middle class males, who were intended to move to the upper class, were promoted.

Choson Dynasty

Confucianism became a powerful instrument for recognizing the state and society and for infusing a new discipline into intellectual life in the fourteenth century with the inception of the *Choson* Dynasty (A.D. 1392–1410), which is better known in the West as the Yi Dynasty. Confucian ethics and values came to dominate social structure and behavior through the centuries, developing a society that highly valued academic learning while treating commerce and manufacturing with disdain.

In the late sixteenth century, however, Korea experienced the trauma of a seven-year war with Japan. After the court of the *Choson* rejected a request by the Japanese warlord *Toyotomi Hideyoshi* to make way for his invasion of China, *Hideyoshi* launched a campaign against Korea. Most of the Korean peninsula was devastated, and numerous Korean artisans and technicians were taken to Japan against their will, resulting in a major influence on Japanese crafts, calligraphy, and drawings (Yun et al., 1996).

Family Relationships

In early Korean history, the typical family was large. Several generations often lived together, with the head of the family regarded as the source of authority. All family members were expected to do what was ordered or desired by the family head. Obedience to the superior was regarded as natural and one of the most admirable virtues. Under this patriarchal system, men were traditionally given the responsibility of representing, supporting, and protecting the family as well as the power to command. Order at home was maintained through obedience to superiors, that is, children obeying parents, the wife the husband, the servants the master.

Most men and women married at an early age. During the *Choson* period, marriage at the age of twelve was not uncommon, but as years passed, the more common age for women changed to sixteen. The wife tended to be a couple of years older than the husband, especially among upper-class families. For financial reasons, males of the lower classes tended to marry at a later age. Nevertheless, all people were usually married before the age of 20.

Filial piety was considered the basic component and premise in the forming and shaping of personality. Koreans have always attached importance to the concept of fidelity. Even if her husband died young, a woman was encouraged to be faithful by serving his parents and not remarrying.

Korean Views of Childhood

Traditionally, Koreans have viewed the beginning of a child as when a couple initiates family planning. This period includes the preparation for becoming pregnant as well as cautions and prevention during pregnancy regardless of economic status or social class. An example includes the date prescribed by the lunar calendar when gods bless a good pregnancy (Lee, 1977)

January:	1, 6, 9, 10, 11, 12, 21, 24, and 29
February:	4, 7, 8, 9, 10, 12, 14, 19, 22, and 27
March:	1, 6, 7, 8, 10, 17, 22, and 25
April:	2, 4, 5, 6, 8, 10, 15, 18, 22, and 28
May:	1, 2, 3, 4, 5, 6, 12, 13, 14, 15, 20, 25, 28, 29, and 30
June:	1, 3, 10, 13, 18, 23, 26, 27, 28, and 29
July:	1, 11, 16, 21, 22, 23, 24, 25, 26, 27, and 29
August:	5, 8, 13, 18, 21, 22, 23, 24, 25, and 26

September:	3, 6, 11, 14, 19, 20, 21, 22, and 24
October:	1, 4, 7, 14, 17, 18, 19, 20, 22, and 29
November:	1, 6, 11, 14, 15, 17, 26, and 29
December:	4, 9, 12, 13, 14, 15, 16, and 24

The reasons for these dates are unknown, but the dates have historically been faithfully maintained. Further, a couple would not be allowed to stay in the same room together until their physical and mental conditions were right for becoming parents. For example, during a period of mourning or of extraordinary happenings when the couple's situation might be somewhat difficult or abnormal, the head of the family would prohibit the couple from staying in the same room. Remnants of these early views of pregnancy and child rearing have remained, even into the present.

Depending on the economic conditions, the couple, especially a prospective mother, takes in nutritious foods, minerals, and herbs, which are believed to result in the best conditions. Koreans have believed that psychological peace is as important as physical health; therefore, they pray for a hundred days for a healthy and righteous baby prior to pregnancy. When pregnancy occurs, there are many rules and taboos that must be observed to ensure a healthy child and a safe delivery. The woman must not approach others or do anything considered unclean. She must not kill anything nor do other mischievous things. A well-known publication, *Innate Principles* by Ms. Lee[1] in the 1300s, recorded the following (Lye, 1990):

> The placenta is the basis of the nature of human beings. Once it forms, it is almost impossible to be changed. The temper is inborn (innate), but the personal character of human beings are postnatal. Therefore, people can educate good-tempered-child as long as they dedicate themselves to prenatal education.

In addition to this period, there is a renowned proverb that says, "It is more effective to be educated during the ten months[2] of pregnancy rather than the ten years of education after birth." Since Koreans have believed that a peaceful mind as well as physical health is essential to being an ideal parent, the temper and characteristic of a child is believed to be decided before conception. This view reflects Koreans' unique perspective on childhood education, assuming that even a child's innate nature can be affected by the preparation of the prospective parents, and this extends the prenatal education far from pre-pregnancy. Even embryo and fetus are viewed as already independent human beings that could be enlightened by the physical and psychological practices of the parents. Children are the objects of socialization, who should be directed, taught, and educated as Korean, who should carry out Korean traditional values, social ethics, and cultural taboos.

The birth of a baby implies the participation of all—family members, relatives, and neighbors. The family of a newborn baby hangs a taboo rope on the front door of the home for twenty-one days, which announces the birth of a child as well as a prohibition of visits. This provides an exhausted mom peaceful and quiet rests from unnecessary visits and protects the infant from outside germs, which could be possibly carried by visitors.

On the hundredth day after the baby's birth, the family members and relatives get together to celebrate the survival of the infant. This celebration also indicates the shift of responsibility for child rearing and education. To keep the young mother healthy, the role of surrogate mother is frequently given to a grandmother who has rich experience and time. The grandmother becomes involved in the physical care as well as facilitating physical development by providing appropriate activities as the infant grows. For example, as the infant spontaneously moves his or her neck, the grandma repeats rhythmical words *Do-ri, Do-ri*, which is believed to promote eye-ear-neck coordination. As time passes, words like *Chak-chak-kung* (eye-hand coordination), *Gon-ji-gon-ji* (eye-finger coordination), *Ka-kung* (object consistency), and *Dan-ji-pal-gi* (toilet training) are demonstrated.

The birth of younger siblings takes the grandma away from the young child, and the educational role is handed over to a grandfather, who usually develops especially close relationships with grandsons. The grandson is taken wherever the grandfather goes, eats meals with him at the same table for table manners and good balanced diets[3], sleeps with him in the same room for the development of sleeping, dressing, combing, and cleaning habits, learns honorable expressions and the history of blood/clan relationships, and is given advice regarding conflicts with siblings or friends. When children play with peers, any adults who witness misbehavior are expected to admonish the children for their carelessness.

Generally, the concept of "childhood" as a separate group from adults did not historically exist in Korea. By the time young children (infant and toddler years according to the western concept) were trained in physical self-control, children leaped into the adult world by staying with elders, by practicing anticipated roles as males or females, and by engaging in early marriage.

This exposure to the adult world at a young age promoted an earlier maturation of human beings without the concepts of childhood and adolescence.

Seo-dang : A Private Institution for Males

Seo-dang was started at the close of the *Koryo* Dynasty (A.D. 1300) and carried out formal education only for multi-aged males, ranged in ages six to sixteen—some of whom were already married (Lye, 1990). A *Seo-dang* was a private institution run by a tutor, himself a philanthropist of the community, or a scholar of a clan[4].

The teacher called *Hoon-jang*,[5] who reached a high degree of scholarly work and had high respect from residents, was in charge not only of the children's in-class behaviors but also of their activities and attitudes outside the class, even at home. Corporal punishment by *Hoon-jang* was/is commonly accepted in society during instruction. Since multi-aged males studied together in the same room, individualized instruction and mastery learning were used for reading, translation, and calligraphy of Chinese characters.

Even though *Seo-dang* was not required by the government, the practice resulted in several highly regarded functions such as teaching literacy and fulfilling basic Confucian ethics. *Seo-dang* was widespread at the beginning of the Japanese annexation of Korea (at the beginning of the twentieth century), but gradually disappeared due to the coercive reform imposed by Japan as well as the Korean ardent desire to learn the "up-to-date" education methods of the West.

Education for Females

Under Confucianism, the proper relationship between the sexes is based on one of the five human relationships, that of husband and wife. Historically, children have played and grown up segregated by sex, as illustrated in the proverb: "Boys and girls at the age of seven should not be allowed to sit in the same room." The strict application of these rules resulted in severe restrictions on women while relative freedom was allowed for men. For women, there were three obedience principles: obedience to the father before marriage, to the husband upon marriage, and to the son after the husband's death. The women's role was "within," that is, within the home, which was her domain. It was the woman's duty to care for children, to help her husband with the farmwork, to prepare the meals, and to make the family's clothes. The female role was firmly established, and women were expected to adhere strictly to that role.

Under these circumstances, girls were educated at home by their mothers or other adult females around them. The content of their education revolved around ethical deeds as a good daughter, submissive daughter-in-law, loyal wife, and self-sacrificing mother. In general, girls did not have opportunities for group study outside the home. Aristocrats were occasionally taught by well-educated female relatives at home prior to marriage. Instruction involved how to be an ethical woman under Confucianism.

Development of Kindergarten in Korea

Early childhood education was introduced in Korea by Christian missionaries from the United States during approximately the same historical period in which Korea was annexed by Japan, two events that cannot be separated from each other. These events constituted a view of childhood and education that perpetuated both control and survival.

Missionary Schooling in Korea: Mental Colonization by the West

It was Lulu E. Frey, an American missionary and fourth administrator of *Ewha*[6] girl's school (high school for girls founded in 1886) from 1904–1921, who believed that kindergarten should be initiated in Korea by a person who had expertise in early childhood education. She made a personal visit to several kindergarten training schools in her sabbatical year in 1912 and found Charlotte G. BrownLee at Cincinnati Kindergarten Teacher Training School. BrownLee made a promise to work in Korea after her graduation and entered Korea in December 1913 as a Cincinnati female missionary. In 1914 she initiated the first kindergarten, *Ewha* kindergarten, for sixteen Korean kindergartners and established *Ewha* kindergarten teacher training school in 1915. To ensure the quality of kindergarten teachers, only women who had high school diplomas, were talented in music, and most of all, had a love for children were admitted. The curriculum of *Ewha* teacher training school was similar to that of the Cincinnati Kindergarten Teacher Training School (Lee, 1995) and included physical training, music, mud craft, drawing, nature study, literature or tales, child study, psychology, games, gifts, occupations, kindergarten programs, mother play, and education of man.

In 1918, E. VanFleet, who graduated from the Cincinnati Kindergarten Teacher Training School and had a bachelor's degree from the university, joined *Ewha* kindergarten teacher training school. Rooted in the Progressive Kindergarten movement, she adapted her expertise to this school and defined the aim of the kindergarten as the following: physical development, intelligent development, appropriate experience for young children, variety of expressive activities, the power of self-control, development of Christianity, satisfaction, and happiness. Her philosophy and practices were consistent with those of Charlotte BrownLee, who had created a "child-centered" approach that went beyond original Frobelian concepts.

Clara Howard, a graduate of Andrew University in Georgia as well as Peabody and Columbia graduate schools, joined the previous two missionaries in the further development of the Korean kindergarten. The focus of the curriculum was on play, music and song, handwork, and storytelling. Compared with traditional Korean education, in which multi-aged students sat in the same room and practiced reading, writing, and calligraphy with books and pens, kindergarten curricula were entirely different (see Table 1).

TABLE I: COMPARISON BETWEEN KOREAN AND MISSIONARY EDUCATION

	Traditional Korean Education	U.S. Missionary Kindergarten
Teaching material	Books and pens	Concrete play materials; gifts and occupations
Teaching strategy	Recitation, handwriting, memorization, mind practice	Hands-on activities such as play, dance, handwork, and storytelling
Role of children	Recipients of social regulations	Inquirers about the world
Role of the teacher	Social regulation administrator Moral ethics transmitter Tutor	Facilitator Provider
Teaching focus	Teacher-directed method Acculturation of children into the society	Child-centered method Modification of social concepts on childhood

Additionally, the three missionaries introduced new literature on teaching materials, curriculum, and instruction from the United States. They translated eleven texts, including "Conduct Curriculum," written by Patty Smith Hill for use with Korean children. Further, they organized "Mother's Associations" that focused on Korean child rearing as ignorant and resulting in high infant/child mortality. They made frequent home visits and conducted monthly meetings, baby contests, child bathing practice sessions, and workshops on preparing food for children.

Japanese Occupation of Korean Education: Physical and Educational Colonization

With the Japanese physical annexation of Korea in 1910, a "Korean Education Act" was put into place proclaiming that the Korean language was banned except in Korean language courses. By 1938, with increased Japanese control, even the Korean language courses were abolished; in 1940 all Korean names were discarded and changed to Japanese forms; finally, in 1945 all Korean schools except elementary were closed in order to send students to war.

Resistance

As other institutions disappeared under the control of Japan, enrollment in public education increased. However, the number of public schools administered by the Japanese could not keep up with the Korean demand for education. Only 50 to 60 percent of Korean applicants were able to attend the schools. This phenomenon resulted in the development of proxy institutions—kindergartens and *Seo-dang*—for lower elementary education.

More importantly, the prohibition of Korean language use in public schools accelerated the development of institutions that were not prohibited from fostering Korean language usage. Mainly because they were for very young children who were of little concern to the Japanese, kindergartens were considered unimportant and were free from regulation of curriculum content. This educational freedom resulted in enthusiastic participation by Koreans who used it to teach Korean language, songs, and historical tales. Since kindergarten could be established and managed by donations from philanthropists or charities, the schools spread to all parts of the country.

Korean intellectuals proposed that Korean songs and tales told in kindergartens were the last defense of Korean nationalism, Korean spirit, and Korean identity for the future of the country. Many wrote songs, which could be sung by kindergartners, that described the future of Korea as independent, glorified, and blessed. The following is an example:

Spring in My Native Village

(Words by Won-su Lee & Music by Nan-pa Hong)
The native village where I lived
Is in the valley where flowers bloom,

A village decorated like a palace of flowers,
With multi-color blossoms
Of peach, apricot, and young azaleas.
I long for the days when I played amongst them

Finally, cooperative kindergarten activities spread throughout the nation and resulted in public performances that created a sense of Korean homogeneity. These public stages of kindergarten activity were not simple presentations of educational outcomes; rather they provided a public place where Korean culture could be legally displayed. Since it was the only occasion that activities were performed in the Korean language from the beginning to the end, attendees were not simply the parents of the kindergartners but all Koreans who were anxious about the future. The representative song, *The Flower of Korea*, was repeated several times prior to each public performance, and was embedded with messages of concealed resistance.

The Flower of Korea

The light of spring sun is coming
From the valley of rugged mountains
Blooming buds are we, flower of Korea
Blooming buds are we, flower of Korea

The flower is blooming at the hill today
Spreading the fragrance around the whole country tomorrow
Blooming flower are we, flower of Korea
Blooming flower are we, flower of Korea

Being exposed to the storm on an open field
Though trees are blown down on the mountain
Coming out flower are we, flower of Korea
Coming out flower are we, flower of Korea

Summary: Resistance and Colonization

As discussed previously, the first Korean kindergarten was initiated by three missionary "experts" from the United States and followed in the steps of the

Progressive Movement in teacher training, teaching strategies, and parenting education. These new ideas changed the traditional Korean view of childhood, constructing "children" as learning through concrete play and hands-on activities instead of books, pens, and mind practice. Further, the period of childhood was extended by creating kindergarten years and by delaying the young person's passage into adulthood through continuous contact with elders. U.S. missionaries had been eager to introduce their beliefs about childhood and learning without any considerations for Korean culture, values, family relations, or social structures. U.S. childhood educational beliefs as well as child rearing practices were presented as superior to that of Korea, an undeniable form of mental and psychological colonization (Cannella & Viruru, 2000; Smith, 1999; Loomba, 1998).

However, Japanese invasion and the policy of Korean culture extermination placed Koreans in a position in which they had no choice. Although Koreans were unaware that so-called "western" beliefs about children and education would continue to dominate psychological views of themselves and learning until the present day (which is an issue that must be addressed), U.S. missionaries created an avenue in which Koreans used education for their advantage to actually perpetuate Korean language and culture and resist physical extermination. The complexities of colonization, the remnants of colonization, and the importance of critique and resistance cannot be denied. The Korean intersections with Japanese, American, and other cultures became very important and are extremely complex. These intersections must be unmasked and revealed as we form opinions and make decisions with/for diverse groups of children, families, and communities.

■ Notes

1. Traditionally, females spent a short period at their birth home and were raised to be a wife, daughter-in-law, and mother in the prospective family. Therefore, first names were not generally given to them. Rather, they kept their last name after marriage and were called by that name (e.g., Ms. Kim), or their birthplace (e.g., Ms. Seoul), or as one's mother after giving birth. The above reference does not have year, first name, or page numbers. The last name (Lee) and the time period, the end of the Koryo Dynasty (A.D. 918–1392), are given.

2. Koreans begin the first month of pregnancy on the first day of a woman's last menstrual period. The two weeks following menstruation are considered part of the ways a woman's body prepares for pregnancy.

3. Traditionally, adult males were served first, then females with children.

4. Among Koreans there is a strong bond between relatives and clan members. In the past, the clan were usually those who lived in the same town. Generally, *Hoon-jang* taught male clans for free, with the families providing living goods.

5. Koreans have believed that men of virtue, usually scholars, do not attend to economic conditions. Therefore, if a scholar sat in a room studying all the time and ignored the poverty of his family, he was still respected and called a "man of morality."

6. *Ewha* girl's school was initiated as a day school by American missionaries in 1886. During the first twenty years, there was no formal curriculum. Rather, the purpose was to keep females from being ignored. *Ewha* started middle school courses in 1904, and subsequently high school programs, which provided the foundation for establishing kindergarten (Lee, 1995).

■ References

Cannella, G. S., & Viruru, R. (2000). *Education and dominant teaching methods: Postcolonial critique*. Paper presented at the Bergamo Conference on Curriculum Theory, Dayton, OH.

Lee, K. T. (1977). *Mind structure of Koreans*. Seoul. Moon-lee-sa.

Lee, S. K. (1995). *History of Korean kindergarten before 1945: Its introduction and establishment*. Seoul. Yang-seo-won.

Loomba, A. (1998). *Colonialism/postcolonialism*. London: Routledge.

Lye, (1990). *Traditional early childhood education in Korea*. Seoul. Kyo-moon-guk.

Nahm, A. (1989). *Introduction to Korean history and culture*. Seoul. Hollym.

Nahm, C. A., Johns, B.J., & Lee, G. (Eds.) (1991). *I love Korea!* Seoul. Hollym. Co.

Smith, L. T. (1999). *Decolonizing methodologies: Research and indigenous peoples*. London: Zed Books.

Yun Seung-yong, Jun Won-Cheol, Kim In-soo, Choi Joon-sik, & Kim Chong-ui. (1996). *Religious culture in Korea*. Seoul: Hollym.

CHAPTER 8

Postcolonial Ethnography:
An Indian Perspective on Voice
and Young Children

Radhika Viruru, Texas A&M University

For several years now, if asked what the motivation for my research was, I would have probably included the word "voice" somewhere in my answer. In my field of early childhood education, dominant discourses are often criticized for representing a predominantly Euro-Western perspective on learning and development (Cannella, 1997; Silin, 1995) and for not giving "voice" to other groups (Polakow, 1992). But as I set about this process of discovering voices, it, too, seemed a well-intentioned but problematic concept. Questions like "if one gives voice to others, is it really their voice that emerges?" started to appear. Further, the privileged view of conferring or giving voice itself is fraught with colonial ideas. This paper thus attempts to look at the concept of voice, as it relates to young children, from a postcolonial point of view, which suggests that the very concept of voice itself reflects Euro-Western biases on speaking and listening (Mohanty, 1993).

Throughout this chapter, I will be using examples from an ethnographic study of a nursery school that I conducted in India. The school was located in a major metropolitan city in South India and served 115 children from various cultural backgrounds and ranging in age from two to five. The school administrators' perspective on voice would certainly question whether it is through voice, or silence, or even other forms of human representation that one is heard.

What Does Voice Mean?

The issue of voice seems closely related to the question of whose knowledge is seen as legitimate or valuable and informs dominant discourses. As Lincoln (1993) suggests, although research literature has begun to reflect increasing interest in and attention to nonmainstream concerns and issues, there is still "a paucity of research on those whose voices have been silent" (p. 29). The silent as a research category have been broadly defined to include nonmainstream gender, classes, and races (Weis, 1988; Giroux, 1991). Such groups are described as marginal, living at the margins, who have had their lives defined and circumscribed by texts which reflect white, male, middle-class biases (Bleier, 1986). It is interesting to note that children are not included within this definition, although they enjoy perhaps even less power than any of the other groups mentioned above.

The concept of voice, especially as seen in feminist writings from the 1980s, seems to have multiple meanings, but seems to be commonly used as a metaphor for freedom, power, assertiveness, and self-determination (Eurich-Rascoe & Kemp, 1997). Although dominant practices in early childhood education certainly claim to promote all of the above, many others suggest that by constructing children as beings whose development has to be carefully prescribed and monitored in all areas (Silin, 1995), these ideas have been reduced to meaningless dimensions. My son's kindergarten class, for example, is allowed "free art" time. Is giving children this kind of freedom, freedom at all?

Gilligan (1982) uses the term "voice" to signify the capacity to declare one's methods and principles of moral decision making: Thus, as a process voice is a person's ability to declare, to stand in, and to stand for one's own experience. The idea of voice has become such an established part of feminist discourses that it has evolved into a research method of interpretive analysis (Brown & Gilligan, 1992). This voice-centered method of research provides a "means of naming and holding the relational nature of psychological analysis" (Taylor, Gilligan & Sullivan, 1995).

Questioning Voice

The concept of voice thus seems an eminently reasonable one: for it allows the silent to speak. But as Fine (1992) points out, the concept presents numerous problems. She points out that social research confers on researchers the privilege of editing others' voices, without having to reveal how one does this editing. As related to young children, this is a major issue. For example, Piaget based his theory of logical reasoning on conversations with children (Walkerdine, 1988). However, it has also been illustrated that Piaget indulged in selective editing—focusing on the portions of dialogue that interested him and ignoring, or repressing, others. Thus, the early focus of Piaget's work discouraged what Egan (1988) calls the "other energetic and evident features of children's thinking...Their romance and fantasy were considered merely contaminants to his attempt to chart the growth of what he calls intelligence" (p. 23).

Fine also points out that even when researchers take the time to seek out other voices, they are often reproduced as though they were relatively uncontaminated and free of power relations. As Foucault has argued, all voices contain and negotiate power relations, for "oppressed informants are neither free from nor uncontaminated by dominant perspectives" (Fine, 1992, p. 219). In the preschool in India, and in my interactions with the school teachers, I could not help feel how our "voices" were contextualized by the dominant perspectives, which I, from a quasi-Western background, was seen as representing. Getting people to talk about things like the curriculum or multilingualism without comparisons to "Western countries" being invoked was difficult, and usually these comparisons resulted in Indian ways being seen as deficient or lacking. For example, Indian schools were usually criticized for being too academically oriented, since they did not have enough "play." Thus, the voices of the people in India, although they spoke and were heard, did not speak outside the context of power and history.

Lincoln (1993) suggests that the issue of voice, too, has been constructed as an either/or dichotomy, whereas it ought to be seen more as a process, for "it sometimes takes an extended amount of time for the silenced to seek and find their voices since the would-be narrators may have to find the shape and form of such stories, and a language and imagery for telling them" (p. 35). Thus, at the very least, the silenced must create their own constructions of voice, for it to be a "voice" rather than an echo.

more concretely...?

Postcolonial Perspectives on Voice

Postcolonial scholars are concerned with issues of discourse, agency, representation, identity, and history (Spivak, 1996) and how these have been used by colonizing groups to subjugate others. Mohanty (1993) examines the concept of voice from a postcolonial point of view and suggests that prominent discourses based on the idea of voice also produce Western subjects as the only legitimate subjects of struggle, while those from the so-called "Third World" are heard as "fragmented, inarticulate voices in (and from) the dark" (p. 42). The central issue, Mohanty suggests, is not just allowing different voices to be heard, which leads only to a benign vision of harmonious pluralism. Such an approach bypasses the issues of power as well as history that have created this difference. Different voices, she suggests, may bring conflict, struggle, and the threat of disruption.

I would like to provide an example of one of these "different voices." Although the emphasis in my study in India was not to seek or provide contrasts to practices in early childhood education in the West, many sharp differences emerged between the two systems. For example, in contrast to Western emphases on educating the "whole child," this school focused mainly on academic subjects such as English and different kinds of math. These curricular choices seemed to reflect not only societal values as to what constituted a proper education but also a belief in the right of children to control their own lives. By restricting its scope to academic subjects, the school provided the children with opportunities to make real choices in their lives. Social development, for example, was not something that the school officially concerned itself with: the children, on the other hand, seemed very involved in their social lives and relationships, which they directed in ways they wanted. This perspective on learning challenges and disrupts dominant discourses about early education.

The concept of voice has also been seen as reflecting ethnocentric biases. Lazreg (1988) asks the question "Isn't the whole point to have a voice?" and suggests that research in postcolonial settings should be about "seeing their lives as meaningful, coherent and understandable instead of being infused 'by us' with doom and sorrow" (p. 82). Lazreg argues that research has tended to see postcolonial subjects as existing "for us" rather than "for themselves"; their individualities have been fractured to fit the generalizing categories of "our" analyses, a process which is an assault on their integrity and their identity.

Parry (1996) points out that the project of a postcolonial critique is to deconstruct and displace the "Eurocentric premises of a discursive apparatus which constructed the Third World not only for the west but also for the cultures it represented" (p. 84). For example, in the preschool that I studied, the one message that the adults in the school seemed to constantly stress was not to trivialize their lives, by using Western standards that had no place there. The children, too, would not want, I think, others to underestimate or somehow disregard the joy and vigor with which they approach and negotiate schooling or the authenticity of their learning, no matter how "inappropriate" their environment might appear to Western eyes.

Bhabha (1996) indicates another dimension in which colonizing discourses "take over" people's voices: They produce the colonized at once as an "other" and yet entirely knowable and visible (p. 41). The voices of the colonized, it would seem, can be instantly understood now that they have been allowed to speak. With young children, we assume that if we could but listen to them enough, we would understand what "they are about." This assumption is in itself an example of the colonization that has been part of children's lives; privileged by a superior state, the adult has only to listen to understand.

Finally, postcolonial critics question the idea of voice in terms of the "essential untranslatability" of local discourses into imperialist languages (Chow, 1996, p. 128). Spivak (1988) indicates that speaking itself belongs to an already well-defined structure and history of domination. Thus, at the very best, postcolonial voices are translated versions of original thoughts. Spivak (1996) further points out that those postcolonial critics such as herself, who do speak, are able to communicate, to exchange, and "to establish sociality" because they have access to the "culture of imperialism" (p. 204).

Voice itself thus can be seen as part of colonizing discourses. In my study, I very quickly realized that any time an issue was identified as particularly important, it would not be brought out into the open—the issue would not be "spoken." The important issue would be hinted at, concealed behind layers of often contradictory messages, but would not come out into the open. One had to pay more attention to what was not said than what was said. There were times that I, the very Westernized participant observer, would force the issue out into the open. When the children looked particularly nice or said something interesting I would comment on it quite openly; at such times, my comments sounded, even to my own ears, as rather artificial and silly.

Breaking the silence did not stop with being artificial and silly. There were times when I would comment on more serious matters which immediately felt like an act of violence, forcing someone to abandon the discourses within which they functioned and enter mine, by using their voices. Perhaps the best example of this is a conversation that I had with a mother who had just enrolled her child in the school. For the first three weeks that the child was there, she cried from the time she arrived to the time she went home, all the while holding on to her lunch basket, from which she refused to be parted. The mother never said anything. She stoically came each morning, dropped off the child, knowing that her daughter would spend the next few hours crying her eyes out. She then picked up the still-crying child hours later. All morning, the teachers tried everything they could but the child could not be comforted. Throughout the weeks that the child cried, I never heard the mother say anything about the child's behavior. Eventually, the child settled down and became very comfortable in school. A few weeks later, the child became the star of the School Day function. One day, I accidentally met the mother and said something about how well her daughter had settled down. Still, the mother said nothing, but her face said it all. In one look, the lines on her face told me about her pain and doubt. Finally, she said, "It took her three weeks; she is really exceptional." I am sure that she would not have said those words to anyone else. By putting her in a position where she felt obliged to speak and otherwise express things that she had kept silent, I felt like a colonizer. It was as though she was somehow suspect because she had chosen not to speak about her emotions: She had to prove that she was "normal" by expressing them, by using her voice.

Alternative Expressions

If voice, too, is found lacking, then the next question is, "What are the alternatives?" There cannot be any one answer except to suggest that people must choose their own forms of representation to be represented at all. The following is a "story" from my study that seems to suggest alternative possibilities.

The Competition

During the early part of the school year, the school holds an annual recitation and fancy dress competition for the children. Those entering the fancy dress competition must "dress up" as something: a cowherder or a bride, for example, and be "judged." The recitation competition demands that the children recite, from memory, a poem or monologue, in any one of three languages. It was never quite clear why they had such a competition, but it seemed to be one of those activities held for the parents' sake. On the other hand, Gita Aunty, the school principal, told me that they take care to hold the competition on a weekday; otherwise, there would be too many siblings getting involved in the affair. Gita Aunty says that if it were held on a weekend the crowd would be impossible and so would the crowd involvement.

The competition was held on the school grounds, but was by no means a small production. It seemed to assume the air of a wedding: An enormous tent was erected; chairs were hired with the name of the renting company on them; a sound system was installed, but as often is the case in India, it arrived late and when it did arrive, it did not work properly. There were also two judges who were not associated with the school. The judges were seated so that they could get an unobstructed view of the small stage, which had been erected for the children to parade on. As soon as the children arrived at the school, they had to "register" with their teacher so that they had an accurate record for the judges. Each class was judged separately, the two-year-olds going first, followed by the older children. As each child's name was called, the parent would lead the student to the stage for a minute, to either display the costume or to recite the chosen piece. The judges would rank them on the spot and then they could get off the stage. Some children, even though they were all dressed up, refused to get on the stage; others entered the stage and performed without hesitation. Although obviously a competition, every child received a prize for participating.

The costumes obviously represented a great deal of parental effort, for they were all homemade and the recitations were very well rehearsed. The children, as was to be expected, looked quite adorable. I was, however, the only one to say so out loud.

This story, since it was the school's own construction, seems to represent their perspectives better than any conversation or interview could. Neither the parents nor the school were in the habit of praising the children for their appearance or their abilities, or for anything else. Those feelings were not expressed in speech, but, I conjecture, through this production, which allowed the parents to present their children to the community. This seemed one way for the parents to express not only their pride in their children but through the attention paid to the costumes, to demonstrate what good parents they were. The school did not openly talk about parent involvement as important, and did not expect the parents to demonstrate their commitment to their children by volunteering or otherwise helping out in the school. However, the entire affair seemed to be arranged for the parents' benefit. The children seemed to flourish in all the attention they received. Nobody told them how good they looked or how much they were valued. I do not think, however, that they ever doubted it.

■ References

Bhabha, H. (1996). The other question. In P. Mongia (Ed.), *Contemporary postcolonial theory: A reader*. London: Arnold.

Bleier, R. (1986). *Feminist approaches to science*. New York: Pergamon Press.

Brown, L. M., & Gilligan. C. (1990). *Listening for self and relational voices; A responsive/resisting reader's guide*. Paper presented at the Annual Meeting of the American Psychological Association, Boston, August.

Cannella, G. S. (1997). *Deconstructing early education: Social justice and revolution*. New York: Peter Lang.

Chow, R. (1996). Where have all the natives gone? In P. Mongia (Ed.), *Contemporary postcolonial theory: A reader*. London: Arnold.

Egan, K. (1988). *Primary understanding: Education in early childhood*. New York: Routledge.

Eurich-Rascoe, B. L., & Kemp, H. (1997). *Femininity and shame: Women, men and giving voice to the feminine*. Lanham, MD: University Press of America.

Fine, M. (1992). *Disruptive voices: The possibilities of feminist research*. Ann Arbor: University of Michigan Press.

Gilligan, C. (1982). Introduction. In C. Gilligan (Ed.), *In a different voice*. Cambridge, MA: Harvard University Press.

Giroux, H. A. (1991). *Postmodernism, feminism and cultural politics: Redrawing educational boundaries*. Albany, NY: SUNY Press.

Lazreg, M. (1988). Feminism and difference: The perils of writing as a woman on women in Algeria. *Feminist Studies, 14*:81–107.

Lincoln, Y. S. (1993). I and thou: Method, voice and roles in research with the silenced. In W. G. Tierney (Ed.), *Naming silenced lives: Personal narratives and processes of educational change*. New York: Routledge.

Lincoln, Y. S., & E. Guba, (1985). *Naturalistic inquiry*. Beverly Hills, CA: Sage.

Mohanty, C. T. (1993). On race and voice: Challenges for liberal education in the 1990's. In B. W. Thompson & S. Tyagi (Eds.), *Beyond a dream deferred: Multicultural education and the politics of excellence*. Minneapolis: University of Minnesota Press.

Parry, B. (1996). Resistance theory/theorizing resistance or two cheers for nativism. In P. Mongia (Ed.), *Contemporary postcolonial theory: A reader*. London: Arnold.

Polakow, V. (1992). Deconstructing the discourse of care: Young children in the shadows of democracy. In S. Kessler & B. B. Swadener (Eds.), *Reconceptualizing the early childhood curriculum: Beginning the dialogue*. New York: Teachers College Press.

Silin, J. G. (1995). *Sex, death and the education of children.* New York: Teachers College Press.

Spivak, G. C. (1988). Can the subaltern speak? In C. Nelson & L. Grossberg (Eds.), *Marxism and the interpretation of culture.* Urbana: University of Illinois Press.

Spivak, G. C. (1996). Poststructuralism, marginality, postcoloniality and value. In P. Mongia (Ed.), *Contemporary postcolonial theory: A reader.* London: Arnold.

Taylor, J. M., Gilligan, C., & Sullivan, A.M. (1995). *Between voice and silence: Women, girls, race and relationship.* Cambridge, MA: Harvard University Press.

Walkerdine, V. (1988). *The mastery of reason: Cognitive development and the production of rationality.* New York: Routledge.

Weis, L. (1988). *Class, race and gender in American education.* Albany, NY: SUNY Press.

■ C H A P T E R 9 ■

A National System of Childcare Accreditation: Quality Assurance or a Technique of Normalization?

Susan Grieshaber, Queensland University of Technology

The Australian government entered the debate about quality daycare in Australia in 1990 when it proposed a mandatory system of quality assurance (Wangmann, 1994). Formal involvement occurred later that year with the establishment of an Accreditation Consultative Committee, and in late 1991, the Interim National Accreditation Council was established (Wangmann, 1994). In 1993 the first edition of the document *Putting Children First: Quality Improvement and Accreditation System Handbook* was published by the National Childcare Accreditation Council (NCAC). The foreword of the document indicates that "Australia is the first country in the world to develop a national child care quality improvement system, initiated, funded and supported by the Commonwealth Government." The way in which the accreditation process operates is analyzed in this chapter to show that it is a technology of management and organizational procedures for long-day childcare centers in Australia. These management and organizational procedures incorporate a manual of instruction and associated practices that have the effect of constructing particular understandings of children, parents, staff, and norms of child rearing.

Putting Children First: Quality Improvement and Accreditation System Handbook uses fifty-two principles constructed by the NCAC and is one of several recent curriculum developments occurring within early childhood education in Australia. In this chapter, I argue that politicians, with the aid of economic rationalist principles, have formed a successful alliance with bureaucrats resulting in interventions into early childhood education that have not been seen before in Australia. This alliance has been instrumental in the production of educational devices aimed at the creation of docile yet productive child and adult bodies that are constantly being subjected to the law of normalization (Foucault, 1980). The most recent spate of educational techniques of discipline includes the somewhat familiar Foucauldian (1977) methods of observation, surveillance, recording, classification, regulation, calculation, and training. These more recent developments are being applied progressively to younger children, and in the case of long-day care, are being applied to areas that were formerly the domain of the family and, therefore, located in the private, rather than the public, sphere.

Recent developments in curriculum have occurred in several Australian states as well as nationally, and most states have published outcomes-based curriculum guidelines, curriculum frameworks, or professional development materials for the compulsory and the noncompulsory years of education. Several of these curriculum changes in early childhood education have been legislated at the national and state levels and accompanied by the economic rationalist rhetoric of efficiency, effectiveness, and improved educational outcomes. For example, the rationale for introducing a national system of compulsory accreditation for all long-day care centers in Australia was that an increasing number of children were spending large chunks of their lives in childcare and that some form of quality assurance was required (Foreword, NCAC, 1993).

Dahlberg, Moss, and Pence (1999) have affirmed that the current dominant language of early childhood education is the "language of quality" (p. 1). They argue that the notion of quality is intrinsically modernist and as such the issue of quality is dominated by "techniques that will ensure standardization, predictability and control…a desire for a clean and orderly world, devoid of messiness and complexity" (Dahlberg et al., 1999, p. 2). Focused on quality assurance, the Australian accreditation document (NCAC, 1993) is an attempt to demonstrate that quality in long-day childcare can be assured through a system of specifying indicators and outcomes. However, these indicators of quality and outcomes are portrayed as "universal and objective, identifiable through the application of expert knowledge and reducible to accurate measurement given the right techniques" (Dahlberg et al., 1999, p. 5). The prescribed outcomes are applied to all long-day care centers in Australia, as all centers are required to participate in the process and are measured against the standards specified in fifty-two principles (NCAC, 1993). This means that what are considered to be issues of quality assurance (by the NCAC) have been standardized and applied to all long-day care centers in Australia. A panel of experts designed the accreditation process and disseminated it to the childcare field. The very idea of a national accreditation system and the detailed process involved lend credence to the notion that the complexity of what happens in long-day care can be reduced to the measurement of fifty-two principles (outcomes) and the contents of a staff self-study workbook. The process of accreditation is presented as a neat and tidy, self-contained package. However, when examined, the package is permeated with technical and bureaucratic procedures and features such as a trail of auditing devices, performance indicators, and outcomes which are characteristics of outcomes or competency-based approaches to education.

Competency-Based Education in Australia

Politicians throughout Australia have embraced moves to competency-based education by endorsing across state and commonwealth levels of government the *Common and Agreed National Goals for Schooling* (Australian Education Council, 1989). These agreed goals have since been used for the development of national curriculum statements and national curriculum profiles in eight key learning areas: English, health and physical education, languages other than English, mathematics, science, studies of society and environment, technology, and the arts (see, for example, Curriculum Corporation, 1994). Furthermore, these eight key learning areas have been sanctioned again in the *National Goals for Schooling in the Twenty-first Century* (Ministerial Council on Education, Employment, Training and Youth Affairs, 1999). The national curriculum statements identify the content of the curriculum in the eight key learning areas, and the curriculum profiles distinguish six levels of attainment, with sublevels (strands) incorporated within the six levels. Teachers are required to measure children's achievements against the standards identified in the levels and strands and plot each child at a particular level. The national curriculum statements and profiles have been used by the states to develop outcomes-based syllabi for the eight key learning areas for the compulsory years of schooling. In addition to the support for outcomes-based approaches to education at the primary and secondary levels, state and national legislation of curriculum documents pertaining to early childhood education has occurred in both the compulsory and noncompulsory years. For example, legislation of the *Preschool Curriculum Guidelines* (Queensland School Curriculum Council, 1998) occurred at the state level. This document is a curriculum guideline for children in the year *before* compulsory schooling, contains outcome statements, and has been made mandatory for all teachers in the public school system. The focus of analysis in this chapter, *Putting Children First* (NCAC, 1993), has been legislated at the national level for all long-day childcare centers in Australia, thus affecting those children aged birth to five years who have center-based care, their parents, and those who staff the centers.

The national curriculum profiles have been used as a blueprint for much recent syllabi and curriculum work in the compulsory years of education. The profiles of achievement for each of the eight key learning areas contain specific levels of achievement and precise descriptions of what is to be accomplished before students can be identified as operating at a particular level. However, this model has permeated the noncompulsory years as well. For example, outcomes and the idea of statements indicating how each outcome is achieved have been incorporated in the South Australian document for children aged three-to-five years, *Curriculum Frameworks for Early Childhood Settings: Foundation Areas of Learning* (Department for Education and Children's Services [DECS], 1996). Here outcomes are specified and indicators are provided to enable staff to know how children are progressing incrementally toward the outcomes, as well as when children have achieved the outcomes. Like several other documents produced for the noncompulsory years (such as the Preschool Curriculum Guidelines [QSCC] 1998), *Curriculum Frameworks for Early Childhood Settings: Foundation Areas of Learning* (DECS, 1996) also identifies content in major areas that are similar to the eight nationally agreed key learning areas. Although different in content emphasis, the accreditation document (NCAC, 1993) is based on the achievement of fifty-two specific outcomes (principles) through efficiency and effectiveness in the educational endeavor.

Disciplinary Power and Docile Bodies

Recent analysis of competency-based education in Australia relating to early childhood education has shown that competency-based education provides the means through which systems of classification can be made even more specific (Grieshaber, 1997). Ashby and Grieshaber (1996) have explained the links between economic rationalism and outcomes-based education, and shown that *Putting Children First* (NCAC, 1993) is an illustration of outcomes-based education applied to the childcare sector. In this chapter, I argue that the accreditation document is an example of government intervention (a technique of normalization), as opposed to quality assurance, as is claimed. By government intervention I mean that the management of childcare in Australia, according to *Putting Children First* (NCAC, 1993), is a way of regulating and normalizing children, parents, staff, and the childcare sector itself.

Jackson (1993) has argued that competency-based education is a mechanism through which "the educational enterprise can be defined, measured and evaluated in the interests of employers, administrators and policy makers" (p. 155). According to Jackson (1993), "competency-based education and training transforms the relations of both curriculum design and program administration, using elaborate documentary information systems" (p. 155). Elaborate documentary information systems are what is encountered with the accreditation document. It is through these complex technical systems that children, staff, parents, and curricula, as well as the educational enterprise, can be defined, measured, and evaluated.

Significant to this analysis are the contingent circumstances in which these recent curriculum documentary systems (such as the accreditation process) came into being. They are devices to meet the events of particular historical circumstances. In this understanding, the role of the state is not an instrument of coercion. Instead, the state exercises administrative technologies. As Hunter (1994) indicated, the state "rules through specific instruments of government: systems of economic management and military security, health and education systems, bureaucratic and legal officialdoms" (p. xix). Furthermore, Hunter (1994) stated that

> these technologies, of which the school system is a prime example, ...work by deploying a special knowledge of the domain to be governed, and their objective is typically the optimal development of its resources, especially its human resources (p. xx).

Schools become then a "key technology of government, responsible for the moral and social training of the population," and are legitimated as "expert system[s] of civic governance" (Hunter, 1994, p. xx). In addition to the formal years of schooling, those institutions of early childhood education dealing with children prior to the compulsory years of schooling have become part of the key technology of government. They are now responsible for the moral and social training of a major proportion of the child population, and by inference, the parent population.

The accreditation document (NCAC, 1993) makes truth claims about specific aspects of pedagogy relating to young children, parents, and staff in early childhood settings. The document establishes "criteria for what is to count as truth" (Rose, 1985, p. 8) about early childhood curricula, the involvement of parents, and the role of staff. The document also "define[s] and defend[s]" (p. 8) the particular regimes of truth established through reference to the role of the NCAC in advising the Minister for Family Services (among other things), about matters related to good quality in Australian child care (Appendix, NCAC, 1993). A "whole technology" (Rose, 1985, p. 8), consisting of devices such as "manuals of instruction, testing and assessment procedures, rules of diagnostic practice and classification" (Rose, 1985, p. 8), is constructed through the document and its accompanying processes. It produces apparatuses to classify, regulate, and administer persons, and therefore has the effect of reinforcing dominant understandings of children, parents, staff, and norms associated with early childhood education, parenting, and child rearing.

Putting Children First (NCAC, 1993), its truth claims, and associated procedures or grids of specification are examples of what Foucault (1977) referred to as disciplinary power. Dreyfus and Rabinow (1982, p. 134) portray disciplinary power as a "technology of the body as object of power" that is formed progressively in a variety of local sites: the daycare center, the preschool, and the early years of schooling. Disciplinary power is aimed at the production of human beings who can be treated as docile bodies:

> Discipline may be identified neither with an institution nor its apparatus; it is a type of power, a modality for its exercise, comprising a whole set of instruments, techniques, procedures, levels of application, targets; it is a "physics" or an anatomy of power, a technology. And it may be taken over either by "specialized" institutions...or by institutions that use it as an essential instrument for a particular end (schools...) (Foucault, 1977, pp. 215–216).

Here the process of disciplinary power operates by identifying norms of conduct, that is, the criteria that are to count as truth. Procedures to remedy deviations from the norm are also established through the criteria that count as truth. Rectification occurs through the normalizing of judgment by, for example, staff at childcare centers in relation to children's behavior, or reviewers and moderators who assess the center as part of the accreditation external review process.

The aim is to turn individuals into obedient subjects through using methods such as observation and surveillance, recording what has been observed, and training children, staff, and in some cases parents, to meet the specified requirements. Both staff and children are implicated in this process, as disciplinary power operates by identifying norms of conduct and establishing procedures to remedy deviations from the norm. Through techniques such as surveillance and assessment strategies employed by outcomes-based education, the individual child, staff members, and parents have become accountable via a variety of processes such as registration, classification, and categorization.

Foucault (1977) talked about the process of becoming accountable as the constitution of the individual. He argued that this has occurred in two particular ways. First, as a

> describable, analyzable object, not in order to reduce him [sic] to "specific" features...but in order to maintain him in his individual features, in his particular evolution, in his own aptitudes or abilities, under the gaze of a permanent corpus of knowledge; and, secondly, the constitution of a comparative system that made possible the measurement of overall phenomena, the description of groups, the characterization of collective facts, the calculation of the gaps between individuals, their distribution in a given "population" (Foucault, 1977, p. 190).

The technologies of assessment require that children and staff members' features and performance be mapped according to the dictates of the relevant corpus of knowledge. In addition, the final award of one, two, or three years' accreditation makes it possible to compare centers throughout Australia. *Putting Children First: Quality Improvement and Accreditation System Handbook* (NCAC, 1993) distinguishes its corpus of knowledge through fifty-two principles or norms of conduct for staff and center operation, and the standards at which staff should be operating to ensure continuation of government benefits.

Accreditation as a Technique of Regulation and Normalization

Although recent curriculum documents have many similarities in the ways that they operate as technologies of power, the means by which *Putting Children first* (NCAC, 1993) operates as a technology of power is through its elaborate documentary information systems. To illustrate how this occurs, I discuss some aspects of the manual of operation and some associated procedures and processes. The aim is to show how the document is an example of educational devices being used to create docile child and adult bodies, constantly subjected to the law of normalization. One way of doing this is to show how children, staff, and each center can be mapped onto a "grid of specification" (Foucault, 1977) and ranked according to gaps identified. I begin by describing the steps in the accreditation process and showing how staff and others in the childcare field are regulated as their actions are proscribed by the process of accreditation. I then discuss how the fifty-two principles are classified to indicate the complexity of this elaborate documentary information system and the way in which the standards can determine the actions and behaviors of staff. This system of classification is also a grid on which the staff at the center can be mapped and categorized according to how well they have achieved the standards specified. Finally, I discuss briefly the notion of resistance to the accreditation process. I begin with the steps involved in the accreditation process.

Steps in the Accreditation Process

There are five steps in the accreditation process. These are (1) registration, (2) self-study, (3) external review, (4) recommendation by moderators, and (5) the decision by the NCAC. Centers are required first to register with a registration fee. The self-study aspect is the second step, requiring the formation of a committee at each center, the composition of which is specified by the NCAC (1993) and must include parent members.

From their literature review of parent involvement in early childhood education, Hughes and Mac Naughton (1999) have argued that much of this literature positions parents as "others," thus "preventing the creation of equitable parent-staff relationships" (p. 1). They identify three main views about parental involvement and maintain that the Australian accreditation system falls into the category where parental knowledge is seen as supplementary to professional knowledge, as "subordinate and of secondary importance"

(Hughes & Mac Naughton, 1999, p. 3). The accreditation system requires staff to involve parents in other ways, not only as part of the accreditation committee. For example, guidelines for children's behavior are to be negotiated with parents (Principle 4). According to Hughes and Mac Naughton (1999), the requirement to involve parents as part of daily center operations presents two problems: "It undermines the status of staff as professionals and it threatens parents with state intrusion" (p. 4). In relation to the latter, negotiating guidelines for children's behavior (Principle 4) means that parents must indicate their own values and expectations. As Hughes and Mac Naughton (1999) point out, this involves disclosure of child-raising techniques that are then subject to the "'expert' judgement of early childhood staff" (p. 4). If found wanting in some way, parents are then susceptible to correction of their parenting and child-raising skills through official representatives of the state — "the more a family collaborates with early childhood staff, the more it risks exposure to the state" (Hughes & Mac Naughton, 1999, p. 4).

As part of its task, the committee of staff and parent members coordinates Principle 2, the self-study aspect of the accreditation process. The self-study process involves

> assessing the quality of care provided and comparing this with the standards of care set out in this Handbook. Where the quality of care is below the standards set for accreditation, the Committee must develop and implement a Plan of action to improve the quality of care towards these standards (NCAC, 1993, p. xv).

Accordingly, the self-study report appears to be an exercise in self-regulation as the committee is required to assess the quality of the care provided in the center and compare it with the standards in the manual. Knowing the standards and that self-assessment is required can, therefore, have the effect of regulating staff actions and behavior according to what is desired, that is, what is stated in the fifty-two principles at the acceptable level for accreditation. In time, the effect of the accreditation document as a technology of power ensures that staff become self-regulating (Foucault, 1977), able to observe, judge, and discipline their own actions in accordance with the standards that are set in the document.

The self-study and self-referral by the committee for the next stage is reminiscent of Foucault's (1982) discussion about the secular confession of the individual subject through self-reflection, writing, or speech. McHoul and Grace (1993) refer to the confessional as a "versatile technology" (p. 79) and "a ritual that always unfolds within a power relationship" (p. 80). The confessional is now employed in institutions such as the family and the early childhood field, areas that existed previously in the private domain and, therefore, on the periphery of the state apparatus. The self-study can be seen, therefore, as a type of confessional through which the committee members disclose their self-assessment to "the authority who requires the confession, prescribes and appreciates it, and intervenes in order to judge" (McHoul & Grace, 1993, p. 80). In this case, the authority is the National Childcare Accreditation Council, and it is responsible for prescribing the process through which the self-study report progresses, as well as making the final decision about the level of accreditation granted.

Referring to segments from the book *Preschool in Three Cultures* (Tobin, Wu, & Davidson, 1989), Blacker (1998) has discussed how "deeply ingrained the confessional ethos has become in Western culture" (p. 354). Tobin et al. (1989) documented how Japanese and American teachers differed in their approaches to what is said and done by staff in an American preschool when a fight occurred with children aged five and six years in the block corner (p. 152). The American teacher focused on encouraging the children involved to say things with words and to express how they felt when other children grabbed blocks. Blacker (1998) explained this action as an example of how "in a typical American preschool, children constantly are encouraged to verbalize, to exteriorize, their feelings" (p. 354). Tobin et al. (1989) indicate that this type of exchange was frequently witnessed in their study and that the Japanese teachers were surprised at the deliberate and very explicit focus on emotions and feelings.

Yet this behavior by American preschool teachers is the very type that is endorsed by the Australian accreditation document. For instance, Principle 5 states, "Staff are responsive to children's feelings and needs." Principle 5 provides indicators for preschool children such as the following: "Staff help children verbalize feelings and deal constructively with negative feelings" (NCAC, 1993, Principle 5, Good quality, Preschoolers). Use of such techniques means that "more about us is seen; we are opened up, laid bare, and exposed to ever more greater degrees of institutional intervention and penetration" (Blacker, 1998, p. 354). Blacker's (1998) aim is to question or make problematic what is regarded in such preschool (confessional) rituals "as simply good common sense — uncomplicatedly 'normal' (p. 355). In relation to the Australian example, setting standards where staff are required to encourage children to verbalize their feelings and emotions is one way of ensuring that such principles become common sense, accepted, and understood as normal behavior. Another way of understanding normal behavior is through what Foucault (1977) called disciplinary power.

Dreyfus and Rabinow (1982, p. 134) talk about the process of disciplinary power as a "technology of the body as object of power," which is formed progressively in a variety of local sites such as the childcare center. Disciplinary power is aimed at the production of human beings who can be treated as docile bodies. What makes the difference in the case of discipline is that the exercise of discipline has produced a "natural" rule or norm (Smart, 1983, p. 85). Disciplinary control ultimately results in the creation of docile yet productive bodies that are constantly subjected to the law of normalization—we learn to take action according to what is considered normal or appropriate as childcare workers. What is considered normal or appropriate is specified in the fifty-two principles.

According to the manual, the committee decides when to make application for the third stage, the external review. However, the apparent location of the decision with the committee is deceptive as the manual states that time limits apply for existing and new centers to engage in the next step. The imposition of time limits is another example of the prescriptive nature of what is required as part of the process. The external review involves a suitably qualified person, the reviewer-judge, who assesses the center through visits to validate the Self-Study Report and provide comments on the plan of action if the center required one. In the process of validating the Self-Study Report, the external reviewer uses the fifty-two principles as the norms against which to make judgments about the center, identifying where the standards set for accreditation have been achieved and where they have not. This process is consistent with Foucault's (1977) understanding of normalization processes in education, where normalizing judgments are based on examination and assessment. Where deviations are identified, remediation and correction occur. Hence, the external reviewer assesses and ranks each of the fifty-two principles in a report that details both where the requirements for accreditation have been achieved and where they have not, and the specific level achieved for each of the principles. This report is then forwarded to the moderation panel.

The fourth step, the recommendation by moderators (moderator-judges), involves the moderators in examining a center's self-study report and plan of action (where required), and the reviewer's report. The moderation panel makes a recommendation to the National Childcare Accreditation Council as to whether the center should be accredited and the level that is advocated. Moderators also provide advice regarding action necessary to achieve the required standards, indicating the correct or preferred way of doing this. The fifth and final step, the decision by the National Childcare Accreditation Council, is just another in the series of checking devices that make up this complex documentary information system. The decision by the NCAC involves evaluations of the self-study report, the reviewer's report, and the report and recommendation from the moderation panel. This lengthy and complex process of auditing is focused on the initial self-assessment (confession) of the staff and center committee and the series of reports or checking devices that follow (external reviewer, moderation panel, and final decision by NCAC).

Finally, accreditation is granted for one, two, or three years, or special arrangements are made if centers are unable to achieve the one-year standard. The determination of one, two, or three years is made according to the level reached in the complex measuring and checking process. The NCAC states the conditions for award of a certificate of accreditation for one, two, or three years. For example, the standard required for award of a certificate of accreditation for one year is as follows:

> Good quality standard for 32 Principles (60%), including all 20 of the Core Principles and 12 chosen by the center, and Basic standard for the remaining 20 Principles (40%) (Appendix 1, National Childcare Accreditation Council, p. viii).

The calculation of gaps between centers is made explicit because of the differences in rating awarded. Accreditation for three years is the longest time available between reviews and, therefore, is more prestigious. Some centers have used the highest ranking (three years' accreditation) to attract clients through advertisement. In selecting a center for their children, parents are likely to inquire about the ranking achieved and use this information when making decisions about where they will place their children. Many centers display the length of time they have been awarded accreditation in a prominent place in the center.

If centers are deemed to be operating below the standards required, special conditions are imposed to ensure they meet what is necessary within specific time frames. Power-coercive mechanisms such as penalties against deviant centers include the possibility of advising the "Minister for Family Services. Following such advice, the Minister can name the centre in Parliament" (NCAC, 1993, p. xvii). Such mechanisms are consistent with the way in which the accreditation system was introduced. When the scheme began, the threat of withholding government benefits from centers that were not registered for the process meant that there was little choice in compliance. Speaking against the accreditation scheme meant contesting the prevailing discourse of quality. The dominant view supports the idea that the accreditation system is an attempt to provide a guarantee of quality and that this is what is needed in long-day childcare in Australia, given the rapid expansion of the field during the 1980s and early 1990s. Parents, then, are constituted and positioned to value the provision of such services because government agencies are the technologies of power through which discourses operate in order to render bodies docile (Foucault, 1977).

The Fifty-two Principles

The accreditation manual of instruction (NCAC, 1993) identifies fifty-two principles. All aspects of center operation are categorized into four major areas. Further categorization ensures that the system becomes much more complicated than dividing the principles into four areas. The four areas include:

1. adult-child and adult-adult interactions (Part A: Principles 1–15);
2. the program (Part B; Principles 16–33);
3. nutrition, health, and safety practices (Part C; Principles 34–47);
4. center management and staff development practices (Part D; Principles 48–52).

Additional classification occurs as the manual identifies four standards of care for most of the principles (44 of the 52). These four standards are unsatisfactory, basic, good quality, and high quality. The procedure becomes further compounded as 20 of the 52 principles have been identified as core principles, which means that the achievement of "good quality" on these 20 principles is mandatory for successful accreditation. The intricacy of the requirements is apparent in this excerpt from the manual:

> In most of the Principles (44 out of the 52), the highest standard described and which, therefore, can be achieved is High quality. However, in the other eight principles the higher standards are not specified because the Principles relate to fundamental and/or routine activities. Of these eight, five have

Good quality as the highest standard described and thus achievable (Principles 22, 23, 24, 38 and 42) and the remaining three have Basic (Principles 39, 45 and 46) (NCAC, 1993, p. vii).

Unsatisfactory, Basic, Good and High quality standards are described for most of the principles, enabling specific mapping of staff actions according to the four levels of quality achievable.

Children are also categorized according to what the manual describes as the "three developmental stages," which are "Infants, Toddlers and Pre-schoolers" (National Childcare Accreditation Council, 1993, p. ix). The manual does remind readers that "these three groups do not necessarily reflect groupings within a given long day care centre. Rather they reflect the developmental stages of the children attending the centre" (NCAC, p. ix). Children, then, can be mapped according to their developmental stage in accordance with relevant principles. Specific indicators in each of these categories (infants, toddlers, etc.) are identified in many of the fifty-two principles (particularly those in areas 1 and 2 noted above). This means that normal developmental levels of children (infants, toddlers, and preschoolers) are supplied so that staff and parents can be aware of what is considered appropriate or normal for each group. As well as specifying what is developmentally normal for infants, toddlers, and preschool children, the manual designates specific activities in which staff are required to engage.

Putting Children First: Quality Improvement and Accreditation System Handbook (NCAC, 1993) is based on what is known as developmentally appropriate practice (Bredekamp, 1987). Bredekamp and Copple (1997) have acknowledged this in the revised edition of *Developmentally Appropriate Practice in Early Childhood Programs* (p. x). The developmentally appropriate practices endorsed in both these documents (Bredekamp, 1987; Bredekamp & Copple, 1997) represent the values of the dominant culture (white, middle-class values) as normal, positive, and universal (Delpit, 1988; Lubeck, 1994). Thus, white middle-class values have become the natural or the normal rule, or regime, of truth by which judgments are made about what is acceptable and what is not. Although there have been many critiques of developmentally appropriate practice (see, for example, the volume edited by Mallory and New, 1994), the salient argument in this analysis remains culture. Lubeck (1994) has argued that through developmentally appropriate practice, much child development research has been used to endorse the belief that "some cultural practices are preferable (and others, if not 'deficient,' certainly less desirable)" (p. 20). In addition, Lubeck has said that the focus in developmentally appropriate practice on individuals has been used "in an effort to rectify social ills" (p. 20). This has the effect of maintaining the status quo, of keeping the more powerful in their positions of power (Delpit, 1988) by identifying those without the preferred cultural practices as deficient.

In the Australian system, preferred practices are those which are tagged with the good and high quality indicators, while those that are undesirable are named as basic and unsatisfactory. By specifying aspects of children's development in the categories of infants, toddlers, and preschool, staff can also make judgments about whether individual children are progressing according to developmental norms. The very act of listing fifty-two principles with different standards means that certain ways of thinking about and enacting curriculum are privileged and others are excluded.

The first nine principles begin with the word "Staff," thereby establishing staff as directly responsible for enacting each of these nine principles. For example, Principle 4 states, "Staff use a positive approach in guidance and discipline" (NCAC, 1993). An explanation of what this means is provided and the section concludes with the statement "There are several important methods of guidance" (NCAC, 1993, Principle 4). These methods are identified as indirect, direct, verbal, and emotional guidance. Specific information is provided for infants, toddlers, and preschool children in relation to indirect, direct, and emotional guidance. For example, one of the indicators for the good quality standard required for this principle (and hence successful accreditation) indicates that staff need to have a set of behavior guidelines that have been developed in consultation with parents. Relevant indicators of staff action and behavior for infants, toddlers, and preschool children are then stated. It is this specific information that is instrumental in reinforcing the preferred norms of staff action and behavior and in emphasizing the developmental norms of infants, toddlers, and preschool children. Furthermore, because all long-day care centers in Australia are involved in the process, these preferred norms of staff action and behavior and the developmental norms of young children are endorsed as being universally applicable. By inference, these preferred norms are also applicable to families, especially given the point made by Hughes and Mac Naughton (1999) about the risks involved if parents disclose child rearing practices that are different from those by which staff are operating.

Principles 10 through 15 do not locate the word "staff" at the beginning of each statement. However, there is an implicit message that staff members are responsible for ensuring that the action described in each principle actually occurs. For instance, Principle 17 states, "The program incorporates learning experiences appropriate for each child, as indicated by individual development records maintained by the staff" (NCAC, 1993). The pedagogic practices associated with this principle are explicated, including

> In order to plan sensitively and appropriately for each child, it is essential to keep written developmental records to which all staff can contribute. Detailed developmental records allow staff to set goals for each child, devise strategies to achieve the goals, keep track of the child's progress and plan appropriate experiences for further learning and development. Every week, staff should closely observe some children during different activities and make a record of their level of development (NCAC, Principle 17).

Following this, suggested methods for recording observations are listed. Detailing pedagogic requirements in this way makes it very easy to classify, administer, and, where necessary, remediate staff. The techniques described also enable staff to identify children whose learning and development differs from what is considered normal, as much of the document is taken up with indicators that make possible the classification of staff, children, and parents. Identification of preferred versions of child rearing (such as Principle 4) and distinguishing curriculum and pedagogic imperatives (such as maintaining developmental records and how to do it) are both explicit and implicit in the document. These are the regimes of truth (Foucault, 1977) of the accreditation document, where what counts as truth is established.

Resistance

Foucault's notion of disciplinary power is closely connected to other key features of his philosophy such as power, discourse, and subjectivity. Intertwined with his understanding of power-knowledge is resistance, for where there is power, there is also resistance (Foucault, 1979). The existence of power relationships "depends on a multiplicity of points of resistance" (Foucault, 1979, p. 95). Like power, the best place to begin an examination of resistance is in the everyday operation and routine application of power/resistance. Starting at the micro level or the extremities where power is applied enables observation of forms of resistance. One place to start, therefore, is the body.

Foucault (Smart, 1983, p. 76) identifies one of the functions of the body, amongst others, as conducting resistances:

> The body is molded by a great many distinct regimes; it is broken down by the rhythms of work, rest and holidays; it is poisoned by food and values, through eating habits or moral laws; it conducts resistances.

There is much anecdotal evidence of staff resistance to the accreditation process. Documentary evidence was gathered by Grieshaber, Halliwell, Hatch, and Walsh (2000), included one director of a child care center, Shauna, who indicated that the volume of written observations required for individual children (required in Principle 17) was unattainable, given the current economic climate affecting long-day care centers in Australia:

> Written work on the individual is not achievable in the current climate. We need to look at ways of making our profession value the information in our heads, rather than words on paper (Grieshaber et al., 2000, p. 48).

Furthermore, Shauna noted that observations are frequently completed to satisfy accreditation requirements, implying that staff just "play the game" of child observation:

> But I know that the majority of people don't do anything until observations are due the week before [the external reviewer assesses the center] and then they make up a year's worth. They're just playing the game (Grieshaber et al., 2000, p. 49).

Playing the game in this way is, therefore, one way of meeting the requirements of the accreditation process on your terms. Recent Commonwealth government policy in Australia has meant that long-day care services are now competing with each other for their market share. This has been further complicated by an oversupply of available places for children in centers, causing Shauna to state that working conditions are stressful and centers are struggling to survive (Grieshaber et al., in press, p. 20). Given these circumstances, it is likely that resistance will continue in a variety of forms.

Conclusion

Government regulations such as the accreditation system reduce the decision-making responsibilities and possibilities for staff and parents under the pretext of providing quality assurance. The National Childcare Accreditation Council (1993) document is an example of regulatory mechanisms becoming more specific in the area of families and childcare. For example, while the accreditation process operates under the auspices of fiscal and institutional support for families, it is an interventionist technique because it is embodied with national legislation and is thus able to prescribe specific ways of providing long-day care for young children. It represents a move into the domain formerly considered to be the responsibility of the family, or something negotiated between the family and the daycare center. Benhabib (1992) has argued that movement from the private to the public domain has occurred because of changes in economic and social conditions. As an instrument of regulation and normalization, the document defines and controls conceptions of parenting, child rearing, and early childhood curriculum. Implementation of *Putting Children First: Quality Improvement and Accreditation System Handbook* (NCAC, 1993) has the effect of sanctioning long-day care and creates the public impression that the government has ensured that all children placed in long-day care centers in Australia will receive quality care.

Any system which sets out to standardize, order, and control something as diverse as quality in all the long-day childcare centers in Australia must be based on particular values and beliefs (regimes of truth). *Putting Children First: Quality Improvement and Accreditation System Handbook* (NCAC, 1993) survives on the assumption that its standards (principles and indicators) are universal and objective, have been identified through expert knowledge, and that the quality provided can be measured accurately if the correct techniques are used. However, when the standards endorse the values of the dominant culture and are accepted as normal, taken for granted, and therefore unable to be questioned, the notion of what is considered quality assurance needs to be addressed. Furthermore, the implicit exclusion of certain ways of thinking about and enacting early childhood curriculum means that creative and divergent ways of dealing with issues such as diversity (culture, ethnicity, gender, class, sexuality, etc.), as well as contexts (global, local, and geographical), situations, and circumstances (community, environments, resources, etc.), are potentially lost. This is a loss that the early childhood field cannot afford.

■ References

Ashby, G. & Grieshaber, S. (1996). Culture and early childhood curriculum in Australia. *Early Child Development and Care*, 123:127–141.

Australian Education Council. (1989). *Common and agreed national goals for schooling in Australia*. Melbourne: Curriculum Corporation.

Benhabib, S. (1992). *Situating the self*. Cambridge: Polity Press.

Blacker, D. (1998). Intellectuals at work and in power: Toward a Foucaultian research ethic. In T. S. Popkewitz and M. Brennan (Eds.), *Foucault's challenge: Discourse, knowledge, and power in education*, pp. 348–367. New York: Teachers College Press.

Bredekamp, S. (Ed.) (1987). *Developmentally appropriate practice in early childhood programs serving children from birth through age 8*. Washington, DC: National Association for the Education of Young Children.

Bredekamp, S., & Copple, C. (1997). *Developmentally appropriate practice in early childhood programs* (Rev. Ed.). Washington, DC: National Association for the Education of Young Children.

Curriculum Corporation. (1994). *Technology—A curriculum profile for Australian schools*. Carlton, Victoria: Curriculum Corporation.

Dahlberg, G., Moss, P., & Pence, A. (1999). *Beyond quality in early childhood education and care: Postmodern perspectives*. London: Falmer.

Delpit, L. (1988). The silenced dialogue: Power and pedagogy in educating other people's children. *Harvard Educational Review*, 58(3), 280–298.

Department for Education and Children's Services. (1996). *Curriculum frameworks for early childhood settings: Foundation areas of learning*. South Australia.

Dreyfus, H. L., & Rabinow, P. (1982). *Michel Foucault: Beyond structuralism and hermeneutics. With an afterword by Michel Foucault*. Brighton: The Harvester Press.

Foucault, M. (1977). *Discipline and punish: The birth of the prison*. Trans. A. Sheridan. Harmondsworth: Penguin.

Foucault, M. (1979). *The history of sexuality 1: An Introduction*. London: Allen Lane.

Foucault, M. (1980). *Power/knowledge: Selected interviews and other writings 1972–1977*. (Ed. C. Gordon). (C. Gordon, L. Marshall, J. Mepham, K. Soper, Trans.). Brighton: Harvester.

Foucault, M. (1982). The subject and power. *Critical Inquiry, 8*, (4):777–789.

Grieshaber, S. (1997). Back to basics: The Queensland year 2 diagnostic net. *Curriculum Perspectives, 17* (3), 28–38.

Grieshaber, S., Halliwell, G., Hatch, J. A. & Walsh, K. (2000). Child observation as teachers' work in contemporary Australian early childhood programs. *International Journal of Early Years Education, 8*(1):41–55.

Hughes, P. & Mac Naughton, G. (1999). Consensus, dissensus or community: The politics of parent involvement in early childhood education. Paper presented at the 8th Interdisciplinary Conference on Reconceptualizing Early Childhood Education: "Politics, identity and practice." Columbus, OH. 24–27 June 1999.

Hunter, I. (1994). *Rethinking the school: Subjectivity, bureaucracy, criticism.* St. Leonard's, NSW: Allen & Unwin.

Jackson, N. (1993). Competence: A game of smoke and mirrors? in C. Collins, (Ed.), *Competencies: The competencies debate in Australian education and training* (pp. 154–61). Canberra: The Australian College of Education.

Lubeck, S. (1994). The politics of developmentally appropriate practice: Exploring issues of class, culture, and curriculum. In B. Mallory and R. New (Eds.), *Diversity and developmentally appropriate practices: Challenges for early childhood curriculum* (pp. 17–43). New York: Teachers College Press.

Mallory, B., & New, R. (Eds.) (1994). *Diversity and developmentally appropriate practices: Challenges for early childhood curriculum.* New York: Teachers College Press.

McHoul, A., & Grace, W. (1993). *A Foucault primer: Discourse, power and the subject.* Melbourne: Melbourne University Press.

Ministerial Council on Educaiton, Emplyment, Training and Youth Affairs (1999). *National goals for schooling in the twenty-first century.* http://www.curriculum.edu.au/mceetya/nationalgoals/index.htm.

National Childcare Accreditation Council. (1993). *Putting children first: Quality improvement and accreditation system handbook.* Canberra.

Queensland School Curriculum Council. (1998). *Preschool curriculum guidelines.* The State of Queensland.

Rose, N. (1985). *The psychological complex: Psychology, politics, and society in England, 1939–1969.* London: Routledge and Kegan Paul.

Smart, B. (1983). *Foucault, Marxism and critique.* London: Routledge and Kegan Paul.

Tobin, J. J., Wu, D. Y. H., & Davidson, D. (1989). *Preschool in three cultures: Japan, China, and the United States.* New Haven, CT: Yale University Press.

Wangmann, J. (1994). Accreditation of child care centres. *Every Child,* 1:11–13.

■ CHAPTER 10 ■

Children's Linguistic/Cultural Human Rights

Lourdes Díaz Soto & René Quesada Inces, Pennsylvania State University

> *"The school took away my language."*
> *(Yazmin, eight-year-old, eastern Pennsylvania, Soto, 1998)*

This chapter relays how the political climate of a nation can affect children's cultural and linguistic human rights. The political reality of unequal access to power has meant that when children are deprived of linguistic human rights they are also silenced. Silenced children are the least able to participate in the political process of a nation, and are prevented from enjoying additional rights such as equal access to education, access to information, freedom of speech, and the ability to maintain cultural practices capable of enhancing intergenerational communication.

In spite of the fact that many nations of the world provide for the protection of minority languages and that a variety of international documents provide guidance for the protection of linguistic human rights, issues of equity, justice, power, and cultural democracy continue to plague children's daily realities. Our goals in this chapter are to (a) explore the concept of linguistic human rights, (b) analyze the ways that English-only movements have/are denying those rights to children, and (c) explore selected international models that provide hope and possibility.

What Constitutes Linguistic Human Rights (LHRs)?

Linguistic human rights can be observed at both the *individual* and the group level. At the individual level, children have the LHRs to learn their home language and at least one of the dominant languages of the nation. At the *collective* human rights level, LHRs imply (a) the right to establish and maintain schools that include home language, home culture, and second-language learning, (b) the guarantees of representation in political affairs, and (c) that there is autonomy with regard to issues of culture, religion, education, information, and social affairs (Skutnabb-Kangas, 1995).

In some countries the forced inclusion into a monolingual and (not so) monocultural system has meant that children throughout the world have been punished for speaking their home language. The punishment can be physical (Kurds in Turkey), psychological and economic (Skutnabb-Kangas, 1995; Skutnabb-Kangas & Phillipson, 1995), emotional (Latino children in Steeltown, Soto, 1997), and even likened to "cultural genocide."

Skutnabb-Kangas (1995) provides just some of the concrete examples of issues of LHRs that children face: A Turkish-Kurd child born abroad and who has a Kurdish name cannot get a Turkish passport because Turkish authorities do not record Kurdish names. Another example is when a guest worker who does speak the language of the host country and is in pain in the hospital cannot communicate with the nurses. Desperately in pain, he jumps from a fifth floor window. A child in Kenya (as in many other countries) is punished physically and humiliated for not speaking the official school language. The international community views the English-only language amendments in the United States along with the treatment of the Kurds in Turkey as the most extreme and assimilation-oriented (Skutnabb-Kangas & Phillipson, 1995).

Many national constitutions do provide protection for minority languages, as illustrated in Finland (Swedish speakers and Sami), Spain (Basque Normalization Law), South Africa, and India. A variety of international documents have also begun to provide guidance for the protection of LHR. Examples include the following:

(a)   *The Charter of the United Nations* (1945) commits its member nations to promoting "universal respect for...human rights and fundamental freedoms for all without distinction as to race, sex, language, or religion" (paragraph 6.11,   p. 55).

(b)   *The Universal Declaration of Human Rights* (1948) states in the second paragraph, "Everyone is entitled to all the rights and freedoms set forth...without distinction such as race, colour, sex, language, religion, political or other opinion." In the 26th paragraph this document calls for the "full development of the human personality" and the right of parents to "choose the kind of education that shall be given to their children."

(c)   *The International Covenant on Civil and Political Rights* (1966) in article 27 states, "persons belonging to such minorities shall not be denied the right to enjoy their own culture, to profess and practice their own religion, or to use their own language."

(d)   *The U.N. Convention on the Rights of the Child* (1989) emphasizes the importance of the "development of respect for the child's parents, his or her own cultural identity, language and values (Art. 29.c)...and due regard shall be paid to the desirability of continuity in a child's upbringing to the child's ethnic, religious, cultural and linguistic background (Art. 20.3)."

Dominant Perspectives in the United States

In the United States, the Lau v. Nichols (1974) Supreme Court decision states that there is no equality of treatment merely by providing students with the same facilities, textbooks, teachers, and curriculum, for students who do not understand English are effectively foreclosed from any meaningful education.

This decision has not, however, helped children to maintain their home language and culture. The advent of English-only policies demonstrates that there is "considerable confusion as to what constitutional rights to language are guaranteed, and that there is little understanding of bilingualism on the bench" (Skutnabb-Kangas & Phillipson, 1995, p. 87).

The political reality of unequal access to power by those who are multilingual can be largely attributed to two myths generated by English-only proponents. First, they declare that monolingualism is somehow helpful to economic growth and second, that minority rights pose a threat to the nation. Some international evidence actually reveals that not granting rights to minorities is more likely to lead to secession attempts (i.e., French Canadians), while second-language learning actually enhances possibilities. At the same time that dominant perspectives and beliefs about language and culture should be challenged, children do need to be taught the language(s) of government and dominant culture to ensure their access to multiple opportunities.

Issues of equity, justice, power, and cultural democracy continue to plague educational institutions in the United States. The idea that "an individual can be bicultural and still be loyal to American ideals" (Ramirez & Castañeda, 1974, p. 23) is one that may elude schools in light of the increasingly conservative agenda promulgated by politicians and selected media personalities. Educational issues of language and culture will benefit from an additive philosophy (English-plus) and not mandates by politically motivated personalities who are neither well versed on these issues nor the life circumstances of children in the United States. Linguists (Fishman, 1995; Wong Fillmore, 1992) in the United States are not concerned about children losing their English language skills but rather about the issue of home language preservation.

Schools continue to impose an ideology that totally disregards and disrespects LHRs. The expectation is for total (dis)assimilation of languages other than English. This perspective oversimplifies language and devalues human diversity. Further, issues of language and culture are intertwined, complex, and directly related to the formation of individual and collective identities. Issues of LHRs are directly related to child rearing practices and the family's ability to actively engage in intergenerational family communication. How will children deprived of their home language maintain their family's cultural practices? Have access to information? Participate in the politics of a nation? Have equal access to education?

Yazmin, an eight-year-old Latino child residing in eastern Pennsylvania, confessed sadly in a recent interview that

> The school took away my language, in the Steeltown School, they took away my language. I don't like the school. I'm sad when I think about what they did to me (cries and repeats sobbing). In the Steeltown School, they took away my language (audiotaped interview, summer 1998).

Yazmin dreads attending school and feels that, through no fault of her own, she is forced to see the world through a language and a culture she does not understand. In addition, Yazmin is expected to shed her home language and culture if she expects to participate in the school and the society.

What is evident in the United States is a continued dismantling of programs for children that support bilingualism. A national climate has been created that allows for domination by English-only forces, cultural invasion that disregards the home, culture, and language. Punishing children for speaking their native language continues. In Louisiana, for example, children have been asked to kneel for speaking in a language other than English. In a Texas courtroom a home language speaking mother nearly lost custody of her child. In Pennsylvania, children have been retained a grade for speaking a language other than English and are disproportionately represented in special education classrooms. In California, bilingual programs have been dismantled and children are expected to "prove" their national origin (Soto, 1998).

Research reported elsewhere (Soto, 1997) helped the first author to understand how issues of power can obscure the very voices representing children's best interests. The more powerful elements in Steeltown dismantled an award-winning twenty-year-old bilingual education program. As an English-only program was being implemented, Margarita (a participant in the events and in the research) whispered that in her school, children are not allowed to speak in Spanish: "En esta escuela no se habla español"; while Juan said he felt that he was walking into a "cage with lions and then you put in a little goat." It was evident that schools and policymakers in Steeltown eliminated bilingual programs and support without taking a careful and close look at what bilingual children are experiencing in schools, and what children need in order to become cultural participants.

James Crawford (1989, 1992) relates the historical and political context of bilingual education in the United States. He notes that German language schools prevailed until the twentieth century and that historically significant documents such as the Articles of Confederation were published in German and French. When the United States entered World War I, however, anti-German sentiments created language restrictionism. Several states passed laws banning German speech, with at least 18,000 persons charged under these laws by 1921 (Crawford, 1989). Public attitudes toward languages changed as English-only speech became associated more and more with patriotism. In spite of the Supreme Court's ruling in Meyer v. Nebraska, 1923, against restrictive language laws, minority languages were devalued for the nation. Public schools responded to the climate and the politics of the times.

The federal government mandated that Native Americans teach in English only. Although the U.S. Senate documented that in the 1850s the Oklahoma Cherokees attained English literacy levels higher than the white populations in Texas or Arkansas, by 1879, Native American children were being separated from their families and sent to militarizing boarding schools. U.S. Representative Ben Nighthorse Campbell retells that

> Both my grandparents were forcibly removed from their homes and placed in boarding schools. One of the first English words Indian students learned was soap, because their mouths were constantly being washed out for using their native language (Crawford, 1989, p. 25).

Mexican American and Asian children have been punished under the guise of patriotic English-only speech. An early childhood educator and former migrant worker in California recently relayed a commonly accepted practice in the local public school:

> When our teacher caught us speaking our language, she would lock us in the closet. Sometimes there would be three of us in that tiny space. It was dark and pretty frightening for us. Sometimes it was even hard to breathe in there. Other teachers punished the Spanish speakers at recess, lunch, or with after school "Spanish detention."

The dissemination of information capable of inciting fear and divisiveness has created a climate that devalues children's bilingualism and biculturalism. Jim Cummins (1994) refers to the groups and individuals who continue to spread xenophobic perspectives as new enemies. He compares the United States to the *Titanic*, headed for destruction when dealing with issues of bilingualism. Isolated programs of excellence are shedding light on best practices, yet these programs appear to be the exception and face tremendous barriers from agencies and the public at large.

Ana Ramos-Zayas (1998) advocates reclaiming the linguistic rights that schools steal from children. The staff and students of Pedro Albizu Campos High School in Chicago have attempted to (a) focus on the students' home language and culture and also (b) teach a nationalist agenda of self-determination and political activism. Students at this school do not simply assimilate as expected/assumed by those in power; they graduate from the school with a strong commitment to language, identity, culture, and democratic ideals.

International Models Celebrating Multilingualism

As the children of the "other" are forced to attend school in a language not their own, there are also spaces of hope that illuminate the path commonly denied to the linguistically oppressed. This section provides the reader with a sample of how nations with a more humanistic approach are starting to deal with the issue at hand.

The models that are exemplified here are those of peoples whose language is afforded a lower status as minorities within an oppressive society. Therefore, at some point of time, their linguistic rights have not been properly addressed. The case of the "privileged minorities" differs since a high economic status affords choices for the kind of education they can provide for their children in the host society. The European Schools provide an example in this sense of a model for multilingual education for the children of international workers. This model is remarkably successful in developing bilingual/biliterate students. In fact, Beardsmore (1993) indicates that this model is elitist and expensive. Such a model is not the subject of this paper.

The Centre for Overseas Studies of the School of Education (Mebrahtu, 1987) at the University of Bristol detailed three premises for the role of education: a) education as necessary to develop awareness of, and bring understanding between, the rich and the poor, b) education to bring about harmonious cultural and ethnic coexistence and cooperation, and c) education to preserve cultural identities of nondominant groups while acquiring effective methods for participation in the larger society. The documents from this conference revealed that in order to improve the school success (achievement) of minority students, the consideration of sociocultural and politico-economic variables is vital. Societal perspectives and educational activities from a variety of countries around the world are demonstrating ways in which these variables can be considered.

In South Africa the principle of home language is followed strictly for native speakers of either Afrikaans or English. Native speakers of either one receive instruction in their home language through the twelfth grade, while the non-home language is studied as a second language. Speakers of any of the other languages receive instruction in their home language up to the forth grade and then one of the two official languages becomes the medium of instruction.

Van Rensburg (undated), the project director for *Stepping into the Future: Education for South Africa's Black, Coloured and Indian Peoples*, argues that

South Africa has enacted a national educational policy of multinational development and it is now at the advanced stage of implementation. With the recent history of racism and white supremacy, South Africa is far from a homogeneous society. Skin color coincides with real, deeply rooted, and complex ethnic division. Blacks represent at least nine major culturally different groups with separate languages. "Coloured people" are the descendants of a mixture of different native ethnic slave groups from West Africa and the East Indies now living in the Cape and can be roughly divided in two major groups: Griquas and Cape Malays. Indians represent a third sector of the population. Finally, the white population is also diverse in background and perspective. South Africa has the difficult responsibility of satisfying the needs and aspirations of each one of these culturally diverse groups in a safe and respectful manner. A separate education program using the home language as medium of instruction has been designed for each group. The programs recognize tradition, language, and culture, as well as a modern curriculum for today's world. Instruction in the home language is guaranteed at least to grade 4, 5, or 6. From there on, Afrikaans and English, the two official languages, are used.

In Wales the efforts to revive the ancestral Welsh language are a means to empower the Welsh-speaking communities (Baker, 1996). Beginning in the 1950s and gaining strength after the 1970s, an emphasis on Welsh as a medium of instruction in an anglicized system emerged. A number of elementary and secondary schools have started bilingual programs in both primarily Welsh neighborhoods and with mixed Welsh and English-speaking families. The goal is to preserve the indigenous language and culture.

For many years, Welsh was viewed as the language of low status, unnecessary and inferior to English, which is perceived as the language that facilitates upward mobility. The first bilingual school was opened in Aberystwyth in 1939 and the first bilingual secondary school, Yscol Glan Clwyd in 1956 (Beardsmore, 1993). Twenty-five percent of the primary school children in Wales are taught mostly or partly through Welsh, with classes for learning Welsh required for the rest of the population. Further, typical subjects taught in Welsh are math, science, history, geography, and religion. Even computer science is taught in Welsh in high schools, thus portraying the feeling that English is not necessarily the academic language. Welsh bilingual graduates compete favorably with monolingual English students in the universities.

Artigal (1993) relays how things have changed for speakers of languages that are not dominant in Spain (Catalan and Basque). Catalan is the language spoken in and around Catalonia, Valencia, and the Balearic Islands. Basque is the historical language of the inhabitants in the Basque Autonomous Community, Navarre. Although the two languages are very different, they share the same destiny. Speakers of Catalan and Basque have been the object of political persecution, official oppression, neglect by the media, and domination by Spanish speakers who have migrated to the areas. The result is that in these territories almost 100 percent of the population speaks the dominant language which is Spanish, while only a minority are competent in the more native languages (Beardsmore, 1993).

The recovery of these languages started at the end of the 1970s as a result of a more democratic government in Spain, and expanded in the early 1980s, as support laws were enacted. Since the nineteenth century, Spanish had been the language of schooling. Bilingual education started with the "ikastolas" (Basque) and the "active schools" (Catalan) in the 1960s through the private effort of interested parents and teachers. However, additional supports were needed for successful programs that included teachers who were fully bilingual and biliterate, as well as laws and educational models.

In Catalonia, a 1983 law established that by the end of the Basic General Education (age 14), all children should be bilingual and that the school should attend to the language which is "ill-treated in the environment." Parents were given a language choice for instruction, with 35 percent to 50 percent choosing Catalan (Beardsmore, 1993).

Three models of bilingual education were introduced in the 1980s in the Basque Autonomous Community. There are now virtually no schools teaching in Spanish only. Research conducted on the Basque models coincides with the positive results attained through bilingual education in other countries. Students develop ability in both Basque and Spanish. The curriculum is enhanced because learning is transferred (Beardsmore, 1993).

Byram (1993) describes how the Danish educational authorities have approached the task of educating a German-speaking minority in Denmark. Since political and geographical borders do not necessarily agree with the distribution of cultural, linguistic, or ethnic groups, the demarcation of the border between Germany and Denmark in 1920 left people with German backgrounds in Nordschleswig, Denmark. Since schooling in the German language was abolished after World War II, instruction in German had to redevelop over time. Finally, German private schools received official permission to take Danish examinations. In 1990, this system was serving a total population of 5,246 students, with 18 schools and 24 kindergartens. After completing school (at age 16), students may opt to go to a university in Germany, a Danish university, or a vocational (Nachschule) school.

Two important factors in this context are that the inhabitants of the region are making the conscious decision to preserve their German culture, ethnicity, and language, but at the same time consider themselves politically loyal to Denmark. The schools are successful in producing bilingual students in German and Danish who are also speakers of their dialectal Sonderjynsk.

Leman (1993) explains how nondominant language speakers are treated by the Dutch Language School System in Brussels (Belgium), a multicultural, multilingual city with massive immigration. English and German are widely spoken in some districts; geographic and economic ties are with Dutch speakers on the North (a minority in the city). There are two major European immigrant groups: Spaniards and Italians, and two non-European groups, Moroccans and Turks. Brussels, in the center of a unified Europe, is actually a multilingual and multicultural city where the dominant languages are French and Dutch, which enjoy an official status.

There are two official educational systems, one in French, the other in Dutch. Bicultural education is only offered in the Dutch language system. A recent study (Leman, 1993, p. 90) reveals that kindergarten students may come from a diversity of linguistic backgrounds: 35 percent from Dutch-speaking homes, 30 percent from mixed-language families (one parent speaks Dutch but French is spoken at home), 20 percent from French-speaking homes, and 15 percent from other language families.

This means that if Dutch is chosen as the language of schooling, then it will be a second language for a vast majority of the student body. To address this issue, a project, the Foyer Model, was begun in 1981 to teach the complete curriculum to all students and at the same time to preserve and reinforce children's cultural identity. Dutch is implemented gradually without abandoning either the native language (which could be Spanish, Italian, Arabic, or Turkish) or French. The home language is given support in the early years because of its special social relevance in the life of the child (Beardsmore, 1993). Flemish children continue to develop their Dutch home language while non-Dutch speakers are developing skills in their first languages. In this project, there is a clear desire for an additive, rather than subtractive, model of bilingual education.

Adjustments are made for the Moroccan population since there is a slower rhythm with which Arabic writing is learned. It also takes into consideration differences between standard and dialectal forms of Arabic. The purpose is to offer a bicultural model with intercultural perspective in which trilingualism is the goal. Parents are strongly encouraged to participate in the school activities. Success is considered to be due to parent support and well-trained bilingual teachers whose second language is given high status in the school (Beardsmore, 1993).

A model of bilingual education in the Amazonia in Peru is described by Angel Corbera (1983) and helps to explain how language and education are political, with decisions reflecting the interests of those who bear political power in a country. When a group takes power, decisions and processes may be reverted. Three main languages are widely used in Peru: Spanish, Quechua, and Aymara. There is also plurality of tongues in the Peruvian Amazonia, with at least thirteen different family languages and many dialects represented. Recently, those in power have demonstrated their complex views of language by implementing The General Education Act. Article 40 of the act states that in non-Spanish communities instruction should be started in the native language, while Spanish is the language that citizens need in modern society. However, the act also states that education is responsible for ensuring Spanish dominance over any other language, official or not, but must respect local, zone, regional, and national needs. Teaching Spanish was pursued with respect for the student's language and culture.

Maria del Carmen Fernandez (Corbera, 1983), a pioneer educator in Peru, witnessed that in some indigenous (Runa) villages along the Napo River, there had been no teacher for more than a year and the children were taught only sporadically. The children told stories of the teachers siding with the landlords, punishing the children for speaking Kichwa. One girl explained that a common form of punishment was to have the children kneel on small pebbles. Another girl had to scrub her face with sand, causing bleeding, in order to erase native face paintings if she wanted to attend school. Students may have spent three or more years in the same grade before dropping out. They were in the "transition" program and never reached any other level. The educational system was obviously failing. Fernandez discovered that the Runas were a people who had been able to recognize the constellations for centuries, something that the teachers were not able to do. They needed an education in accordance with their culture, traditions, values, knowledge, and language.

Another educator, Maria de los Angeles Fernandez, decided that effective education among the Napo should be based on native beliefs of the Runas—a conscience of a distinctive group, sharing, younger people taught by those who are older, education from life and for life, and loyalty to their ethnicity, language, and customs. An Assembly of the Napo asked for bilingual education for their children based on their own cultural values to generate free and critical people, able to communicate with other cultures without losing their own. In 1975, bilingual education was proposed that included (a) a special curricula with textbooks specific for each linguistic group and (b) Quechua as a compulsory subject in all levels of education in Peru (Corbera, 1983).

In the Napo region, the bilingual education program was started with twelve schools by training native teachers among those who had finished elementary school and had a desire to help. Training of teachers (fifteen Kichwas, two Witotos, and one Orejon) started on March 15, 1975, and continued as they taught. The teachers were asked to think about one question: "What am I going to teach?" The answer would need to come from the child's reality. The teachers developed the curriculum based on Freire's (1970, 1985) conscientization method in order to pursue an education that would be liberating. The techniques used were those which are more common among the indigenous groups: cooperation and group dialogue. Teachers and older students elaborated on the teaching materials (Corbera, 1983).

Further, linguistic and cultural traditions were believed to involve thought, action, judgment, and struggle, not simply "ways of saying," but "ways of being." Bilingual education was viewed as a bridge to Spanish and assimilation to the greater Peruvian culture. By the early1980s, after six years of the bilingual programs, results were positive. However, political changes in Peru soon ended this Freirian approach to bilingual education.

Sweden has also attracted many immigrants. The Commission on Immigrants and Ethnic Minorities established policies which were approved by the Parliament in 1975 that included equality between immigrants and Swedes, cultural freedom of choice for immigrants, and cooperation and solidarity between Swedes and ethnic minorities (Paulston, 1988). The right of immigrant children to retain their language had been recognized in 1962 when it was considered that home language instruction is important for the child's social, emotional, and intellectual development. The responsibility of education lies with the municipalities that have been given the freedom to implement the model of home language instruction which they consider convenient. In 1982, 60 percent of the immigrant children were receiving some form of home language training through state subsidies in Finnish, Spanish, Turkish, and Greek. Swedish bilingual programs are dominated by familiar models, ranging from traditional second-language "pull-out" experiences to models in which all instruction uses the home language for young children, with the Swedish language progressively introduced in later years.

Conclusion

In this chapter we explored linguistic and cultural human rights and how these issues are related to ideology, dominance, and human respect. We also explored selected international education models that provide hope for nations struggling with these issues. Even though there are multiple options for supporting linguistic diversity, the linguistic/cultural human rights of children remain an illusion. The dream for an equitable and just treatment of children will continue to be just a dream until we can provide children an education that critically analyzes their circumstances and protects their home language(s) and culture(s). Will the children themselves be the ones who will finally garner the wisdom and the courage to lead us away from oppressive "paradigms of shame to paradigms of compassion" (Soto, 1997, p. 89)?

"The school took away my language."
(Yazmin, eight-year-old, eastern Pennsylvania, Soto, 1998)

■ References

Artigal, J. M. (1993). Catalan and Basque immersion programs. In H. B. Beardsmore (Ed.), *European models of bilingual education*. Clevedon, England: Multilingual Matters Ltd.

Baker, C. (1996). *Foundations of bilingual education and bilingualism*. Bristol, PA: Multilingual Matters Ltd.

Beardsmore, H. B. (1993). The European school model. In H. B. Beardsmore (Ed.), *European models of bilingual education*. Clevedon, England: Multilingual Matters Ltd.

Byram, M. (1993). Bilingual or bicultural education and the case of the German minority in Denmark. In H. B. Beardsmore (Ed.), *European models of bilingual education*. Clevedon, England: Multilingual Matters Ltd.

Corbera, A. (1983). *Educacion y linguistica en la amazonia peruana*. Lima, Peru: Centro Amazonico de Antropologia y Aplicacion Practica.

Crawford, J. (1989). *Bilingual education: History, politics, theory and practice*. Trenton, NJ: Crane.

Crawford, J. (1992). *Hold your tongue*. New York: Addison-Wesley.

Cummins, J. (1994). Keynote speech at the National Association for Bilingual Education, Los Angeles, CA.

Fishman, J. A. (1995). On the limits of ethnolinguistic democracy. In T. Skutnabb-Kangas (Ed.), *Linguistic human rights: Overcoming linguistic discrimination*. New York: Mouton de Gruyter.

Freire, P. (1970). *Pedagogy of the oppressed*. New York: Seabury Press.

Freire, P. (1985). *The politics of education: Culture, power, and liberation*. South Hadley, MA: Bergin & Garvey.

Leman, J. (1993). Bicultural programs in the Dutch language school system in Brussels. In H. B. Beardsmore (Ed.), *European models of bilingual education*. Clevedon, England: Multilingual Matters Ltd.

Mebrahtu, T. (Ed.) (1987). *Swann and the global dimension: Education for world citizenship*. Youth Education Service.

Paulston, C. (1988). Ethnic relation and bilingual education: Working papers in bilingualism. No. 6. Toronto: Ontario Instutute for Studies in Education.

Ramirez, M., & Castañeda, A. (1974). *Cultural democracy: Bicognitive development and education*. New York: Academic Press.

Ramos-Zayas, A. (Summer 1998). Nationalist ideologies, neighborhood-based activism, and educational spaces in Puerto Rican Chicago. *Harvard Educational Review*, *68* (2): 164-192.

Skutnabb-Kangas, T. (1995). *Linguistic human rights: Overcoming linguistic discrimination*. New York: Mouton de Gruyter.

Skutnabb-Kangas, T., & Phillipson, R. (1995). Linguistic human rights, past and present. In T. Skutnabb-Kangas (Ed.), *Linguistic human rights: Overcoming linguistic discrimination*. New York: Mouton de Gruyter.

Soto, L. D. (1997). *Language, culture, and power: Bilingual families and the struggle for quality education*. New York: State University of New York Press.

Soto, L. D. (1998). Bilingual education in America: In search of equity and social justice. In J. Kincheloe and S. Steinberg (Eds.), *Unauthorized methods: Strategies for critical teaching*. New York: Routledge.

Van Rensburg, C. (project director) (undated). *Stepping into the future: Education for South Africa's Black, Coloured and Indian peoples*. Johannesburg: Erudita Publications.

Wong Fillmore, L. (1992). Language and cultural issues in early education. In L. Kagan (Ed.), *The care and education of America's young children*. The 90th Yearbook of the National Society for the Study of Education.

CHAPTER 11

(Euro-American Constructions of) Education of Children (and Adults) Around the World: A Postcolonial Critique

Gaile S. Cannella & Radhika Viruru, Texas A&M University

As illustrated in the book *The United States and Decolonization: Power and Freedom* (Ryan & Pungong, 2000), the United States was born out of a "first wave" of decolonization. However, the new country immediately implemented a colonial project in the name of "liberty" (Ryan, 2000) that either removed or eliminated Native Americans and appropriated large amounts of Mexican land. Further, although anticolonial sentiment has dominated thought and Americans have used an idealistic language that would oppose colonialization and oppression, policies toward decolonization have been muted at best (e.g., the reaction to the independence movement in India), grounded in racist doubts about the abilities of dark-skinned peoples to govern themselves (Hunt, 2000), and implemented as if playing the role of parent to problem children (Lucas, 1991). Historians such as Lafeber (1963, 1993; Hunt, 2000) have even proposed that American rejection of colonialism was because formal control or force was not viewed as effective. Informal maintenance of economic interests was felt to be cheaper and even resulting in greater control. Gandhi (1998) has explained that colonialism is not only physical force, but has also been manifested in moves toward cultural enlightenment and reform, in the name of order, civilization, and even freedom. This type of colonization is more insidious, colonizing the minds, hearts, cultural perspectives, and even desires of peoples (Nandy, 1993).

Much of the European-American agenda for education is/may be an avenue (however unintended or subconscious) for informal colonization. The purpose of this chapter is therefore to provide beginning explorations of global colonization (imperialism and/or hegemony, depending on one's definitional perspective) as accomplished through dominant teaching and instructional methodologies. From a critical perspective, we believe that we must take into account that around the world education has been proposed as the "savior" of the poor, less fortunate, and even savage. Further, this exploration is needed as U.S. (or what might be called European-American) constructions of education increasingly dominate. This "educational colonization" is evident in multiple locations, from the massive acceptance of the American-generated "developmentally appropriate practice" for young children, to the construction of "text books" by the World Bank, to presentations by U.S. scholars of "cutting-edge" research on teaching methods in the pejoratively cast "second" or "third" world context, to the privileging of American universities around the world.

Uncertainties and disagreements over words, definitions, concepts, and themes are always with us, especially in research that explores issues of power and dominance. To begin our exploration, we would first attempt to explore the language and ideas used in our work, the discourses that give voice to and create boundaries surrounding our discussions. Second, we explore the dominant themes in education (especially as tied to enlightenment and materialism) and the ways in which individuals and groups of people are constructed within "educational colonialism."

Postcolonial Discourses in the Examination of "Educational Colonization"

To examine dominant teaching and instructional methods as avenues of global colonization, the varieties of postcolonial scholarly discourse and recognition of materialist perspectives, materialisms, and materiality are beneficial for meaning-making. These discourses are fraught with contradictions, challenges, and debate. However, we do not attempt to prove or disprove challenges because we hope to avoid using postcolonial, materialist perspectives, or other discourses, as theories. San Juan (1998) discusses the concept of theory as a Euro-Western construction that has been accepted as truth—a dominant belief theory(ies) are truths to be discovered, revealed, and understood (even if truths that are individual social constructions). To avoid this reification of theory as universal, new relational ways of thinking, border crossings, and forms of multiplicity are necessary (San Juan, 1998). We use these discourses as multiple positions in our search for unthought-of possibilities, not as requiring consistency or truth orientations, but as diverse sights from which we struggle to create meaning.

Postcolonial discourses have been both widely interpreted and widely criticized, issues that we have previously discussed in *A Postcolonial Scrutiny of Early Childhood Education* (Viruru & Cannella, 1999). Most prominent of the criticisms have been tied to the notion that the use of the prefix "post" inaccurately implies that colonization no longer occurs. As Aidoo (1991) states: "Applied to Africa, India, and some other parts of the world, 'postcolonial' is not only a fiction, but a most pernicious fiction, a cover-up of a dangerous period in our peoples lives" (p. 152). Further, Aidoo and others believe that the use of the term masks contemporary political, economic, and discursive inequities. While potentially revealing dominant narratives, the discourse reinforces existing power structures as played out in privileged academic communities and tied to the emergence of global capitalism (Dirlik, 1997; Jacoby, 1995).

The interpretation of their own work by scholars engaged in postcolonial studies, however, tends toward perspectives that read "post" as representing the end of some (although not necessarily all) directly physical colonialisms that are tied to the continued effects of colonial power exhibited through philosophical domination and discursive practices (Mongia, 1996). Although critiqued by European (Schulze-Engler, 1993) and American (Gates, 1994) scholars for de-centering the subject and creating theories that cannot account for agency (which, as criticisms, could be considered interpretations that privilege individualism), Bhabba (1996) addresses ways that colonial discourses create the "Other" (p. 37), producing subject peoples who are lacking. Authority is thus created over the subject peoples and justification emerges for their control. Loomba (1998) has further described colonial violence as epistemic, attacking ideas and value systems, often begun physically but maintained through institutionalized discourse (Tiffin & Lawson, 1994). For example, historians in Africa began years ago (and have continued) to discuss the ways that discourses of "custom" and "tradition" were invented and used by colonizers to control the colonized (Vaughn, 1991). Postcolonial scholars seem to be very aware of the distance between "the subalterns and intellectuals" (Loomba, 1998, p. 257). However, they remind us that members of marginalized, subjugated groups have led the discussions and that borders have been crossed.

Spivak (1996, 1999) has suggested that we underestimate the power of colonizing structures in rewriting intellectual and cultural systems of thought. We agree with Spivak that this power must be considered, not as a truth but as a vantage point (or vantage points) for viewing the world. For these reasons, we choose to use the critical work of postcolonial studies and scholars to examine educational practice, not as truth-oriented theory filled with colonized subjects that lack agency, but as perspectives from which to examine actions, discourses, and power.

Postcolonial perspectives create positions from which unthought-of directions or possibilities can emerge, especially in analysis of education related to global capitalism. Loomba (1998) has explained how modern colonialism (or capitalist colonialism) restructured economies of physically dominated peoples. This restructuring created (a) an imbalance necessary to advance European capitalism, (b) an image of colonized countries as responsible for their own "underdevelopment," and (c) maintenance of dependent markets with women and children as sources of cheap labor. We could very easily discuss this restructuring in terms of education (and will provide examples in the next section).

However, capitalist ties to postcolonialism are even more complex than restructuring. Dirlik (1997) explains that postcoloniality is incomprehensible without reference to the material circumstance of capitalism, especially global capitalism. He notes that the border challenges evident in export-oriented economies, the successes of diasporic populations with capitalism (e.g., India, China), and the hybrid conditions of life experienced by intellectuals identified as representing the "Third World" lead to a celebration of shifting and reconstituted identities, notions dominant in discussions of the postmodern condition. This does not, however, make world traders, diasporic peoples, or postcolonial critics postmodern agents of global capitalism. However, a complicity (even if unintended) between postcolonialism and global capitalism is revealed. Dirlik (1997) proposes that the postcolonial predicament is ripe with critical possibilities, but only if past and future histories and complicity with capitalism are acknowledged and critiqued as related to changing patterns of class relations. For critique, ties to capitalism cannot be denied.

Finally, we cannot discuss postcolonial scholarship, education, and the inevitable tie to capitalism without at least briefly addressing concepts of materialism, whether materialism as scientific theory and/or the materiality of individual lives. Grounded in a complete acceptance of science as truth (however evolving and changing), materialism at the turn of the millennium proposes that the origin of the cosmos was a violent event in a "boundless natural order and that terrestrial life randomly evolved from the inorganic materials of the solar system" (Vitzthum, 1995, p. 219). Humanity is believed to be rooted in this natural material order and the evolutionary instinct for survival. Materialism gives human emotion and desire high priority (in a physical sense), but makes no claim to understanding the "why" of existence. Materialism takes existence as truth, claiming that "empirical and logical evidence is as trustworthy as anything can be" (p. 222). The material order is accepted as the true reality, with human thoughts and feelings reducible to physical energy flow. As materialism has evolved from the classical to the millennial, ties to material conditions have also been generated. For example, the United States is considered prosperous while moving toward a material secularism—perhaps closely related to the concept of capitalism. (Actually, some have directly tied materialism to capitalism—Eisenberg, 1967—and many have illustrated the influence of Enlightenment bias on materialism.) Materialism prefers no particular moral code but focuses on the physical as natural and social fact. Using this concreteness, the physical as fact, education as constructed through "enlightened" science and embedded in capitalism emerges as savior, the savior of the formerly colonized.

Education as Savior of Individuals

Dominant views of education and historical ties to controlling particular groups of people have been well defined and discussed (Cannella, 1997; Goodman, 1992). From a postcolonial perspective, however, we would suggest that the construction of the concept of education as necessary savior and the use of Americanized teaching methodologies (which are increasingly being adopted all over the world) are forms of neocolonization; colonization is no more about "guns, guile, and disease" but maintained through more indirect methods (Tiffin & Lawson, 1994, p. 3). This indirect colonization can be illustrated by examining the focus on individualism, materialism, and intellectualism.

The concept of individualism is so tied to teaching methods that only those techniques that are not individually oriented are named as such; for example, cooperative learning is specifically categorized as cooperative, but standardized testing is not named as "individual" testing. The norm is assumed to be the individual, whether the individual student, learner, or agent. Such strategies, viewed from postcolonial perspectives, emphasize the Western divide between the individual and his or her group, and disempower other ways of functioning.

Further, dominant views of education privilege the construction of individual learner needs; for example, the need for "lifelong learning" and a "love of books," the kinds of needs that self-actualized individuals are thought to have. Although these ideas have served to empower some people in their lives, the universalization of needs and the notion that without such needs and desires an individual is incomplete and functioning at a "lower level" require critique. Perhaps most damaging is that colonized people (such as children) come to accept that these needs exist (as universal truth rather than cultural construction) and spend their lives trying to fulfill them. For example, in India, after retiring from work, older people have not traditionally considered it necessary to develop new interests or habits. This time period in life has been understood as one during which one gradually learns to give up attachments to the world of material objects. However, such attitudes are now being replaced with more Western ideas of lifelong learning; to avoid "growing old," one must try and do new things. Historically in India, growing old has had few negative connotations; age has been welcomed as bringing wisdom and social status. Perspectives, however, are now changing; growing older is increasingly tied to the material circumstances of lifelong learning.

Loomba (1998) has used Gramsci's notion of hegemony to analyze how needs are created among the colonized, mostly with their consent, stressing all the while that colonial conditions differ in many ways from the European ones in which Gramsci formulated his theories. From a postcolonial perspective, the focus is on how colonial regimes achieved domination through creating partial consent, or "involving the colonized peoples in creating the states and regimes which oppressed them" (Loomba, 1998, p. 31).

In modern capitalist societies, hegemony is achieved through "Ideological State Apparatuses" such as schools, the family, and the media. These apparatuses are seen as perpetuating the dominant system by creating subjects who are conditioned to accept the values of the system. Students and older people are given the message that unless they are learning something all the time and that the learning is through the material world, they are somehow becoming static (which is an undesirable state). For example, parents and teachers of young children are often told to surround them with books in as many places as possible: in the bathtub, at bedtime, in each and every learning center in the classroom. Children are thus constantly given the message that books are both important and valuable things to have: "quality" time with children is often seen as time during which adults read to children. Worldwide, these ideas are gaining popularity, creating more and more parents obsessed with the need to read to their children. All this of course has material consequences: creating books that can be read in the bathtub, and to toddlers; creating books in different languages to disseminate worldwide (not to mention, the requirement to learn English to be able to read). Global materialist/capitalist possibilities are endless. This focus on dominant needs, linked as they are to systems of power which make them seem natural and utterly innocent (Which rational person, it is argued, could question the value of reading to children?), continues to marginalize other ways of knowing and viewing the world. When time is spent on reading and exploration of concrete objects, what is being replaced? What of those knowledges that do not lend themselves to the form of the written word? Why would someone feel incomplete if they were not learning something all the time? What about the educational hierarchies that are perpetuated?

Materialism is obviously embedded in the dominant discourses of education and teaching methods. To illustrate, the National Association for the Education of Young Children has listed sixty-two examples of what it sees as representing "appropriate" care for infants (Bredekamp & Copple, 1997); thirty-seven of those examples involve the use of materials of some kind (toys, supplies, lighting, music, and diapers, to name but a few). The use of infants as the particular example is deliberate. Among all children, infants are perhaps seen as the least human or civilized, the "other" in most need of care and education. The message that emerges is that being educated into the real human world is being socialized into the proper use of things. The guidelines make only brief mention of how infants are part of any kind of social structure (family, community, cultural groups, or even childcare center participant). Through connecting infants mostly with material possessions and objects, dominant images of what it means to be educated and cared for are underscored and enforced.

A hallmark of more "primitive" ways of organizing the world was the use of fewer material objects as compared with the necessity for goods created by science. As Loomba (1998) has pointed out, the colonizing processes of classifying and organizing people involved the use of material resources as well as institutions and facilities. Photography, for example, was extensively used to support notions of difference; at the same time it created new employment opportunities for those who were already privileged. Colonial representations of the colonized justified the use of arms against people constructed as "violent" but have also been linked to the creation and maintenance of such institutions as "theater and cinema, art, cartography, city planning, museums, educational, legal and medical institutions, prisons and military establishments" (p. 99). The creation of colonial discourses about others thus cannot be distinguished from the materialist economic implications of those discourses.

If we look at schools from this perspective, much of the paraphernalia that becomes essential to educate children can be seen as material objects essential to maintaining the power of the colonizing institution. Perhaps nowhere else is this as evident as in early childhood education, where it is assumed that children cannot learn without "hands-on" experiences with objects. Despite evidence from multiple sites around the world (Viruru, 2001) that children can and do learn in environments with few or no materials, materialist perspectives continue to dominate.

Finally, the dominant construction of what it means to be saved through education is to become an individual who intellectually conforms to notions of scientific progress and advancement. Loomba (1998) has discussed the complex process through which the "rational intellect" has come to be seen as the distinguishing mark of superior humanity. As she points out, a crucial part of this process was the "gathering and ordering of information about different lands" (p. 57). Early European travelers took with them a series of images about foreign lands (such as a view of inhabitants as "wild and hairy men"). Multiple encounters between the West and the non-West led to what Loomba calls a "continuity and reshaping" of these images, continuity in that previously held opinions of European superiority justified the active colonization of these "others," and reshaping in the sense of adjusting images to specific colonial practices. For example, Spanish colonists used a complex composite of images to label the people who resisted colonial rule in the Caribbean and Mexico as cannibals, thus justifying the imposition of brutal colonial practices on those seen as lacking in intellect and reason. The prevalence of stereotypes is justified as scientific, reducing "images and ideas to a simple and manageable form" that results in a "method of processing information" (Loomba, 1998, p. 60). The actual purpose is to perpetuate a sense of difference between the "self," endowed in this case with scientific intellectual capabilities, and the "other," who at best organizes his or her world in a primitive and disorganized fashion.

Construction of the scientific intellect has been partly based on interactions with colonized groups of human beings. During interaction between the colonizer and the oppressed, many of the ideas of the colonized are appropriated, reshaped, and used against them. This approach accounts for the unique nature of many of the teaching methods that are used in American schools today. On the one hand, the methods are claimed to be child or student centered and based on studies of "how children learn"; on the other hand, techniques are reshaped to construct a view of those who are younger as "undeveloped" and lacking full intellectual capabilities. For example, the method of "whole language instruction" assumes that children are capable of creating their own ideas about literacy and its relation to multiple social contexts while at the same time suggesting that they will not acquire literacy unless whole language methods are used. Furthermore, as Delpit (1995) has pointed out, such process-centered approaches are based on studies of how mostly white, middle-class children organize their world and are considered as the most "appropriate" way in which to educate all groups of children.

Perhaps the most obvious reflection of the importance given to the individual scientific intellect is the widespread use of testing with school children. Concepts such as "IQ," which represent almost entirely Western middle-class male perspectives on what it means to be intelligent, are used to colonize children by perpetuating the dominant view of what it means to be intelligent and also by labeling diverse groups of children as "dumb," despite their varied capabilities (Kincheloe, Slattery, & Steinberg, 2000). As DeYoung (1989) has suggested, following the dictates of science that "separates individuals from their cultural context," the relegation of children who are poor and non-White to "low" ability groups, based on standardized test scores, is considered necessary for the smooth functioning of the school (Kincheloe, Slattery, & Steinberg, 2000, p. 97). One reason is that testing is a multimillion-dollar industry that dictates teacher salaries, scholarships, and college admission, clear ties to colonialist privileging of one group over others.

Education as Colonizing Bodies

The obvious method through which colonization is accomplished is when one group places restrictions on the human bodies of another group, controlling what oppressed bodies can do and what spaces they are allowed to inhabit and navigate. Although arguments are continually made that physical colonization no longer exists, dominant views of education and teaching methodologies colonize younger human beings by prescribing and controlling their physical bodies and constructing the spaces, times, and distances within which they must function.

Tobin (1997) has suggested that "just as colonialism is based on a dualism—the white colonizers associated with mind and culture and the dark skinned colonized with body and passion," so too are women and children thought of as "prisoners of body and biology" (p. 18). The implication is that these two "groups" have to be liberated from their bodies and taught to control them, to recreate bodies in the image of the "controlled" adult male. As we have suggested elsewhere, the most fleeting glimpses of life in schools are hauntingly evocative of colonial conditions, especially when it comes to disciplining young bodies (Viruru & Cannella, 1999). When children enter daycare as infants and toddlers, "all leaky bodies and unregulated desire, fluids pouring out of orifices insufficiently closed to the world," they are subjected to multiple methods designed to teach them control, to move them from "unbridled expressions of bodily pleasure to socially sanctioned forms of play, from excessive pleasure to good clean fun" (Tobin, 1997, p. 19).

The control of the body is also linked by Tobin to indulging only in sanctioned forms of pleasure, especially those that advance the interests of capitalism. "Citizen-consumers with a particular constellation of desires" are essential to maintaining the capitalist system (p. 19). Citizens in the neo-colonial late capitalist world are controlled by a system that requires the endless manufacture of consumer desire for new objects and experiences. Reproducing this system requires that children learn through materialist, regulated schooling to consume rather than produce passion. According to Tobin:

> The American kindergarten's daily routine of worksheet activities alter-
> nating with learning center times, snacks and recess, imitates and antici-
> pates the cycle of adult pleasureless office work broken up by packaged
> pleasures in the form of shopping expeditions, coffee and lunch breaks and
> vacations (1997, p. 18).

Smith (1999) has suggested that the ways in which space has been
defined for colonized people (within which we would include those who are
younger) is yet another example of establishing the dominance and assumed
superiority of Western ways of knowing. In many languages there are no special words for the concept of space; for example, the Maori word for space
and time is the same. Western ideas about time and space are, however,
encoded in much of its philosophy and many of its languages and have been
imposed on others in a variety of contexts. The Western concept of space consists of lines which are either parallel or elliptical. From these ideas, disciplines
of study have emerged (mapping and geography, measurement and geome-
try, motion and physics). The notion of space as composed of lines is also linked
to the construction of the idea of compartmentalization, resulting in categories like public, private, city, country, work, and play.

Compartmentalizing classroom space is also a major component of
the dominant discourses tied to the education of young children. According
to Johnson, Christie, and Yawkey (1999), a key issue in arranging the early
childhood classroom is whether space should be "open" or "partitioned."
Open arrangements help children to move around the classroom easily.
However, partitioning space has been seen as the better arrangement, since
it "reduces noise and distractions making it easier for children to concen-
trate and stay focused on activities" (p. 253). Interestingly, the authors suggest that one of the advantages is that partitions discourage "rough-and-tumble"
play. Partitioned spaces are linked to verbal interaction, cooperation, pretend
play, and activity with educational materials, whereas open spaces are linked
to "rowdy, withdrawn and random behavior" (Johnson, Christie, & Yawkey,
1999, p. 254). The implications seem clear—to control and partition space is
to control and "civilize" the bodies that function in that space.

Johnson et al. also maintain that "the issue of open versus partitioned space is closely connected with the notion of spatial definition" (p.
254). They quote the work of Moore (1987), suggesting that classroom space
should be organized into well-defined behavior settings or areas that are
clearly marked as apart from "circulation space" and where only certain

kinds of activities are tolerated. Neumann and Roskos (1993) suggest that the boundaries between classroom space ought to be marked with both "physical" and "symbolic" cues, which provide children with the "locational detail they so often need to signal and guide their behaviors" (p. 106). Partitions are justified on the basis of child need; children left to themselves would not know to organize their space so must have control imposed upon them. They "need" to be controlled in space. The parallels between this argument and the logic of colonization as civilizing mission are obvious. The concept of classroom space seems to fit with what Smith (1999) sees as one of the main features of Western constructions of space, that it is something to be controlled and tamed.

Smith's most devastating critique of Western notions of space is that it is linked to control through a colonialist constructed vocabulary. Embedded within this vocabulary are three concepts—the line, the center, and the outside. Historically, the line was used to mark the limits of colonial power; the center meant orienting oneself to the system of power; and the outside was in opposition to the center. Those who were in opposition did not exist because they were outside the system. The lines or boundaries of schooling are clearly marked, both physically and in a curricular sense. The central system of power can be seen in schools when all children in the school are controlled by certain "schoolwide" policies (such as when an entire school or school system adopts a particular "discipline" policy). Children are expected to respond to the center, to the system, without opposition.

Finally, Smith (1999) has suggested that one of the first reactions that Western observers have about non-Western people regards their use (or lack thereof) of time. "Natives" have often been characterized as "lazy, indolent and with low attention spans" (p. 53). Colonizers, in varied parts of the world, tried hard to inculcate in natives such habits as eating at "proper" meal times, and reorganizing family patterns to enable men to work at some things while women worked on others (ibid). This obsession with time resembles our insistence on getting children (especially younger children) scheduled and into predictable routines. The argument is that young children "need a schedule" or they "need to know what to expect," otherwise there will be complete chaos. Time must be arranged predictably and regularly for a child to feel comfortable. A safe, predictable routine is in many ways reified into a universal need. In other words, dominant constructions of how to best use one's time are imposed onto the bodies of those who are younger.

When one controls a person's concept of both space and time, human beings can be distanced from their physical environments and communities. Furthermore, colonial rule was essentially something that functioned from a distance, separating the individuals in power from the subjects that they governed. Distance in turn leads to power being seen as something impersonal and rational; removing human faces from the colonizer's rules made them appear all the more as rules that were enforced for the "good" of the colonized.

We would suggest that much the same holds for dominant teaching methods. Techniques are presented as distant from human feelings and desires and isolated from culture and human endeavor. Although it is true that in some cases methods have been linked to particular human beings (e.g., Madeline Hunter), in general they assume the guise of representing a scientific conception of how children ought to be taught. Often, they seem to be based on scientific theories of learning, which seem to create an even further distance between them and the children they influence. This distance seems to work in favor of those in power, who can present the methods as impersonal, objectively based tools.

Final Thoughts: Can Education Become Decolonization?

The notion that education has been (and currently is) colonization cannot be denied. Historic reasoning and contemporary practice illustrate the intrinsic tendency for education to be conceptualized as control of the "other" (whether physically, socially, intellectually, or in the construction of desire), especially regarding those who are younger. Some very well-meaning liberal educators would respond to our suggestions with hurt and dismay that we would propose that the "thirst for knowledge" could actually be limiting and controlling. Others, perhaps more conservative responders, might insist that the world is a better place because of Euro-American constructions of education (even if those views are imposed on others through yearly testing, control of curriculum content, and scientific teaching methods). Most recently, those who seem to want to hear the voices of all involved have suggested that education should be reconceptualized to provide increased possibilities for great numbers of people, social activism, and the expectation of diversity. We believe that all of these perspectives are important and should be examined and thoroughly considered, especially when we consider the diverse materiality of human life in a capitalist, power-oriented world. Actually, much of our work can be placed into somewhat liberal and definitely reconceptualist perspectives. We would not suggest the elimination of education or schooling.

However, we do believe that education should be placed into a position in which (a) intrinsic power, domination, and control issues within the concept are perpetually revealed, and (b) continual contextual critique occurs. This positioning would continuously challenge the construction of education as an "intellectual savior." To illustrate, education as an institution (whether viewed as reading books, passing standardized tests, obtaining a high school diploma, lifelong learning, or learning about one's community and diverse cultures) constructs desire within individuals and groups. Whether that desire is to test well, know facts, or work with others collaboratively, the construction of desire is a form of control. Even the work of individuals such as Freire that has challenged particular forms of colonization may produce certain desires that colonize individuals—and perhaps as we interact with and share values with others, colonization is unavoidable. We do not have answers as to how an intrinsically colonizing practice such as education can be conceptualized to avoid control (in some form) over others. However, we propose that education should be examined as dangerous, not only because of "liberatory" tendencies toward Western enlightenment, but also because of the way that those tendencies have denied diverse knowledges and ways of being in the world. Finally, we suggest that the multiple forms of colonization be further explored in education and that decolonization become a major focus of our struggle as educators.

■ References

Aidoo, A. (1991). That capacious topic: Gender politics. In P. Mariani (Ed.) *Critical Fictions*. Seattle: Bay Press.

Bhabba, H. (1996). The other question. In P. Mongia (Ed.), *Contemporary postcolonial theory: A reader* (pp. 37–54). London: Arnold.

Bredekamp, S., & Copple, C. (1997). *Developmentally appropriate practice in early childhood programs*. Washington, D.C.: NAEYC.

Cannella, G. S. (1997). *Deconstructing early childhood education: Social justice and revolution*. New York: Peter Lang.

Delpit, L. (1995). *Other people's children*. New York: The New Press.

DeYoung, A. (1989). *Economics and American education*. New York: Longman.

Dirlik, A. (1997). *The postcolonial aura: Third world criticism in the age of global capitalism*. Boulder, CO: Westview Press.

Eisenberg, R. (1967). *The east-west conflict: Psychological origin and resolution*. New York: Diplomatic Press.

Gandhi, L. (1998). *Postcolonial theory: A critical introduction*. New York: Columbia University Press.

Gates, H. L. (1994). Critical Fanonism. In R. Davis & R. Schleifer (Eds.), *Contemporary literary criticism*. New York: Longman. Also published in *Critical inquiry, 17*: 457–470.

Goodman, J. (1992). *Elementary schooling for critical democracy*. Albany, NY: SUNY Press.

Grove, R. H. (1995). *Green imperialisms: Colonial expansion, tropical island Edens and the origins of environmentalism 1600–1860*. Cambridge: Cambridge University Press.

Hunt, M. H. (2000). The decolonization puzzle in U.S. policy: Promise versus performance. In Ryan, D., & Pungong, V. (Eds.), *The United States and decolonization: Power and freedom* (pp. 207–229). New York: St. Martin's Press.

Jacoby, R. (September/October, 1995). Marginal returns: The trouble with post-colonial theory. *Lingua Franca*, 30–37.

Johnson. J. E., Christie, J.F., & Yawkey, T.D. (1999). *Play and early childhood development*. New York: Longman.

Kincheloe, J. L., Slattery, P., & Steinberg, S. (2000). *Contextualizing teaching*. New York: Addison, Wesley and Longman.

Lafeber, W. (1963). *The new empire: An interpretation of American expansion, 1860–1898*. New York: Cornell University Press.

Lafeber, W. (1993). *Inevitable revolutions: The United States in Central America*. New York: W. W. Norton.

Loomba, A. (1998). *Colonialism/Postcolonialism*. London: Routledge.

Lucas, W. S. (1991). *Divided we stand: Britain, the U.S., and the Suez crisis*. London: Hodder & Stoughton.

Mongia, P. (1996). Introduction. In P. Mongia (Ed.), *Contemporary postcolonial theory: A reader* (pp. 1–19). London: Arnold.

Moore, G. (1987). The physical environment and cognitive development in child-care. In C. Weinstein & T. David (Eds.), *Spaces for children: The built environment and child development* (pp. 41–72). New York: Plenum.

Nandy, A. (1993). *The intimate enemy*. Delhi: Oxford University Press.

Neumann, S., & Roskos, K. (1993). *Language and learning in the early years: An integrated approach*. New York: Harcourt Brace.

Ryan, D. (2000). The United States, decolonization and the world system. In Ryan, D., & Pungong, V. (Eds.). *The United States and decolonization: Power and freedom* (pp. 1–23). New York: St. Martin's Press

Ryan, D., & Pungong, V. (Eds.) (2000). *The United States and decolonization: Power and freedom*. New York: St. Martin's Press.

San Juan, E. (1998). *Beyond postcolonial theory*. New York: St. Martin's Press.

Schulze-Engler, F. (18 May 1993). Universalism with a difference: The politics of postcolonial theory. Paper read at Karl-Franzens University, Graz, Australia.

Smith, L. T. (1999). *Decolonizing methodologies: Research and indigenous peoples*. London and New York: Zed Books.

Spivak, G. (1996). Poststructuralism, marginality, postcoloniality, and value. In P. Mongia (Ed.), *Contemporary postcolonial theory: A reader* (pp. 198–223). London: Arnold.

Spivak, G. (1999). *A critique of postcolonial reason: Toward a history of the vanishing present*. Cambridge, MA: Harvard University Press.

Tiffin, C., & Lawson, A. (1994). *De-scribing empire, postcolonialism and textuality*. London: Routledge.

Tobin, L. (1997). The missing discourse of pleasure and desire. In J. Tobin (Ed.), *Making a place for pleasure in early childhood education* (pp. 1–37). New Haven: Yale University Press.

Vaughn, M. (1991). *Curing their ills: Colonial power and African illness*. Stanford: Stanford University Press.

Viruru, R. (2001). *Early childhood education: Postcolonial perspectives from India.* New Delhi: Sage.

Viruru, R., & Cannella, G.S. (1999). *A postcolonial scrutiny of early childhood education.* Paper presented at the JCT Conference, Dayton, OH, October 1999.

Vitzthum, R. (1995). *Materialism: An affirmative history and definition.* New York: Prometheus Books.

EDITORS
& CONTRIBUTORS

GAILE S. CANNELLA is an Associate Professor in the Department of Educational Psychology at Texas A&M University. She is a former early childhood and elementary teacher who received a master's degree from Tennessee Technological University and a doctoral degree from the University of Georgia. Dr. Cannella has served on the faculties of Louisiana State University, the University of Northern Iowa, and St. John's University in New York. She is the author of *Deconstructing Early Childhood Education: Social Justice and Revolution* and coeditor (with Sue Grieshaber) of *Embracing Identities in Early Childhood Education: Diversity and Possibilities*. Her interests are the construction of a broad-based field of "childhood studies" that includes critical advocacy, poststructural and feminist perspectives, and recognition of political, historical, and multicultural contexts.

JOE L. KINCHELOE is Bell Zeller Chair of Public Policy and Administration, CUNY Brooklyn College and Graduate Center. Dr. Kincheloe is a former public school teacher with a Ph.D. from the University of Tennessee. His multiple publications include the recent *Rethinking Intelligence: Unauthorized Methods, White Reign: Deploying Whiteness in America, Measured Lies: The Bell Curve Examined,* and *Kinderculture: The Corporate Construction of Childhood.* Most recently, he has authored *Getting Beyond the Facts: Teaching Social Studies in the Twenty-First Century* and *The Sign of the Burger: McDonald's and the Culture of Power*.

SUE BOOKS, a former journalist, is now an associate professor in the Department of Educational Studies at the State University of New York at New Paltz. She teaches courses in education and poverty, literacy and learning, and the social and philosophical foundations of education. The editor of *Invisible Children in the Society and Its Schools* (1998) and coeditor (with Valerie Polakow) of a special issue of *The Journal of Educational Studies* on schooling and poverty (Fall 2001), Sue has been writing about poverty, schooling, and education throughout her academic career.

LOURDES DÍAZ SOTO is a Professor of Education at Pennsylvania State University. She has authored numerous articles and book chapters. Her books include *Language, Culture, and Power: Bilingual Families and the Struggle for Quality Education; The Politics of Early Childhood Education;* and *Making a Difference in the Lives of Bilingual/Bicultural Children* (forthcoming).

JANICE A. JIPSON is Professor of Education at National Louis University, where she teaches in the doctoral program in Curriculum and Social Inquiry and in the Interdisciplinary Studies Program. Her scholarly interests include early childhood curriculum and issues of identity, intersubjectivity, and representation in narrative research. Her recent books include *Resistance and Representation: Rethinking Childhood Education* (2001) with Richard Johnson; *Intersections: Feminisms/Early Childhoods* (1998) with Mary Houser; *Daredevil Research: Re-creating Analytic Practice* (1997) with Nicholas Paley; and *Questions of You and the Struggle of Collaborative Life* (2000) with Nicholas Paley.

SUMANA KASTURI is the author of *Entering the Magic Kingdom: Childhood, Cultural Pedagogy, Disney, and the Internet* (forthcoming). She has written and presented papers on media, education, and culture. She formerly worked as a journalist, documentary filmmaker, and editor of *Teacher Plus* (a resource periodical for school teachers). Her research interests include children's communication and cultural pedagogy. Currently, she is taking a break from her Ph.D. to be with her baby daughter.

NICHOLAS PALEY is Professor of Education in the Graduate School of Education and Honors Professor in the Liberal Arts at George Washington University. His work explores the relations—in theory and in practice—of arts-based approaches to issues of educational inquiry. His most recent book (with Janice Jipson), examining the dimensions of the collaborative research experience, is titled *Questions of You and the Struggle of Collaborative Life*. He is currently Visiting Fellow at the Pembroke Center for Teaching and Research on Women at Brown University, where he is studying, as a member of the Pembroke Research Seminar, "The Question of Emotion."

RENÉ QUESADA INCES is a doctoral candidate at Pennsylvania State University. Currently, she is writing her dissertation, which is an analysis of the Costa Rican educational system. SUSAN GRIESHABER lives and works in Brisbane, Australia. She completed her Bachelor and Master's of Education degrees at the University of Queensland and her Ph.D. at James Cook University of North Queensland. Dr. Grieshaber taught young children in before-school and regular education contexts for thirteen years in rural, urban, and isolated communities before moving into academic life. She works currently in the School of Early Childhood at Queensland University of Technology, with approximately twenty other early childhood academics who provide preservice and in-service teacher education programs. Her research interests include early childhood curriculum, early childhood policy, families, and gender. She is the editor of the journal *Contemporary Issues in Early Childhood* (with Nicola Yelland) and has edited (with Gaile Cannella) the book *Embracing Identities in Early Childhood Education: Diversity and Possibilities* (2001).

DOMINIC SCOTT is a native of Ireland who has lived in New Mexico for ten years. He is a doctoral student in Curriculum and Instruction at New Mexico State University. He previously studied in Europe at Oxford, Edinburgh, and the University of Ulster. Dominic has been a middle and high school teacher in the UK, Ireland, and the United States He has a deep interest in disaffected and marginalized adolescents, and in developing educational programs and opportunities that address the needs, hopes, and aspirations of excluded youth. He is an evaluator for an innovative, nonprofit, alternative school for marginalized Chicano/a youth. His other interests are education as a liberatory experience, social justice, cultural studies, social studies education, multicultural education, critical pedagogy, and teacher training. He loves to travel and has visited thirty countries, where he has observed the impact of globalization and cultural imperialism firsthand. In his travels he finds a reaffirmation of the goodness of humanity. Along with his wife and eleven-year-old daughter, he enjoys gardening, crafts, simple living, and the search for a more conscious expression of human potential.

MEE-RYOUNG SHON is Assistant Professor at Morehead State University, focusing on early childhood education with an emphasis in critical theory and multicultural children's literature. She completed her master's degree at Ewha Woman's University, Seoul, Korea, with a thesis titled *The Study of Korean Buddhist Kindergarten,* and undergraduate work at Kyung-book College. While completing her doctoral work in early childhood education at Texas A&M University, she was a teacher in the Texas A&M University Children's Center and was previously a teacher in Si-Yeon Kindergarten, Seoul. Her recent publications include "Child-Centerness as Colonization: Early Childhood Education in Korea" in the *Journal of Curriculum Theorizing* in 1999 and a translation of *Wally's Stories* by Vivian Paley into Korean in 1997. Her dissertation and further scholarly interests include cultural values authenticity in the translation of children's literature (specifically from Korean to English) and historical, crosscultural studies of curriculum for young children.

RADHIKA VIRURU received her Ph.D. in education from Texas A&M University, where she is a lecturer in Early Childhood Education. Her book *Early Childhood Education: Postcolonial Perspectives From India* was published in 2001. Additionally, Dr. Viruru is coeditor (with Gaile Cannella) of the section "Childhood and Cultural Studies," published in the *Journal of Curriculum Theorizing.* Her research interests and publications address issues of postcolonial theory and its relationship to early childhood education.

■ INDEX ■

RETHINKING CHILDHOOD

JOE L. KINCHELOE & JANICE A. JIPSON, *General Editors*

A revolution is occurring regarding the study of childhood. Traditional notions of child development are under attack, as are the methods by which children are studied. At the same time, the nature of childhood itself is changing as children gain access to information once reserved for adults only. Technological innovations, media, and electronic information have narrowed the distinction between adults and children, forcing educators to rethink the world of schooling in this new context.

This series of textbooks and monographs encourages scholarship in all of these areas, eliciting critical investigations in developmental psychology, early childhood education, multicultural education, and cultural studies of childhood.

Proposals and manuscripts may be sent to the general editors:

Joe L. Kincheloe
c/o Peter Lang Publishing, Inc.
275 Seventh Avenue, 28th floor
New York, New York 10001

or

Janice A. Jipson
219 Pease Court
Janesville, WI 53545

To order other books in this series, please contact our Customer Service Department at:

(800) 770-LANG (within the U.S.)
(212) 647-7706 (outside the U.S.)
(212) 647-7707 FAX

Or browse online by series at:
www.peterlangusa.com